W9-AIZ-815

# BY THE NUMBERS

## A Survival Guide To Economic Indicators

Stephen D. Slifer
&
W. Stansbury Carnes

International Financial Press, Ltd.
4743 Cornell Road, Cincinnati, Ohio 45241

BY THE NUMBERS: A SURVIVAL GUIDE TO ECONOMIC INDICATORS. © 1995 by International Financial Press, Ltd.

All rights reserved. No part of this book may be reproduced or transmitted in any form or by any means electronic or mechanical, including photocopying, recording, or any information storage and retrieval system, without permission in writing from the publisher. For information contact International Financial Press, Ltd., 4743 Cornell Road, Cincinnati, Ohio 45241.

FIRST EDITION

Designed by David Davis and Jodi Dellinger

Money
Words and Music by Roger Waters
TRO—Copyright 1973 Hampshire House Publishing Corp., New York, NY
Used by permission of Music Sales Corporation, sole selling agent of Pink Floyd Music Publishing Ltd., for print rights throughout the world.

**Publisher's Cataloging-in-Publication**
(*Prepared by Quality Books Inc.*)

Slifer, Stephen D.
    By the numbers : a survival guide to economic indicators /
Stephen D. Slifer & W. Stansbury Carnes. – 1st ed.
      p. cm.
      Includes index.
      ISBN: 1-887147-03-9.

      1. Economic indicators–United States.   2. Business cycles–
United States–Statistics.   3. United States–Economic conditions–
Statistics.   I. Carnes, W. Stansbury.   II. Title.

HC103.S55 1996               330.973
                          QBI96-20089

Printed in the United States of America.
00 99 98 97 96     5 4 3 2 1

*To Katie*

*—Steve Slifer*

*To my—*
 *Wife, Mary*
 *Children, John, Grant and Ansley*
 *Father, Bill Carnes*
 *Sister, Virginia Rather*

*—Stan Carnes*

# Contents

# Part III

# Federal Reserve Operations

# Appendix

# Index

Money, so they say
Is the root of all evil today
But if you ask for a rise
It's no surprise
That they're giving none away ©

—Pink Floyd

# PART I
## OVERVIEW

Whether you are an investor, broker, financial market economist, business student, or speculator, you want to know the future course of the economy and inflation, the likely response of the Federal Reserve Board to these developments, and, finally, the implications for interest rates. Why are we all so interested? Simply because the combination of these factors is going to largely determine the direction of the major financial markets.

This book is a simple, easy-to-use pictorial guide to the economic indicators and the Federal Reserve — the primary factors that move the markets. It describes how these key indicators work and what effect they have and takes a detailed look at the U.S. central bank. Using this book as a guide, you will be better able to interpret the reactions of financial markets to economic news and plan accordingly.

**FIXED-INCOME MARKETS ARE DIRECTLY LINKED TO INTEREST RATES**

Our first look is at the fixed-income markets. These markets are inexorably linked to interest rates because of the inverse relationship that exists between interest rates and the price of a fixed-income security. When interest rates rise, the price of a bond falls and vice versa *(Figure 1-1)*. For example, suppose an investor

Suppose the U.S. Treasury issues a bond at prevailing interest rates, say 8%...

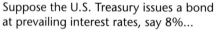

8%          $1000

If interest rates fall to 6%...          $1200

6%

The price of the bond rises because its return is higher than that of a new bond.

10%   But if interest rates rise to 10%...

$800

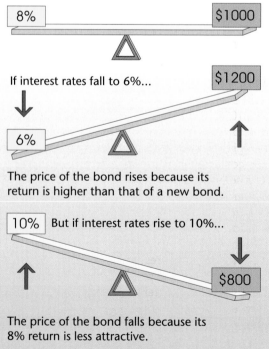

The price of the bond falls because its 8% return is less attractive.

*Figure 1-1*
*How Bond Yields and*
*U.S. Treasury Security*
*Prices Are Related*

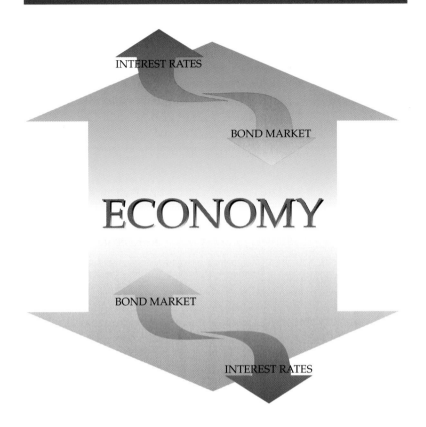

*Figure 1-2*
*How the Economy Affects the Fixed-Income Markets*

holds a Treasury bond that yields 8%. If the economy expands rapidly, inflation will eventually begin to climb — pushing bond yields higher to, say, 10%. In that case, the 8% bond will become less attractive and its price will decline; investors would rather own the new higher-yielding 10% security. Thus, any market force that causes the economy to grow more rapidly, or causes the inflation rate to rise, increases the likelihood that the Federal Reserve will raise interest rates and decrease prices in the fixed-income markets *(Figure 1-2)*. The process works just as well in reverse. Any market force that causes economic activity to decline, or the inflation rate to drop, increases the likelihood that the Federal Reserve will lower interest rates and raise prices in the fixed-income markets. Since the prices of fixed-income securities are so closely linked to interest rates, it is crucial for participants in this market to be cognizant of developments in the economy, the pace of inflation, and implications for Federal Reserve policy.

THE STOCK MARKET IS
TIED TO CORPORATE
PROFITS – PLUS THE
ECONOMY,
INFLATION, AND
INTEREST RATES

Movement in the equity (stock) market is directly linked to the outlook for corporate profits. If profits are expected to rise, then stock prices will also rise. As you can see from *Figure 1-3*, when corporate profits are rising, the stock market also rises. But, when corporate profits drop (such as in the recessions of 1973-74 and again in 1980-82), the stock market also falls. Quite clearly the pace of economic activity plays a major role *(Figure 1-4)*. If the economy dips into recession, corporate profits are certain to

*Figure 1-3*
*How the S&P 500*
*Tracks Corporate*
*Profits*

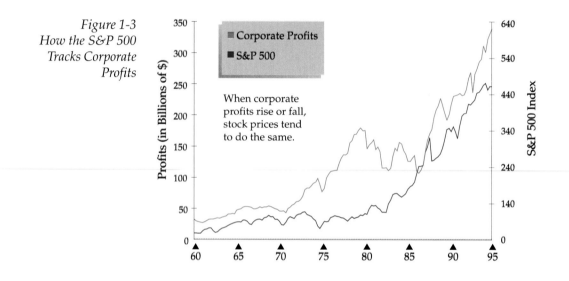

slide — pulling the overall stock market down with it. Inflation also plays a role. To the extent that inflation rises, the real value of earnings and dividends declines — usually prompting stock prices to fall. Thus, a pickup in inflation is also viewed negatively by the equity markets. And if interest rates rise, the increased cost of borrowing by corporations reduces earnings. There is no question that other factors can play a role in establishing stock prices *(Figure 1-5)*. At the micro level, management changes, technological developments, and the implementation of more sophisticated cost control procedures are important in determining the price of an individual company's stock. And, if the company is large enough, it can influence the overall level of stock prices. Nevertheless, the economy, inflation, and interest rates are critical factors in determining the future path of the stock market because of their correlation with profits. Thus, if you can come to terms with the macroeconomic environment, you are well on your way to becoming a better stock market investor.

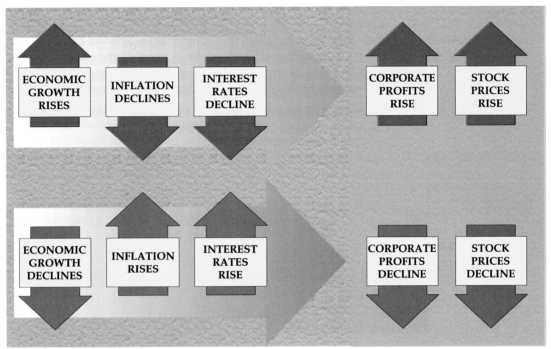

Figure 1-4
How the Macroeconomy Affects Corporate Profits and Stock Prices

Figure 1-5
Factors Affecting the Stock Market

No matter what market you are most closely associated with, it behooves you to have a working knowledge of what drives the economy, what produces inflation, and what factors are going to cause the Federal Reserve to change policy. Ultimately, you need to forecast the direction of interest rates.

GDP = C + I + G + X - M
CONSUMPTION
INVESTMENTS
GOVERNMENT
EXPENDITURES
EXPORTS
IMPORTS

We have found that most market participants have a reasonably good theoretical knowledge of the economy and how it functions. Yet, these same market participants seem to have difficulty interpreting the series of economic indicators that are released each month and figuring out the implications for the economy or inflation. And who would not? Back in that Economics 101 class, you learned that GDP represents the sum of consumption spending, investment, government expenditures, and exports minus imports (or the old GDP = C + I + G + X - M equation) which is shown pictorially in *Figure 1-8*. It turns out that almost every one of the economic indicators fall into one of these categories, and each one is useful for the information it provides about the overall economy. We will consider, for example, where construction spending fits into this framework, what the purchasing managers' report means, and try to sort through the employment report. When we consider inflation, we will explain the difference between the implicit price deflator, the fixed-weight deflator, the CPI, and the PPI, and what you should expect when one of these numbers is released.

The first part of the book deals with the various economic indicators. For each series we want to focus on three things:

*What the indicator means*. Why do we care what happens to it? What does it tell us about the economy? What does it tell us about inflation, about interest rates, about the Federal Reserve's policy? What other things are important about this indicator?

*The background of each indicator*. Who publishes the series? When is it released? How reliable is it? How do economists form their expectations about what that indicator will do for any given month?

*The market's response to each indicator*. How will the fixed-income markets react to a higher-than-expected figure for GDP growth? What will happen to the equity markets? What will happen to the foreign exchange market?

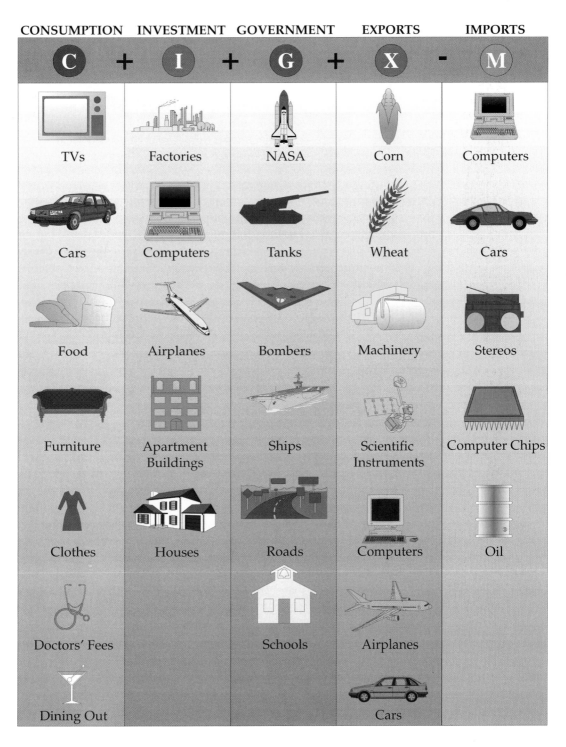

*Figure 1-8  Gross Domestic Product Components*

EACH ECONOMIC INDICATOR TELLS US SOMETHING ABOUT THE ECONOMY OR INFLATION

As we've mentioned, each economic indicator is associated with a part of the GDP = C + I + G + X - M equation (*Figure 1-9*). The construction spending indicator referred to above, for example, falls under the "I" category as it provides us with information about residential and nonresidential spending — both of which are important parts of the investment component of GDP. The construction spending report is also included under the "G" category because it tells us something about state and local government spending. Some reports, such as the monthly employment report, the purchasing managers' survey, leading indicators, and quarterly GDP, tell us nothing about the various components of GDP. Rather, these reports tell us about GDP itself. They are broader indices that more appropriately apply to the economy as a whole, and not to its parts.

Some indicators — such as the PPI, the CPI, and the fixed-weight and implicit price deflators — do not refer to what is happening with GDP, but to inflation. Later in the text, we will highlight the differences between these various inflation measures and the advantages and disadvantages of each.

As we noted at the outset, any market indicator that points towards a faster pace of GDP growth or higher inflation is generally regarded as a negative for the fixed-income markets because it implies higher interest rates and, hence, lower bond prices. Similarly, once you understand what is happening to the economy and what that suggests for interest rates, the appropriate response of the equity and foreign exchange markets can be determined.

THE MARKET REACTS WHEN THE ACTUAL CHANGE OF AN INDICATOR DIFFERS FROM THE MARKET CONSENSUS

While it is clearly important to understand what an indicator tells us about the economy or inflation, it is also extremely important to recognize that the market's reaction is going to be determined more by how it compares to the market's consensus forecast than by the absolute change in an indicator. For example, suppose that the market believes that GDP growth for some particular quarter is going to rise only 0.5%. If the Commerce Department data reveal that growth was actually 1.0%, the fixed-income markets probably will decline because GDP was more rapid than had been expected, *even though* a 1.0% growth rate is still quite slow. The equity markets probably will also decline because the higher-than-anticipated GDP advance reduces the likelihood that the Federal Reserve will ease monetary policy and, hence, interest rates may not decline in the near future.

$$GDP = C + I + G + X - M$$

| | | | | | |
|---|---|---|---|---|---|
| Quarterly GDP (Ch. 2) | Car Sales (Ch. 4) | Housing Starts | Construction Spending (Ch. 17) | Merchandise Exports (Ch. 20) | Merchandise Imports (Ch. 20) |
| | | Building Permits (Ch. 11) | | | |
| | Retail Sales (Ch. 8) | | | Merchandise Trade Balance (Ch. 20) | |
| Initial Claims (Ch. 3) | | | | | |
| | | Durable Goods Orders (Ch. 13) | | | |
| NAPM (Ch. 5) | Consumer Sentiment (Ch. 10) | | | | |
| Employment (Ch. 6) | | | | | |

**INFLATION**

Implicit Deflator (Ch. 2)

| | | |
|---|---|---|
| | PCEs/ Personal Income (Ch. 14) | New Home Sales (Ch. 16) |
| Industrial Production/ Capacity Utilization (Ch. 9) | | |

Fixed-Weight Index (Ch. 2)

| | |
|---|---|
| | Construction Spending (Ch. 17) |
| Leading Indicators (Ch. 15) | Factory Orders (Ch. 18) |

PPI (Ch. 7)

CPI (Ch. 12)

Business Inventories (Ch. 19)

Nonfarm Productivity/ Unit Labor Costs (Ch. 21)

*Figure 1-9*
*The GDP Formula*

The employment report for May 1990 is a classic example of how the markets reacted to a figure that was different from expectations. On Friday, June 1, the Bureau of Labor Statistics reported an increase in payroll employment for May of 164,000. The street consensus was for a gain of about 200,000. In addition, the April rise in payroll was revised downward from an *increase* of 64,000 initially, to a *decline* of 23,000. The combination of a smaller-than-expected increase for May *and* a sharp downward revision to April increased the likelihood that the Federal Reserve would ease in the relatively near future and that interest rates would decline. As a result, the bond market rose by nearly two points the same day, causing the yield on 30-year bonds to decline 16 basis points from 8.58% to 8.42%. The stock market also reacted to the prospect of lower rates — the Dow Jones Industrial average rose 24 points, closing above 2900 for the first time. The point is simply that the market's short-term reaction is determined by whether a number is higher or lower than expected, rather than by the absolute value of the number. In our discussion of each indicator, we try to include several factors that economists look at in order to make forecasts. The sum of these views becomes the street's "consensus" — the benchmark by which a number is deemed to be stronger or weaker than expected.

**AN INDICATOR'S VALUE IS PARTLY DETERMINED BY ITS RELEASE DATE**

It is also important to understand that an indicator's value is determined, to some extent, by its release date. With the exception of the GDP report, which is presented first because it is so important, our discussion of the various economic statistics is presented in chronological order for a typical month. We have ranked the importance of each using a "star" system whereby:

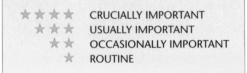

Figure 1-10 provides you with a list of the indicators' approximate release dates. The first hard data that we receive for any given month are initial claims for unemployment insurance, which are released on Thursday *of each week*. With the exception of the Johnson Redbook data, which are discussed in the chapter on retail sales (and which are not particularly useful), these are the *only* hints about economic activity that we see during the course of that *same* month. Once that month ends, however, and we move into the beginning of the *following* month, the data flow accelerates. On the first business day of that next month, we see the purchasing managers' report and most of the car and truck sales data. Then, generally on the first Friday of each month, we view the employment report — providing our first fairly complete sense of what happened to the economy during the prior month. A week later, the producer price index (PPI), retail sales figures, and industrial production data are released. This continues until several weeks later when we receive data on business inventories and the trade deficit for goods and services — invariably the last indicators for any given month. There is no question that information released *first* is much more valuable than the *last* data to be published, simply because the new information tells us something that we did not know previously. When we have already seen 16 indicators for a given month,

*Figure 1-10 Release Dates for Economic Indicators*

| Report | Chapter | Release Date |
|---|---|---|
| Initial Unemployment Claims | Ch. 3 | Every Thursday for week ending previous Saturday |
| Car Sales | Ch. 4 | 1-3 business days after end of the month |
| Purchasing Managers' Report | Ch. 5 | 1st business day of following month |
| Employment | Ch. 6 | 1st - 7th of following month |
| PPI | Ch. 7 | 9th - 16th of following month |
| Retail Sales | Ch. 8 | 11- 14th of following month |
| Industrial Production/ Capacity Utilization | Ch. 9 | 14th - 17th of following month |
| Consumer Sentiment | Ch. 10 | 13th - 20th of following month |
| Housing Starts/ Building Permits | Ch. 11 | 16th - 20th of following month |
| CPI | Ch. 12 | 15th - 21st of following month |
| Durable Goods Orders | Ch. 13 | 22nd - 28th of following month |
| GDP | Ch. 2 | 21st - 30th of following month |
| Personal Income/ Consumption Spending | Ch. 14 | 22nd - 31st of following month |
| Leading Indicators | Ch. 15 | Last business day of the following month |
| New Home Sales | Ch. 16 | 28th - 4th for two months prior |
| Construction Spending | Ch. 17 | 1st business day for two months prior |
| Factory Orders | Ch. 18 | 30th - 6th for two months prior |
| Business Inventories/Sales | Ch. 19 | 13th - 17th for two months prior |
| Trade Balance | Ch. 20 | 15th - 17th for two months prior |
| Nonfarm Productivity/ Unit Labor Costs | Ch. 21 | 7th - 14th of midmonth of quarter for previous quarter |

what marginal value do the 17th and 18th indicators have? Not a lot. By the time the last indicators are published, we are anxious to see what happened in the following month.

## IF AN INDICATOR IS EXTREMELY VOLATILE, ITS VALUE IS REDUCED

One final point concerning the indicators should be noted — the *theoretical* importance of an indicator is not always the same as its *actual* value. The classic example is the orders data. Theoretically, if one knows what is happening to orders, and whether the stack of orders on a manager's desk is growing or shrinking, one should be able to make some inference about production in the months ahead. But, unfortunately, the orders data are extremely volatile *(Figure 1-11)*. If a $3 billion aircraft order happens to be included in one month's data, durable goods orders can rise by 2.5 percentage points in that month. The next month, when orders return to normal, durables will decline by 2.5%. Because of these exaggerated swings, it is fruitless to attach a great deal of weight to a single month's data point. Thus, for some types of reports, it's better to take a 3-month moving average that helps smooth the data — and tells us whether there has been a significant change in trends.

## HOW THE FEDERAL RESERVE *DETERMINES* AND *IMPLEMENTS* MONETARY POLICY

After reading Part II of this book, investors will have a better sense of the information that each economic indicator conveys about the state of the economy or inflation and, more importantly, what these indicators tell us about the future direction of interest rates. Part III of this book deals with the Federal Reserve and its critical role in determining interest rates. First, we describe the crucial role that the Federal Reserve plays in influencing interest rates and how it actually determines monetary policy. Second, we explain how the Federal Reserve controls short-term interest rates but not long-term rates and how changes in monetary policy are transmitted to the economy through changes in interest rates. Finally, we explain how the Federal Reserve actually implements that policy. There are several steps to this process that can sometimes be rather technical. But you should spend the time reading this portion of the book because you will discover how monetary aggregates and bank reserves are related and how the level of borrowings from the discount window essentially determines the level of short-term interest rates.

*Figure 1-11 Durable Goods Orders: Month-to-Month Versus Three-Month Moving Average*

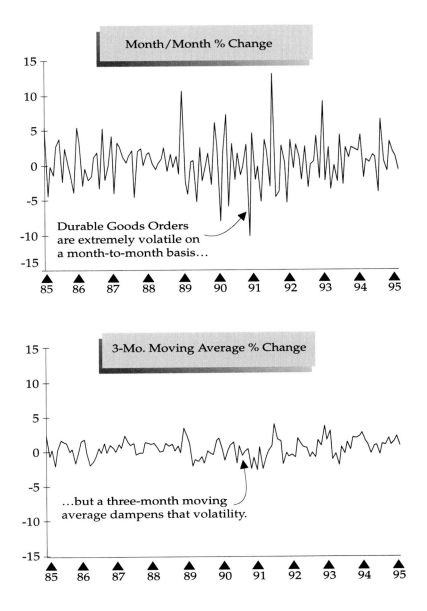

THE FEDERAL
RESERVE
DETERMINES
SHORT-TERM
INTEREST RATES BUT
NOT LONG-TERM
RATES

The first thing to understand about the Federal Reserve is that, through its open market operations, the central bank has total control of the overnight federal funds rate — the rate at which banks borrow or lend reserves. This means that, for all practical purposes, the Federal Reserve determines short-term interest rates. However, it does not have as much control over long-term interest rates such as bond yields or mortgage rates — those rates depend more upon GDP growth and inflation. This distinction is important because short-term interest rates *do not* always move in the same direction as long-term rates. We noted earlier that changes in the financial markets are closely tied to changes in interest rates. For example, if interest rates rise, the prices of fixed-income securities fall and the bond market declines. If interest rates rise, the stock market usually falls and the value of the dollar generally climbs. But what happens if short-term interest rates do not move in the same direction as long-term rates? When this occurs, it is not clear what investment or trading strategy you should pursue. Therefore, you must be aware not only of what is happening to the economy and the inflation rate, which largely determine the direction of *long-term* interest rates, but also of what the Federal Reserve is doing. What this really means is that you, as a market participant, must be aware of the shape of the *yield curve* — which shows interest rate levels for different maturities.

As an example of how short-term and long-term interest rates can move in different directions, *Figure 1-12* shows the yield curve at two different points in time. The bottom curve is the one that existed in early January 1990 when the bond market was very bullish and interest rates were expected to decline further. The Federal Reserve, at that time, pegged the funds rate at almost exactly 8.25%. But the markets were convinced that the economy was heading into a recession and that inflation would recede. This extremely favorable market psychology pushed long-dated bond yields to 8.04%, or 21 basis points (or hundredths of a percent) *below* the funds rate. A few months later, the world turned topsy-turvy as the economic data suddenly became much stronger and oil prices surged. At that point, the Federal Reserve still wanted the funds rate around 8.25%. However, by this time, the apparent strength in the economy had pushed inflationary expectations much higher, and bonds yields climbed to 9.0% or 75 basis points *higher* than the funds rate. Throughout this period Federal Reserve policy was unchanged, as evidenced by the fact that the funds rate remained at 8.25%. Yet the dramatic change in market psychology caused bond yields to rise by a full percentage point. Clearly, the Federal Reserve essentially "targets" short-term rates, but the economy and inflationary expectations are the driving forces behind long-term interest rates.

*Figure 1-12*
*Federal Reserve Policy, Long-Term Interest Rates, and Market Psychology*

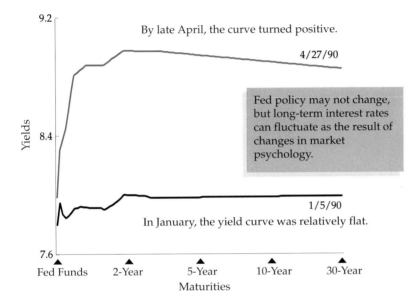

Many traders, salespeople, and investors have a good understanding of the *theoretical* aspects of monetary policy. They know that, as shown in *Figure 1-13*, the Federal Reserve tries to regulate money supply growth by controlling bank reserves. And they recall that, by regulating growth in the money supply, the Federal Reserve can indirectly influence the pace of economic activity and the inflation rate. Many people, however, become confused because they do not fully understand how the Federal Reserve uses open market operations to *implement* monetary policy. This book attempts to clarify this and answer questions such as the following: Why does the Federal Reserve intervene in the market almost every day doing repos or matched sales? What is the importance of a coupon or bill "pass?" What is the difference between a customer and system repo? How can you tell when the Federal Reserve is changing policy? Also, we hope to explain the link between what the Fed is doing in theory — controlling the growth rate of bank reserves — and the direct effect that has on short-term interest rates. As we will soon see, this link is crucial.

THE MARKETS DO NOT FULLY UNDERSTAND HOW MONETARY POLICY WORKS

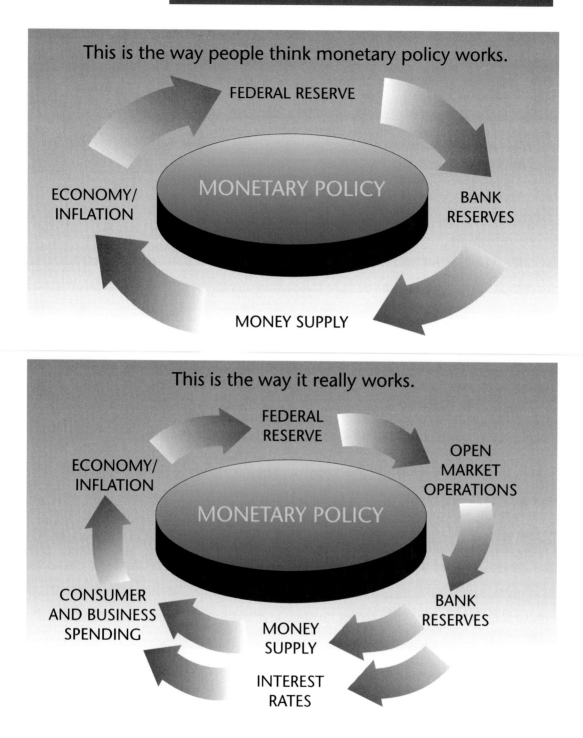

*Figure 1-13*
*Federal Reserve Policy: Theory Versus Reality*

Not surprisingly, you will find that — like the rest of us — Federal Reserve officials look at the economic indicators, the inflation rate, the value of the dollar, and conditions in the financial markets before making policy decisions. These factors are all detailed in the minutes of each Federal Open Market Committee (FOMC) meeting. If the Federal Reserve decides the economy is growing too rapidly and the inflation rate is unacceptably high, it will move to tighten monetary policy. In the *theoretical* world, this means that the Federal Reserve tries to slow down the growth rate of bank reserves in an effort to moderate growth in the money supply. But in the *real* world, we will find that this process has an immediate effect on short-term interest rates, the federal funds rate in particular. The link between the theoretical and real-world aspects of monetary policy, therefore, is interest rates *(Figure 1-14)*. By controlling the rate of expansion of bank reserves, the Federal Reserve influences interest rates. As interest rates rise and fall, firms and consumers alter their spending plans. As a result, changes in monetary policy are transmitted throughout the economy via changes in interest rates.

THE FEDERAL RESERVE TRANSMITS POLICY CHANGES TO THE ECONOMY VIA CHANGES IN INTEREST RATES

What this means for the individual investor or trader is that the Federal Reserve plays an absolutely critical role in determining the future course of interest rates. Certainly, the pace of economic activity and the inflation rate are important, but equally significant is the Federal Reserve's *response to these very same data*! As we noted previously, long-term interest rates may rise or fall depending upon the pace of GDP growth and/or inflation, while the Federal Reserve basically determines short-term interest rates. As these short- and long-term interest rates fluctuate, the shape of the yield curve can change. However, in general, short- and long-term interest rates move in the same direction. It is therefore imperative that market participants understand the crucial role played by the U.S. central bank.

BECAUSE THE FEDERAL RESERVE PLAYS A MAJOR ROLE IN DETERMINING INTEREST RATES, MARKET PARTICIPANTS MUST UNDERSTAND HOW IT WORKS

In Chapter 24, we show you exactly how the Federal Reserve carries out monetary policy. This is a four-step process that, as noted earlier, can be rather technical. We are not going to delve into technicalities at this point, but it is worth reading this portion of the book as there are important lessons to be learned at each stage in the process. In that chapter, you will see how the various money supply measures and bank reserves are related, how the level of borrowing from the discount window determines the funds rate, why the Federal Reserve intervenes in the

ONCE MONETARY POLICY IS DETERMINED, THE FEDERAL RESERVE MUST IMPLEMENT THAT POLICY

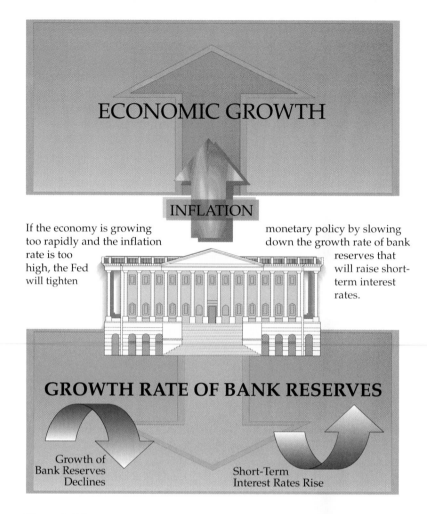

If the economy is growing too rapidly and the inflation rate is too high, the Fed will tighten monetary policy by slowing down the growth rate of bank reserves that will raise short-term interest rates.

*Figure 1-14*
*How the Federal Reserve Puts the Brakes on the Economy*

market almost every day — and how it used to send hints of policy changes to the markets. With this information in hand, you can quickly anticipate the reaction on the part of the financial markets.

# PART II
## THE ECONOMIC
## INDICATORS

### THE HOLY GRAIL OF ECONOMICS

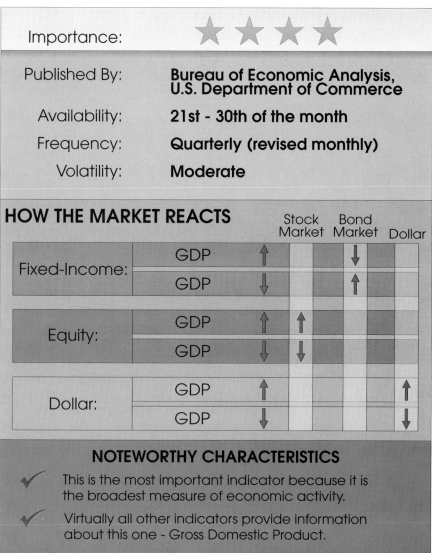

| Importance: | ★ ★ ★ ★ |
|---|---|
| Published By: | **Bureau of Economic Analysis, U.S. Department of Commerce** |
| Availability: | **21st - 30th of the month** |
| Frequency: | **Quarterly (revised monthly)** |
| Volatility: | **Moderate** |

**HOW THE MARKET REACTS**

| | | | Stock Market | Bond Market | Dollar |
|---|---|---|---|---|---|
| Fixed-Income: | GDP | ↑ | | ↓ | |
| | GDP | ↓ | | ↑ | |
| Equity: | GDP | ↑ | ↑ | | |
| | GDP | ↓ | ↓ | | |
| Dollar: | GDP | ↑ | | | ↑ |
| | GDP | ↓ | | | ↓ |

**NOTEWORTHY CHARACTERISTICS**

✓ This is the most important indicator because it is the broadest measure of economic activity.

✓ Virtually all other indicators provide information about this one - Gross Domestic Product.

**GDP IS THE MOST IMPORTANT ECONOMIC INDICATOR**

Gross Domestic Product (GDP) is probably *the* most important report during any given quarter. Real, or inflation-adjusted, GDP is the best single measure of U.S. economic output and spending. Even though GDP is itself one of the economic indicators — which in this book are organized around a typical monthly calendar — we decided to examine GDP first because it is so crucial. In order to fully appreciate the other economic indicators, you need an overall framework or paradigm. And that paradigm is the report on Gross Domestic Product.

Naturally, data contained in the GDP accounts affect the markets because investors, analysts, traders, and economists get their sense of where the economy is heading from it. But the GDP reports also influence decisions at the highest levels — from Congressional budget staffers and Federal Reserve policymakers to corporate strategic planners and labor negotiators. When all is said and done, GDP is how the nation keeps score — not only domestically, but internationally as well.

**WHAT IS GDP?**

GDP is the sum total of goods and services produced by the United States. Although there are many interpretations (and shortcomings), for our purposes, GDP should be viewed as a measure of demand for U.S. output — the dollar amount spent on a dizzying array of newly produced items. There are four major components included in the GDP accounts — consumption, investment, government purchases, and net exports. In

*Figure 2-1*
*Gross Domestic*
*Product*

CONSUMPTION   INVESTMENT   GOVERNMENT   EXPORTS   IMPORTS

C   +   I   +   G   +   X   -   M

Imports represent a "negative" number when calculating GDP.

The GDP calculation can also be illustrated as follows:

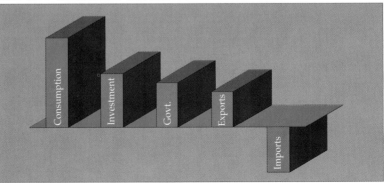

standard macroeconomic parlance, GDP = C + I + G + (X - M) (*Figure 2-1*).

The most important sector of the U.S. economy is consumption, or consumer outlays. Economists generally contend that consumption spending represents about two-thirds of GDP. They arrive at this number simply by dividing the level of personal consumption expenditures by the level of GDP. However, that is not entirely correct. It is important to remember that a portion of consumption spending reflects purchases of imported goods that are not included in GDP. Thus, a more accurate estimate of the consumption component is probably about 58% *(Figure 2-2)*. Either way it is clear that the consumption category is larger than the other three categories combined. These consumer outlays can be segregated into three categories: durable goods — which are items expected to last three years or more (automobiles, furniture, and golf clubs); nondurable goods — which are expected to last less than three years (food, clothing, and aspirin); and services (medical care, haircuts, and legal fees) *(Figure 2-3)*. Durable goods account for about 15% of consumption, whereas nondurable goods account for 31% — more than twice as much. Services provide the remaining 54% *(Figure 2-4)*.

*Figure 2-2*
*Composition of GDP: Consumption*

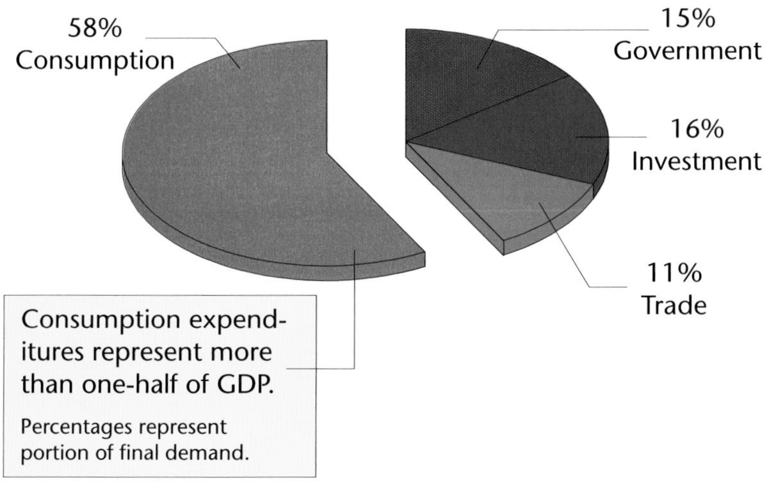

58%
Consumption

15%
Government

16%
Investment

11%
Trade

Consumption expenditures represent more than one-half of GDP.

Percentages represent portion of final demand.

*Figure 2-3*
*What Is Consumption?*

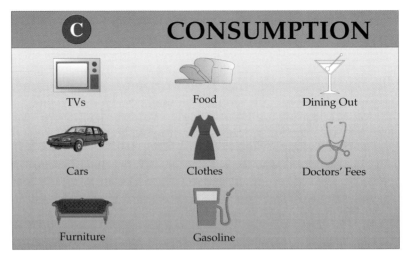

*Figure 2-4*
*Types of Consumption*
*Spending*

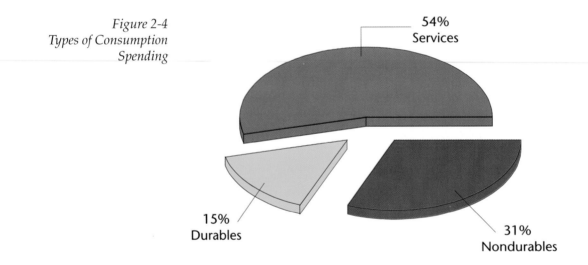

**INVESTMENT (I)**    Known formally as "gross private domestic investment", investment spending accounts for approximately 16% of GDP *(Figure
2-5)*. The two broadest categories of investment are nonresidential and residential. The nonresidential component includes
spending on plant and equipment (auto factories, computers,
and oil rigs). Residential investment is just that: single-family
and multi-family home buildings *(Figure 2-6)*. The third part of
investment spending is the change in business inventories. If
inventories are excluded, our GDP estimate will be incorrect. To
understand why, it is important to recognize that in calculating
GDP we are essentially adding up the dollar amount of goods

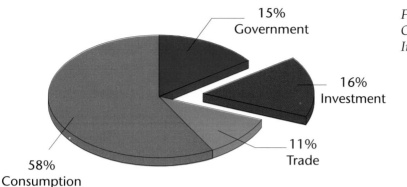

15%
Government

16%
Investment

11%
Trade

58%
Consumption

*Figure 2-5*
*Composition of GDP:*
*Investment*

Percentages represent portion of final demand.

*purchased* by consumers, businesses, and government. But GDP represents the amount of goods *produced*. If, for example, General Electric produces 100 refrigerators but sells only 90, its inventory level will rise by 10 refrigerators. If we merely add up the amounts spent on goods purchased in that quarter, actual production will be understated — we only counted the 90 refrigerators that were sold. The 10 refrigerators, which were produced but not sold, will *not* be counted. Thus, we must incorporate the change in business inventories in our GDP calculation. If inventories are rising, the rise in business inventories is *added to* GDP. If inventories are falling, the fall in business inventories is *subtracted from* GDP.

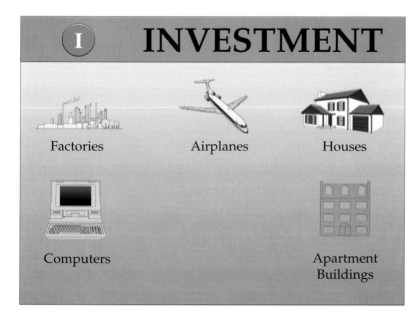

*Figure 2-6*
*What Is Investment*
*Spending?*

GOVERNMENT (G)   The next component of GDP is "G," or government spending. As you are well aware, the government spends a lot of money. While the benefits are sometimes debatable, the Commerce Department assumes that the government's outlays count toward the GDP totals. In other words, government purchases of nuclear weapons, tanks, and highways end up as income for someone (Figure 2-7). Government spending — federal, state,

*Figure 2-7*
*What Is Included in*
*Government*
*Spending?*

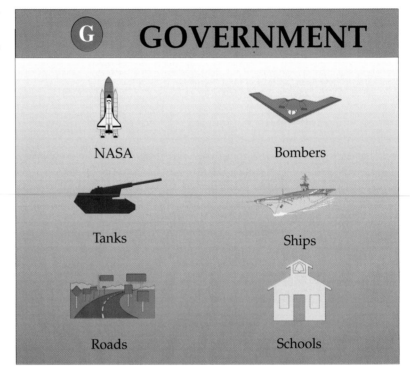

*Figure 2-8*
*Composition of GDP:*
*Government*

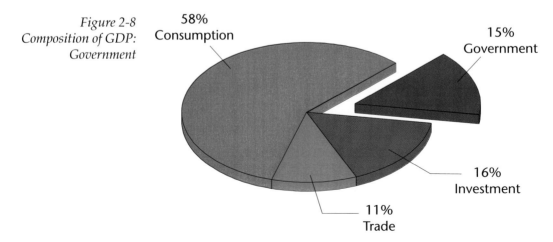

Percentages represent portion of final demand.

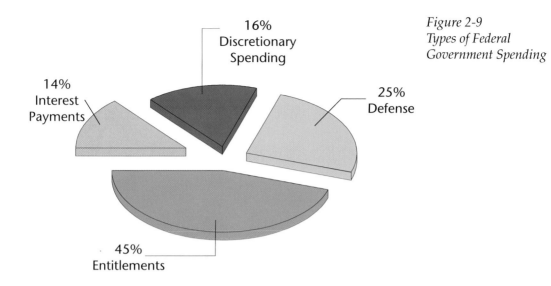

Figure 2-9
Types of Federal
Government Spending

and local — accounts for approximately 15% of GDP *(Figure 2-8)*. Federal spending is roughly 36% of total government expenditures. The major categories in the federal budget are entitlements (Social Security, Medicare, and veterans benefits), 45%; defense (aircraft carriers, bombs, and tanks), 25%; "discretionary" spending (NASA, the Park Service, the IRS, and the FBI), 16%; and interest payments, 14% *(Figure 2-9)*.

**NET EXPORTS (X - M)**

By all rights, the final component of GDP should be referred to as "net imports," instead of the traditional textbook term "net exports," since the United States has not experienced a surplus of exports over imports in quite some time. In any case, exports *add* to GDP because these goods and services are produced here, and imports *subtract* from GDP because they are produced by a foreign country or overseas firm. The principal goods that the U.S. exports and imports are shown in *Figure 2-10*. The importance of the trade sector has increased in recent years, and it now represents about 11% of total spending in the economy *(Figure 2-11)*. The United States currently runs a huge deficit on goods and services (that is, X - M is negative), in the amount of $110 billion per year in current dollars. It should be noted here that the "market-moving" *monthly* trade figures reflect merchandise and services only. In the *quarterly* GDP report, the U.S. net export balance includes "invisibles", such as freight, insurance, and so forth. (See Chapter 20 for more details.)

*Figure 2-10*
*What the United States*
*Exports and Imports*

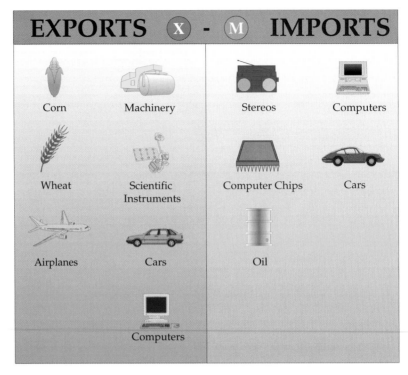

*Figure 2-11*
*Composition of GDP:*
*Trade*

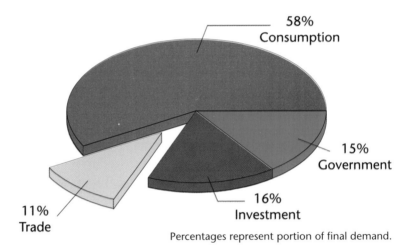

Percentages represent portion of final demand.

**THE PRIMARY
MEASURE OF
PRODUCTION IN
THE U.S. USED TO BE
"GNP"**

Prior to August 1991 the primary measure of production in the United States was GNP rather than GDP. Both measures are defined in terms of goods and services produced, but there is a conceptual difference between the two. Specifically, GDP measures goods and services produced *in the United States*. GNP represents good and services produced *by U.S. residents anywhere in the world*. This means that if a U.S. factory produces goods in

Germany, for example, that output is included in GNP but not in GDP. Similarly, if a foreign firm builds something in the United States, that production is *not* included in GNP (because this concept includes only goods and services produced by U.S. residents), but is counted in GDP (because this measures the goods and services produced in the U.S.). To move from GDP back to GNP, you must *add* the value of goods and services produced by U.S. residents overseas (known technically as "factor income receipts from foreigners"), and *subtract* the value of goods and services produced by foreign entities in the United States (or "factor income payments to foreigners). U.S. officials decided to make this conceptual change for two reasons. First, it makes analysis of the economy a bit simpler because GDP is consistent in coverage with other indicators such as employment, productivity, industrial production, and investment spending. Second, it facilitates comparisons of economic activity in the United States with that in other countries. GDP is the primary measure of production in the System of National Accounts, which is the set of international guidelines that virtually every other country uses. While there is clearly a difference in the two measures conceptually, there is very little difference in terms of dollar levels. This is because, as shown in *Figure 2-12*, net receipts (receipts from foreigners less payments to foreigners) is quite small. Indeed, the level of GDP is only about $7.0B or 0.1% larger than the level of GNP. Some may contend that this is much ado about nothing!

| ITEM | 1994 (Billions of Dollars) |
|---|---|
| Gross Domestic Product (GDP) | $5,344.0 |
| Plus:  Factor income receipts from foreigners | $130.7 |
| Less:  Factor income payments to foreigners | $137.4 |
| Equals: Gross National Product (GNP) | $5,337.3 |

*Figure 2-12*
*GDP Versus GNP*

Prior to 1995 the Commerce Department emphasized a "fixed-weight" measure of GDP constructed by valuing goods and services at prices that existed in some base period and then summing to a total.  But output measures which use fixed price weights tend to overstate growth in the current period.  This tendency is known as "substitution bias."  The Commerce Department provided a simple example using apples and oranges that illustrates this so-called substitution bias.

IN LATE 1995 THE COMMERCE DEPARTMENT CONVERTED TO A "CHAIN-WEIGHTED" MEASURE OF GDP TO ELIMINATE SUBSTITUTION BIAS

|          |          | Expenditures | Quantity | Price  |
|----------|----------|--------------|----------|--------|
|          | Oranges: | $3.00        | 30       | $0.10  |
| Year 1   | Apples:  | 2.00         | 10       | 0.20   |
|          | Total:   | $5.00        |          |        |
|          |          |              |          |        |
|          | Oranges: | $4.00        | 20       | 0.20   |
| Year 2   | Apples:  | 5.00         | 20       | 0.25   |
|          | Total:   | $9.00        |          |        |

**SUBSTITUTION BIAS OCCURS AS CONSUMERS SHIFT THEIR SPENDING PATTERNS IN RESPONSE TO PRICE CHANGES**

In this example, *nominal GDP* rose from $5.00 to $9.00. But part of that additional spending came about because of increases in the prices of both oranges and apples. To calculate *real GDP*, we first have to pick a base year. Suppose we let Year 1 be the base year. This means that we want to value GDP in "Year 1" prices. In that event, real GDP in Year 1, also happens to be $5.00 (in the base year nominal and real GDP are always the same). In Year 2, however, we value the spending on apples and oranges using Year 1 prices. Thus, real orange spending is (20 x $0.10) or $2.00, while real apple spending is (20 x $0.20) or $4.00. This implies that real GDP in Year 2 is $6.00, which represents an increase of 20%.

But suppose now that we use Year 2 as the base. In this case, both nominal and real GDP in Year 2 are $9.00. To calculate real GDP in Year 1, we value the quantity in Year 1 by the prices that existed in Year 2. Thus, real GDP in Year 1 is (30 x $0.20) or $6.00 for oranges plus (10 x $0.25) or $2.50 for apples, or $8.50. The percentage increase is now 5.9% instead of the 20% gain measured with Year 1 as the base year. The reason that the 20% growth rate calculated using Year 1 as the base is higher than the 5.9% growth rate using Year 2 as the base is because consumers substituted apples for oranges between Year 1 and Year 2 as the price of oranges rose much more rapidly than the price of apples — hence, the name "substitution bias".

**UNDER A "FIXED-WEIGHT" SYSTEM GDP GROWTH RATES ARE REVISED EVERY FIVE YEARS**

The first important point to note is that under a fixed-weight system of calculating real GDP growth, the growth rate is dependent upon which base period is selected. Every time the base year changes, GDP growth rates are revised for every single year. For example, one might think that GDP growth in a particular year was 3.0%, but once we get the 5-year revision, it may turn out that growth was only 2.2%. And when we get the *next* 5-year revision, GDP growth could slip still further to 2.0%. This is a problem; we can never state with certainty, for example, that GDP growth in 1993 was 3.2%; it is all subject to revision years after the fact.

There is no question that it is preferable to calculate real GDP using prices that exist in the more recent time period. A more real-world example using automobiles and computers will illustrate this point.

|       |            | Expenditures | Quantity | Price    |
|-------|------------|--------------|----------|----------|
|       | Autos:     | $16,500      | 1        | $16,500  |
| 1987  | Computers: | 16,500       | 1        | 16,500   |
|       | Total:     | $33,000      |          |          |
|       |            |              |          |          |
|       | Autos:     | $20,000      | 1        | 20,000   |
| 1995  | Computers: | 4,500        | 1        | 4,500    |
|       | Total:     | $24,500      |          |          |

In 1987 a car and a computer both had prices of about $16,500. If consumers bought 1 of each in 1987, then both nominal and real GDP in that year would be $33,000. But by 1995 the price of a new car had risen to about $20,000, while the price of a comparable power computer fell to $4,500. Thus, real GDP in 1995 should be $24,500, a decline of almost 26%. But when the Commerce Department calculated GDP in 1987 dollars, it valued both autos and computers using 1987 prices. Doing so implied that real GDP in 1995 was $33,000 or unchanged from what it was in 1987. In reality, real GDP should have fallen 26%. Clearly, the fixed-weight method grossly overstates GDP growth. It seems intuitively obvious that we should not value a computer today at its 1987 price of $16,500 when a comparable power machine costs only $4,500.

This measurement problem with real GDP is known as "substitution bias." In general, when the relative price of a good or service falls, people substitute towards that good or service. Thus, goods and services whose relative prices are declining tend to have the most rapid rate of growth. But because those goods and services are valued at the price in the base period rather than at current prices, those goods and services will be overweighted in years beyond the base year and be underweighted in years prior to the base year.

With a base year of 1987, real GDP growth was biased downwards prior to 1987 and biased upwards in recent years. As shown in the table below, this bias got bigger the farther away from the base year. Switching to a 1992 base year *reduced* the upward bias to recent years but *increased* the downward bias for years prior to 1987.

UNDER A FIXED-WEIGHT SYSTEM, GROWTH IN YEARS BEYOND THE BASE YEAR TEND TO BE BIASED UPWARDS

|      | Real GDP (1978$) | Real GDP (Chain-weighted) | Difference |
|------|------------------|----------------------------|------------|
| 1990 | +1.2%            | +1.2%                      | 0.0%       |
| 1991 | -0.6%            | -0.7%                      | +0.1%      |
| 1992 | +2.3%            | +2.1%                      | +0.2%      |
| 1993 | +3.1%            | +2.5%                      | +0.6%      |
| 1994 | +4.1%            | +3.6%                      | +0.5%      |
| 1995 | +3.2%            | +2.4%                      | +0.8%      |

**SUBSTITUTION BIAS IS A PROBLEM FOR SEVERAL ECONOMIC INDICATORS**

It should be noted that substitution bias is a problem not just for the calculation of real GDP. It affects fixed-weight *price* measures such as the consumer price index (CPI) and the Commerce Department's featured measure of prices, the fixed-weight price deflator. In these measures, prices of various goods and services are weighted according to the amount of each good and service purchased in the base year. Because consumers tend to substitute away from goods and services whose prices are rising most rapidly, these fixed-weight price measures overweight the items with the highest prices and are thus biased upward after the base year. Keep in mind, too, that GDP data are used to assess such issues as productivity, returns to investment, and the long-term potential growth rate of the economy. The CPI data are used to determine the annual cost of living adjustments for Social Security recipients. Thus, minimizing the distortions arising from this so-called substitution bias is quite important.

**SUBSTITUTION BIAS BECAME A SERIOUS PROBLEM IN THE EARLY 1980S AS COMPUTER PRICES FELL SHARPLY**

Prior to the 1970s this bias associated with fixed-weighted measures was small enough to be safely ignored. But then in the early 1980s computers provided a classic case of substitution bias. At that time computers prices began to decline rapidly while computer output surged. Under the then current fixed-weight system of measuring real GDP, each computer produced was valued at its 1987 price. But, as we all know, the prices of computers have fallen dramatically since that time. Thus, the 1987-dollar based series was seriously overstated.

**A CHAIN-WEIGHT GDP MEASURE ELIMINATES SUBSTITUTION BIAS**

To address this problem of having to select a base year, the Commerce Department came up with what it calls a "chain-weighted" index to eliminate this base period bias. In the chain-weighted method of aggregation, these problems are avoided because the change in real output between successive years depends *only* on relative prices in those years, not on relative prices in some base year. To use the oranges/apples example above, we determined that GDP growth in Year 2 was 20% if Year 1 was used as the base period, but 5.9% if Year 2 was the base. The new chain-weighted measure is the geometric mean of growth rates calculated using each of the two base-year choices.

The 20% and 5.9% growth rates are used to calculate a growth rate that is not sensitive to the base year by adding both to the number 1, multiplying them together, and taking the square root. In this case we get: $(1.20 \times 1.059)$ ^ ½, which gives us 1.127, or 12.7%. These annual growth rates are then "chained" together to form a time series for real GDP. This seems a bit complicated, but the growth rate for real GDP can be *estimated* fairly accurately by taking the average of the two growth rates calculated by using price weights for the current year and the prior year, in this case, (20% + 5.9%) / 2, or 13.0%.

Given the apparent advantages of a chain-weighted index, one might ask why we ever adopted a fixed-weight measure to begin with. There are essentially six reasons for this. First, a fixed-weight index is quite simple to calculate. As shown in the example above, we simply multiply price times quantity for every good and service in the base year, and add them up. We then do the same thing for every other year *except* we value the quantities produced using prices that existed in the base year. Second, the index may be stated in terms of real dollars. For example, we can say that real GDP in 1995 was $5,483.0B. Third, any two periods can be compared on a consistent basis. If we know the level of GDP for 1993 and the level for 1995, we can easily figure out the growth rate over that two-year period. Fourth, the components of GDP will always add up to the total. Fifth, by knowing the dollar level for the various components and the total, one can quickly ascertain the importance of any particular spending category. It is easy to determine that consumption spending, for example, is about 60% of real GDP. And, finally, it allows us to compare our GDP level with that of other countries. Thus, there are some clear advantages for a fixed-weight system. Its primary disadvantage, substitution bias, had not been a particularly big problem until lately. But with the recent drastic decline in the price of computers, and the consequent surge in computer sales, this distortion increased to the point where it became a significant problem.

A CHAIN-WEIGHT INDEX SOLVES THE SUBSTITUTION BIAS PROBLEM BUT HAS PROBLEMS OF ITS OWN

A chain-weighted system, as we have seen, eliminates this substitution bias. By calculating a GDP growh rate solely on the basis of prices for the current and previous years, one does not have to pick an arbitrary base year. It has a second advantage in that one gets away from big revisions to GDP growth whenever the base year is changed. But this system also has drawbacks. First of all, instead of a level for GDP of say, $5,483.0B, we have to work with an index number, i.e., something like GDP in the second quarter of 1995 was 118.3 (which means that it was 18.3%

A FIXED-WEIGHT MEASURE HAS SEVERAL ADVANTAGES BUT ONE BIG DISADVANTAGE — SUBSTITUTION BIAS higher than in the base year). Second, because there is not a real dollar level for GDP, it is difficult to compare the size of our economy to that of other countries. Third, for the same reason (i.e., we are dealing with indexes rather than dollar amounts), it is difficult to determine the relative importance of any particular sector. To get around some of these disadvantages, the Commerce Department came up with a 1992 dollar series, which is similar to what we had been getting previously. They also now provide dollar levels for both GDP and its major components, which helps determine the relative importance of various sectors. But one problem here is that those sectors do not add up to the total. They are close, but not quite. Nevertheless, the elimination of substitution bias alone probably justifies the shift. As we go forward and become more familiar with the data, we will probably find that we can live with the shortcomings.

A LOOK BACK   What is the long-run track record of the U.S. economy? What constitutes above-average growth? How do we define a recession? These are some of the questions we discuss in this section. As *Figure 2-13* demonstrates, the average sustainable growth rate for inflation-adjusted, or real, GDP appears to be somewhere between 2.5% and 3%. While the U.S. has periodically enjoyed growth rates in excess of 6%, expansions of this magnitude are usually short-lived. The main reason is inflation. When the economy is growing rapidly, firms — experiencing robust demand for their products and services — invariably raise prices. At some point, price gains begin to exceed wage increases, thereby halting the consumer's ability to spend. Or, if the consumer continues to spend with borrowed money, the Federal Reserve tightens monetary policy — the resulting higher interest rates bring an end to business investment and consumer debt expansion. Usually, some of each scenario takes place and the boom is brought to a close.

In an economic downturn, known as a recession, the reverse is true: There is insufficient demand from consumers, business, and government to sustain activity. On at least seven occasions since World War II the U.S. economy has slipped into recession — defined as two consecutive quarters when real GDP is negative. The most recent recessions occurred in the 1974-75, 1980-82, and 1990-91 periods.

*Figure 2-13 How Real GDP Affects Inflation*

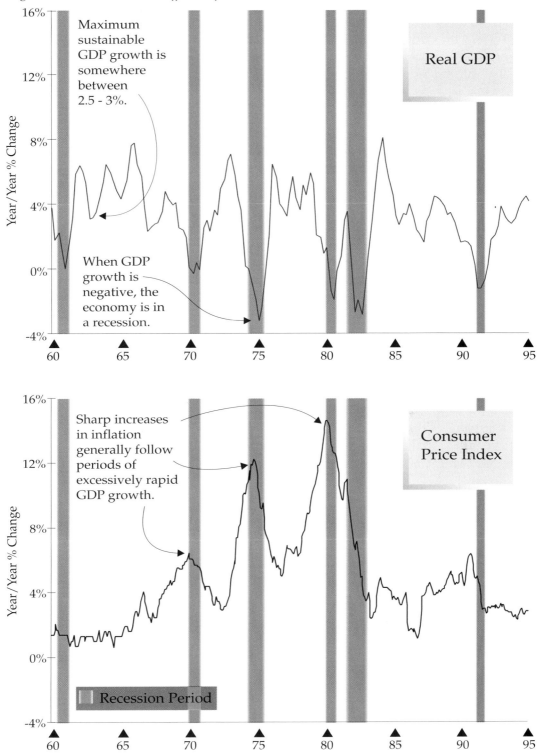

THERE ARE THREE
GDP ESTIMATES FOR
EVERY QUARTER

The monthly GDP report, put together by the Bureau of Economic Analysis (BEA) of the Department of Commerce, is generally released in the third week of the month. For each quarterly GDP number, there are three separate estimates. The initial look at GDP, known as the "advance" report, is released in the first month of the following quarter. This means, for example, that the advance report for the first quarter of the year comes in April. This early snapshot of the economy is based on three months of data for consumption spending and two months of data for most of the other GDP components. Thus, it is relatively incomplete. Furthermore, some of the figures on which the advance report is based — such as retail sales — are subject to large revisions. As you might expect, since this first estimate of GDP growth is not particularly accurate, a GDP "revision game" is played in each of the following two months when BEA provides what are known as the "preliminary" and "revised" estimates. Therefore, analysts and investors get to track a particular quarter's GDP over a three-month period. The difference between the advance report and the final version two months later can be substantial. To complicate matters further, the BEA issues "benchmark" revisions each July in which it recalculates all the numbers going back three years.

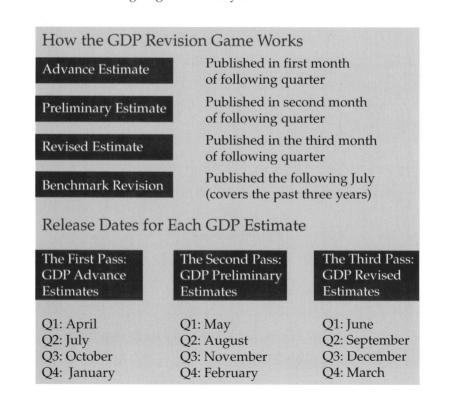

How the GDP Revision Game Works

| Advance Estimate | Published in first month of following quarter |
| Preliminary Estimate | Published in second month of following quarter |
| Revised Estimate | Published in the third month of following quarter |
| Benchmark Revision | Published the following July (covers the past three years) |

Release Dates for Each GDP Estimate

| The First Pass: GDP Advance Estimates | The Second Pass: GDP Preliminary Estimates | The Third Pass: GDP Revised Estimates |
| --- | --- | --- |
| Q1: April | Q1: May | Q1: June |
| Q2: July | Q2: August | Q2: September |
| Q3: October | Q3: November | Q3: December |
| Q4: January | Q4: February | Q4: March |

## THE IMPLICIT DEFLATOR MEASURES PRICE CHANGES AND CHANGES IN SPENDING PATTERNS

Along with GDP, the Commerce Department estimates two price deflators — the implicit and fixed-weight deflators — which are actually two different measures of inflation. The implicit deflator is the one cited most often, but it should be noted that it is *not* a pure measure of inflation. Rather, the implicit deflator measures a combination of price changes *and* changes in the composition of GDP. For example, if prices are absolutely unchanged between one quarter and the next, but GDP is composed of more high-priced goods in the later quarter, the implicit deflator will register an increase *(Figure 2-15).* The classic textbook example is the substitution of butter for margarine: If the prices of butter and margarine do not change, but consumers suddenly feel wealthier and start buying more butter and less margarine, the implicit deflator rises. There is now a larger weight given to the higher priced good. A more up-to-date example is in the housing industry: As plumbers substitute relatively inexpensive plastic pipe for more costly copper tubing, the implicit price deflator declines (or at least has a downward bias). Thus, the implicit deflator provides some information about how consumers and firms respond to inflation by changing their spending patterns. Certainly that information is useful. In fact, some analysts believe that the deflator is a more relevant concept than a pure price measure. Keep in mind, however, that the deflator does not tell us precisely what is happening to inflation.

## THE FIXED-WEIGHT DEFLATOR TELLS US WHAT IS HAPPENING TO INFLATION

The fixed-weight deflator, on the other hand, is a *pure* measure of inflation. It is not tainted by changes in the composition of GDP. Basically, the Commerce Department takes all the goods that are included in the implicit deflator and holds the market weights constant. As a result, the fixed-weight deflator provides a measure of price changes for an extremely large basket of goods and services — over 5,000 items are included. In terms of coverage, the fixed-weight deflator is clearly the most important inflation measure that exists. The number of items dwarfs that of either the PPI or CPI. Nevertheless, this measure does have some significant drawbacks. Because it measures prices on all goods and services produced in the United States, the fixed-weight deflator is, by definition, a strictly *domestic* inflation gauge. What about all the goods that are imported? When the dollar is falling, prices of imported goods and services rise. In this type of environment, as in the 1985-86 period, the fixed-weight deflator

**THE GDP REPORT ALSO CONTAINS INFORMATION ABOUT INFLATION**

Figure 2-15
How the Fixed-Weight
and Implicit Price
Deflators Work

| First Quarter | Margarine | Butter | |
|---|---|---|---|
| Price | $.80 | $1.00 | = $1.80 |
| x Quantity Sold | 10 | 10 | |
| Total Spent | $8.00 | $10.00 | = $18.00 |

Fixed Price Deflator

| Second Quarter | Margarine | Butter | |
|---|---|---|---|
| Price | $.80 | $1.00 | = $1.80 |
| x Quantity Sold | 8 | 12 | |
| Total Spent | $6.40 | $12.00 | = $18.40 |

Implicit Deflator

The *fixed price deflator*, which reflects price changes, shows no change.

The *implicit deflator*, which reflects both price changes and changes in spending patterns, has risen by 2.2% because consumers feel wealthier and therefore buy more of the high-priced goods.

understates the true rate of inflation. During a period of rising (or falling) prices for imported goods, the CPI is a more appropriate measure. It covers a smaller basket of goods — only some 300 to 400 items — but it has the advantage that imported goods are included in proportion to their importance in overall consumer spending *(Figure 2-16)*.

Figure 2-16 Comparison of Inflation Measures

| | Facts | Advantages | Disadvantages |
|---|---|---|---|
| **PPI** | 3,450 commodities Wholesale prices | Broad-based measure | Goods only; No services |
| **CPI** | 365 goods and services | Includes goods as well as services. Includes some imported products. | Small sample size |
| **Fixed-Weight Deflator** | 5,000+ goods and services | Broadest measure of inflation | Domestic measure only. Includes no imported goods. |
| **Implicit Deflator** | 5,000+ goods and services | Captures changes in spending patterns caused by reaction to inflation. | Not a pure measure of inflation. |

In sum, the implicit and fixed-weight deflators are important measures of inflation. Both have drawbacks, but their broad range of coverage enhances their appeal. (See also Chapters 7 and 12).

A good example of how the markets respond to GDP data can be found in the 1.2% growth rate for the second quarter of 1990. As usual, it is important to note what the market was expecting. The consensus view approaching the data release of July 27, 1990, was for Q:2 GDP growth of approximately 1.8%. Not only was the actual pace lower than anticipated, but the Commerce Department simultaneously released benchmark revisions going back to 1987. (Recall that, in July, the benchmark revisions covering the previous three years are released.) Instead of a 1989 growth rate of 2.6%, the Department said it was only 1.8%. Moreover, GDP for the first quarter of 1990 dropped to 1.7% from 1.9%. All this was wonderful news for the bond market — the 30-year Treasury bond yield fell to 8.48% from the prior day's close of 8.55%. By the following day, the yield was down to 8.41%. Short-term rates fell as well. We will see again and again that sluggish growth is taken positively by the fixed-income markets *(Figure 2-17)*.

**BONDS LIKE WEAK GDP GROWTH**

In this example, the GDP news was not well received by the stock market. There had been worries for some time that the economy was flirting with a recession and corporate profits had been sinking for months. The equity market was not pleased to hear that growth was even lower than anticipated. Sometimes the stock market shrugs off indications of weak GDP — if interest rates decline significantly in an environment of decent profits. On this occasion, however, the DOW headed south by some 22 points.

**STOCKS DO NOT**

For the dollar, the new information was bearish. With inflation still relatively high — and with a perception lurking that the Federal Reserve would be forced to ease credit anyway — the greenback declined against most major currencies. Sluggish growth and lower interest rates usually are viewed negatively by those holding long dollar positions. In addition, rates in Germany and Japan, in real terms, were already higher than U.S. rates. Thus, there was an immediate reallocation of so-called "hot money" seeking higher yields elsewhere.

**NEITHER DOES THE DOLLAR**

*Figure 2-17*
*Market Reaction to*
*GDP*

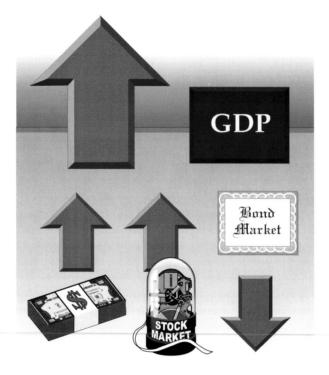

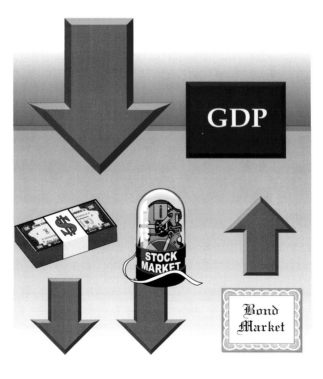

THE FIRST HINT

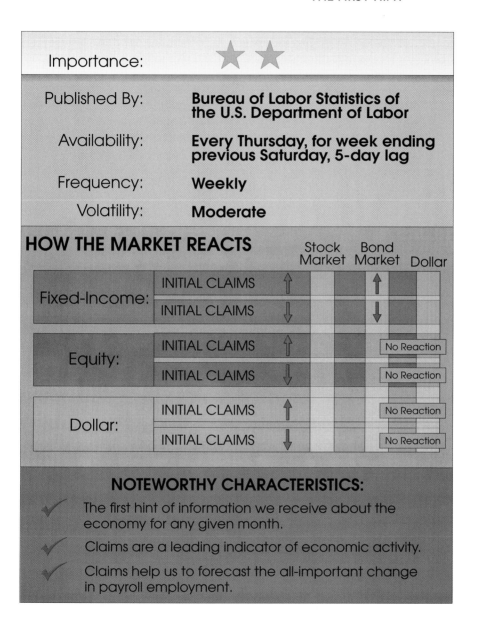

| Importance: | ★ ★ |
|---|---|
| Published By: | **Bureau of Labor Statistics of the U.S. Department of Labor** |
| Availability: | **Every Thursday, for week ending previous Saturday, 5-day lag** |
| Frequency: | **Weekly** |
| Volatility: | **Moderate** |

## HOW THE MARKET REACTS

| | | Stock Market | Bond Market | Dollar |
|---|---|---|---|---|
| Fixed-Income: | INITIAL CLAIMS ⇑ | | ⇑ | |
| | INITIAL CLAIMS ⇓ | | ⇓ | |
| Equity: | INITIAL CLAIMS ⇑ | | No Reaction | |
| | INITIAL CLAIMS ⇓ | | No Reaction | |
| Dollar: | INITIAL CLAIMS ↑ | | | No Reaction |
| | INITIAL CLAIMS ⇓ | | | No Reaction |

## NOTEWORTHY CHARACTERISTICS:

✓ The first hint of information we receive about the economy for any given month.

✓ Claims are a leading indicator of economic activity.

✓ Claims help us to forecast the all-important change in payroll employment.

**INITIAL CLAIMS ARE A MEASURE OF HOW MANY PEOPLE FILE FOR UNEMPLOYMENT BENEFITS EACH WEEK**

Initial unemployment claims are a measure of how many people are filing for unemployment benefits *for the first time* in any given week. As such, it provides an indication of how quickly the ranks of the unemployed are growing. Unfortunately, many people who get laid off and subsequently find a job, will get laid off again in that same year. When they reapply for unemployment insurance benefits, they are no longer counted as a "first-time applicant" and are, therefore, not counted in the initial claims data for that week. But if they meet the requirements for their state, they may still be eligible to receive benefits. If so, they are included in a second series, which is known as "continued claims." This series, therefore, is sometimes known as the number of "people receiving benefits."

**ELIGIBILITY FOR UNEMPLOYMENT BENEFITS IS DETERMINED INDIVIDUALLY BY EACH STATE**

The administration of and eligibility requirements for receiving jobless benefits are determined individually by each state. As a result, coverage can vary. Some states will pay workers who are on strike; others will not. Some states will pay agricultural workers for those periods of time when they are not harvesting crops, but most do not. Similarly, there may be waiting periods of a week or two in some states before one can apply for unemploy-

*Figure 3-1*
*Initial Claims and the Business Cycle*

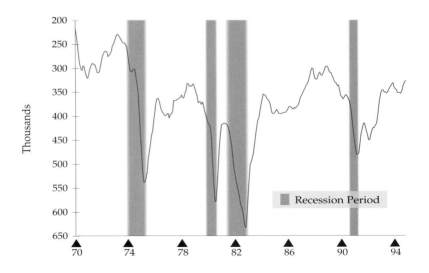

ment insurance benefits, but in other states you can file immediately. There are times when the Federal government becomes involved. For example, when the economy dips into a lengthy recession and unemployed workers are exhausting their state benefits, the Federal government will generally step in. Typically, it will extend the duration of support for the unemployed for up to twice the normal length of coverage. But these extended benefits are only temporary — the Federal government is not involved in providing jobless benefits on a *continuing* basis. This is supposed to be the responsibility of the states. The most recent occasion when the Federal government provided these additional benefits was from August 1992 through December 1993.

Because they are released on a weekly basis, initial unemployment claims are quite timely. Every Thursday morning at 8:30 A.M. eastern time, we learn what happened to claims in the week that ended the previous Saturday. Thus, there is only a very short, five-day lag between the time that a week ends and the time we actually see the data. The only other semi-important pieces of information that are released on a weekly basis are the Johnson Redbook data and the ABC/Money Magazine measure of consumer comfort. The Johnson Redbook provides weekly data on chain and department store sales. However, its relationship to the general merchandise and apparel store sales reported in the monthly retail sales release is quite loose. Thus, we do not believe that this series warrants its own chapter, but we will discuss it briefly in the chapter on retail sales. The ABC/Money Magazine survey of consumer comfort is a reasonably good weekly indicator of consumer sentiment, but it does not receive much attention from the markets. For this reason we believe that it, too, does not warrant its own chapter, but we have included it in the discussion of consumer sentiment in Chapter 10. So, of all the weekly pieces of information, we regard the claims data as the most important.

**INITIAL CLAIMS ARE VALUABLE BECAUSE THEY ARE THE FIRST PIECE OF INFORMATION ABOUT THE ECONOMY FOR ANY GIVEN MONTH**

There is another reason why the claims data are influential — they are a good leading indicator of economic activity *(see Figure 3-1)*. When the economy is in a recession, for example, and a business owner is beginning to sense an improvement, he does not rush out to hire additional workers. But he *may* not be as inclined to lay off someone now as he might have been a month or two earlier. He might need that person a couple of months down the road if his sales begin to perk up. As a result, fewer people show up at unemployment offices each week and, hence,

**INITIAL CLAIMS ARE ONE OF THE ELEVEN COMPONENTS OF THE INDEX OF LEADING INDICATORS**

there are fewer initial claimants. In general, initial claims decline prior to a pickup in payroll employment. Similarly, when economic conditions are deteriorating, some workers are going to be laid off and claims will rise. But other firms will still be hiring and, as a result, employment growth may remain robust for another couple of months. Thus, a rise in claims is an indication that labor market conditions are getting worse and payroll employment may soon fall. Because initial unemployment claims seem to foreshadow changes in the pace of economic activity so well, the Commerce Department has seen fit to include a monthly average of claims as one of the eleven components of its index of leading indicators.

*Figure 3-2 Claims Versus Change in Employment*

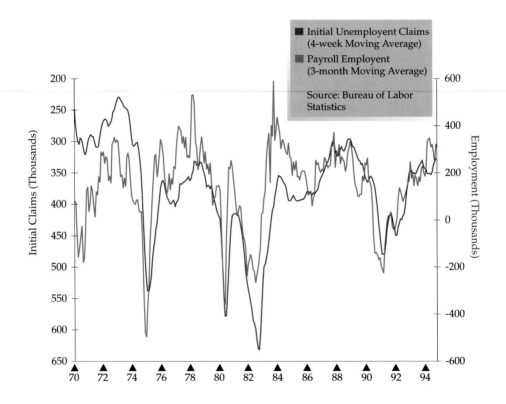

**INITIAL CLAIMS HELP US ESTIMATE PAYROLL EMPLOYMENT**

As detailed in Chapter 6, the most important piece of information we receive each month is the employment report, because it provides an in-depth look at a host of economic sectors. Because initial unemployment claims help us forecast payroll employment — which is probably the most critical piece of information contained in the employment report — they, too, are important.

And since changes in payroll employment can trigger wild reactions in the fixed-income markets, anything that helps us forecast payrolls is, by definition, also important. As shown in *Figure 3-2*, there is a reasonable correlation between a *4-week moving average* of initial unemployment claims and a *3-month moving average* of payroll employment. Thus, the *trends* in these two series are important. But when we use claims to estimate payroll employment on a *monthly* basis, the relationship is far more tenuous. There are simply too many factors that affect payroll employment that may, or may not, be captured in the claims data. Weather, natural catastrophes, and strikes quickly come to mind. The differences in the coverage provided by the various states means that the link between initial unemployment claims and payroll employment is a bit loose. Furthermore, as we noted previously, claims are a *leading* indicator of economic activity, while payroll employment is a *coincident* indicator. Thus, lagged values of claims are also helpful in making our forecasts of payroll employment. Despite these difficulties there is at least a *reasonable* correlation between initial claims and payroll employment. For this reason, economists eagerly await the claims data each Thursday.

Each month people are hired and people are fired. Initial claims provide us with information about the second part of this equation — the number of people who are being laid off — but they tell us nothing about hiring. The number of people receiving benefits, however, should capture both of the ways that employment can change. If someone is hired, the number of people receiving benefits declines. If someone is laid off for the first time, or for the second or third time for that matter, the number of people receiving benefits will rise. One might think that this series would track better with changes in payroll employment but, statistically, we have had slightly better luck with the claims data alone. The benefits data, however, seem to do a better job than the claims data in estimating the unemployment rate.

**THE NUMBER OF PEOPLE RECEIVING BENEFITS SEEMS TO TRACK THE UNEMPLOYMENT RATE FAIRLY WELL**

Weekly data are notoriously volatile. For that reason alone, economists are reluctant to attach much significance to the change for a particular week. Instead, we like to focus our attention on the 4-week moving average of claims, which provides a better indication of changes in the trend rate of employment.

**AS WITH ANY WEEKLY SERIES, THE DATA CAN BE QUITE VOLATILE**

**THE DATA ON CLAIMS AND BENEFITS ARE PUBLISHED WEEKLY BY THE BUREAU OF LABOR STATISTICS**

The Bureau of Labor Statistics, a division of the Department of Labor, gathers data on both initial unemployment claims and the number of people receiving unemployment benefits each week from the various state employment offices. The data are for the week that ends on Saturday and are published by the BLS five days later — on Thursday of the following week.

**A RISE IN CLAIMS HELPS THE BOND MARKET**

An increase in initial unemployment claims is an indication that labor market conditions are beginning to soften, presumably in response to a dropoff in the demand for goods and services. Slower growth is always helpful for the bond market because slower growth implies lower interest rates, and lower interest rates imply higher bond prices *(Figure 3-3)*.

**THE STOCK MARKET RARELY REACTS TO THESE DATA**

While theoretically a rise in claims is an indication that the pace of economic activity is slowing, which could reduce corporate profits, the stock market rarely reacts to the data. Perhaps it is because the data are available weekly and the stock market concludes that an additional week's worth of data cannot be all that important. Or perhaps it is because the numbers are released one hour prior to the opening of the stock market, and by the opening bell the data have been largely forgotten. In any event, the stock market is rarely influenced by the initial claims data except to the extent that the bond market strongly reacts either positively or negatively.

**LIKE THE STOCK MARKET, THE DOLLAR RARELY RESPONDS TO THE CLAIMS DATA**

This is simply not a series that the foreign exchange market considers important. In theory, a rise in claims should suggest to the foreign exchange market that the pace of economic activity is slowing. If one were to believe that the Federal Reserve might ease as a result of this slower growth and that interest rates were going to decline, this should be bearish for the dollar. A drop in claims, which is indicative of a faster rate of growth and higher rates, should be bullish for the dollar. But, more often than not, the foreign exchange market ignores the Thursday ritual.

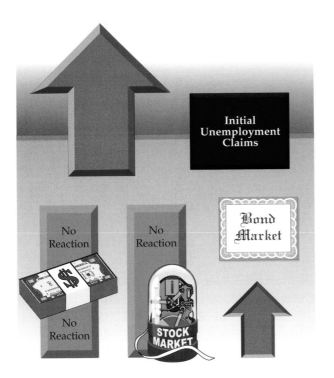

*Figure 3-3*
*Market Reaction to*
*Initial Unemployment*
*Claims*

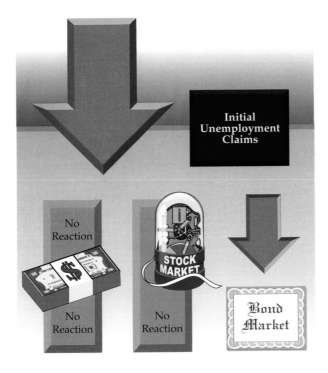

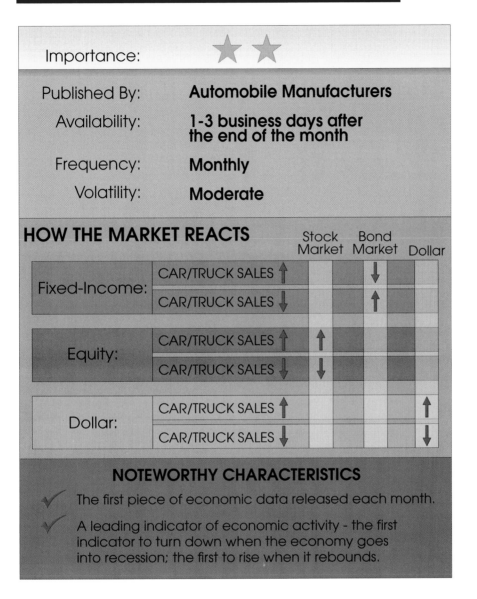

Importance: ★ ★

| | |
|---|---|
| Published By: | **Automobile Manufacturers** |
| Availability: | **1-3 business days after the end of the month** |
| Frequency: | **Monthly** |
| Volatility: | **Moderate** |

## HOW THE MARKET REACTS

| | | Stock Market | Bond Market | Dollar |
|---|---|---|---|---|
| Fixed-Income: | CAR/TRUCK SALES ↑ | | ↓ | |
| | CAR/TRUCK SALES ↓ | | ↑ | |
| Equity: | CAR/TRUCK SALES ↑ | ↑ | | |
| | CAR/TRUCK SALES ↓ | ↓ | | |
| Dollar: | CAR/TRUCK SALES ↑ | | | ↑ |
| | CAR/TRUCK SALES ↓ | | | ↓ |

## NOTEWORTHY CHARACTERISTICS

✓ The first piece of economic data released each month.

✓ A leading indicator of economic activity - the first indicator to turn down when the economy goes into recession; the first to rise when it rebounds.

## VEHICLE SALES PROVIDE AN EARLY HINT OF ECONOMIC STRENGTH OR WEAKNESS

Unit car and truck sales tell us the *number* of cars and trucks that were sold during a particular month and are released on the first business day of the following month. Hence, they are very timely. However, this number used to be even more important because it was released during the course of a month *for that same month*. Specifically, we saw data for each of the three 10-day periods of the month three business days later — it was the *very first* piece of information we saw each month concerning the strength or weakness of the economy. But in January 1994 the automobile manufacturers decided to stop releasing 10-day data and began publishing only on a monthly basis. The timeliness was thereby reduced. To further complicate matters, the data are not all reported on the same day. In the past, all of the automobile manufacturers reported sales data on the third business day of the month. But beginning February 1995, G.M., Chrysler, and most smaller manufacturers began to report their car and truck sales data on the *first* business day of the following month. Ford and Nissan, however, citing reporting difficulties, continue to release their data on the *third* business day of the month. While this arrangement is a bit messy, we have a fairly good idea of car and truck sales on the first business day of the month because the early reporters represent about 70% of the market. It should be noted that there is a private marketing/research firm that continues to provide 10-day data. However, its data for the month as a whole does not square with data that is ultimately reported by the manufacturers. Thus, this is *not* an adequate replacement for the previously reported 10-day data from the manufacturers. Indeed, it can sometimes be quite *misleading*.

## VEHICLE SALES PROVIDE CLUES ABOUT OTHER ECONOMIC INDICATORS

In addition to being relatively timely, car and truck sales have a second great strength. They provide us with an important clue concerning the retail sales and personal consumption expenditures (PCE) data to be released later in the month, both of which can be big market movers. Vehicle sales represent about 20% of retail sales and about 6% of consumption.

Car and truck sales have a third important feature. They give us an early warning signal of an impending recession and tell us when we can begin to expect a recovery. The underlying reason is that automotive sales are very sensitive to changes in interest rates and consumer psychology. If consumers become nervous about the economic outlook, or are bothered by rising interest rates, one of the first things they do is cancel plans to buy a new car. This makes sense because automobiles and housing are obviously the biggest-ticket items in the family budget. If you're going to cut costs, this is the place to start! Historically, the automobile and housing sectors of the economy are the first to turn down when economic conditions deteriorate. They are also the first sectors to experience a recovery *(Figure 4-1)*. Thus, car

**CAR AND TRUCK SALES WARN US ABOUT CHANGES IN THE PACE OF GDP GROWTH**

*Figure 4-1*
*How Real GDP Traces Auto Sales*

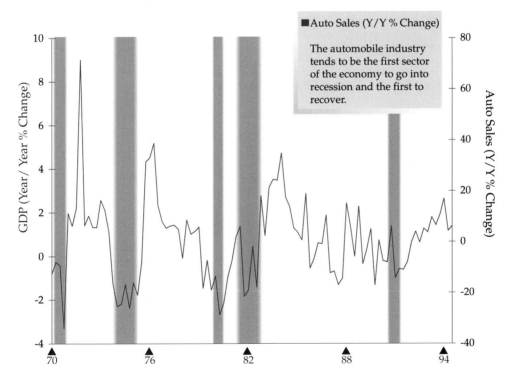

■ Auto Sales (Y/Y % Change)

The automobile industry tends to be the first sector of the economy to go into recession and the first to recover.

and truck sales tend to be a leading indicator of economic activity and can provide some clues concerning when the economy is about to undergo a major directional change. This is why we consider car sales data to be so valuable.

WHEN WE DISCUSS CAR SALES, WE REALLY MEAN CARS AND TRUCKS

It used to be that when market participants analyzed car sales, they specifically meant car sales. But in the past decade or so it has become *very* trendy to have a 4-wheel drive vehicle like a Jeep Cherokee or a Ford Bronco. But these vehicles are not cars. They are classified as "light trucks," and they have been selling like hotcakes. Ten years ago these so-called light trucks were 30% of the market. Five years ago their market share had jumped to 39%. Today it is 45%. In a few more years truck sales will surpass car sales in importance. But because market participants remember the old days when truck sales could almost be ignored, they generally refer to "car sales" when they are really talking about sales of both cars and light trucks. Do not be confused; the terms are generally synonymous!

RAW DATA MUST FIRST BE CONVERTED TO ANNUALIZED SELLING RATES

When unit sales data are released on the first and third business days of the month, sales for each manufacturer will be published. Although these raw statistics must be converted to seasonally adjusted annual selling rates to be meaningful, it's a simple process. The Commerce Department publishes the seasonal factors in advance, which adjust for both seasonal variation and differences in the number of selling days in each period. Analysts simply add up data for the individual manufacturers and divide by the seasonal factor to see what is happening *(Figure 4-2)*.

*Figure 4-2*
*Calculating Car Sales, March 1995*

| | |
|---|---:|
| GENERAL MOTORS | 259,495 |
| FORD | 158,511 |
| CHRYSLER | 80,948 |
| HONDA | 41,936 |
| TOYOTA | 39,729 |
| NISSAN | 35,885 |
| MAZDA | 13,534 |
| MITSUBISHI | 9,237 |
| SUBARU | 5,287 |
| SUZUKI | 417 |
| TOTAL SALES | 644,979 |
| SEASONAL FACTOR | 89.16 |
| SELLING RATE | 7,234T |

At the end of a month, when all the car and truck sales data are available, economists take these adjusted figures and attempt to estimate the automobile component of both retail sales and personal consumption expenditures. There is no question that the unit car sales data *help* in estimating the automobile component of the retail sales figure for the month. However, the relationship is not as close as it could be. First, these data represent *unit sales*, which means that we know the *number* of cars and trucks that were sold. In order to link car and truck sales to retail sales, we want to know the *dollar value* of those sales since the

CAR SALES DATA HELP TO ESTIMATE AUTOMOBILE COMPONENTS OF BOTH RETAIL SALES AND CONSUMPTION

*Figure 4-3*
*Personal Consumption Expenditures Versus Auto Sales*

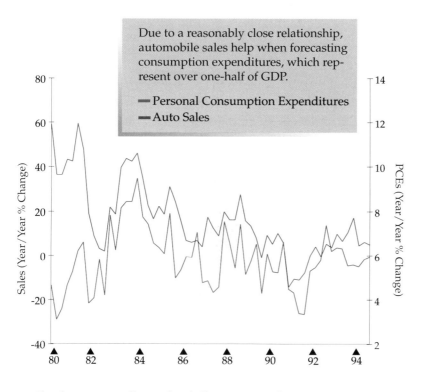

Due to a reasonably close relationship, automobile sales help when forecasting consumption expenditures, which represent over one-half of GDP.

━ Personal Consumption Expenditures
━ Auto Sales

retail sales report tells us the dollar amount that was spent on autos, trucks, and other goods during the course of the month. Second, the automobile component of retail sales also includes used car and truck sales and sales of automobile parts. For these two reasons, the relationship between unit car/truck sales and the auto component of retail sales is a loose one.

It is a bit easier to use the unit sales data to estimate the automobile component of personal consumption expenditures because, unlike retail sales, the consumption data do not include used cars and trucks *(Figure 4-3)*. In fact, the Commerce Department uses those same data, together with an estimate of the average value of new cars and trucks, to come up with its estimate.

CAR SALES CAN MOVE MARKETS

The car sales data are extremely important to the markets for the following reasons:

- · They are timely.
- · They help us to estimate other indicators that will be released later in the month.
- · They are generally a leading indicator of economic activity.

A stronger-than-expected figure on car and truck sales makes the fixed-income markets jittery since interest rates will rise and bond prices will fall *(Figure 4-4)*. A more rapid pace of car sales implies faster growth of both the consumption component of GDP and GDP itself. A pickup in the pace of economic activity could induce the Federal Reserve to tighten monetary policy by increasing interest rates. A slower pace of sales would trigger the opposite reaction.

From an equity point of view, a faster pace of car and truck sales is *usually* a positive event. A pickup in car sales would imply a stronger economy that, in turn, leads to higher profits — a plus for the stock market. The exception occurs when market participants believe that the economy is growing too quickly and fear a Federal Reserve tightening move. In that instance, the stock market reacts adversely.

The impact in the foreign exchange markets depends upon interest rates. If the bond market assumes that the Federal Reserve will tighten credit in response to a faster pace of economic activity, the dollar will strengthen.

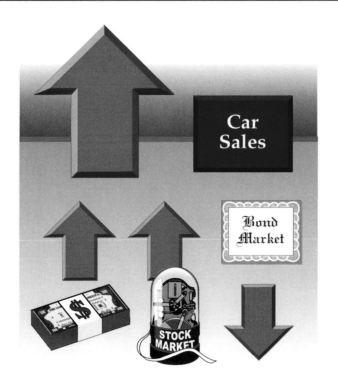

*Figure 4-4*
*Market Reaction to Car*
*Sales*

A VIEW FROM THE TRENCHES

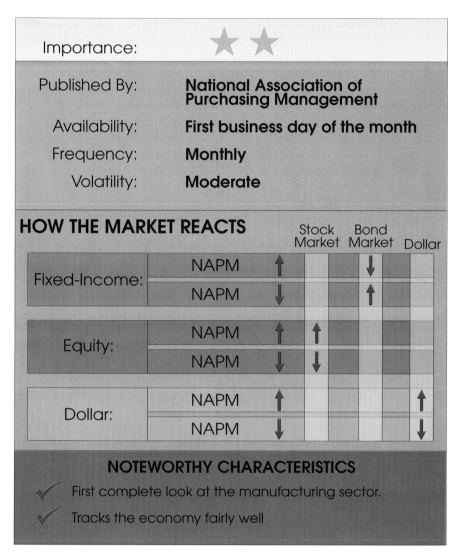

| Importance: | ★ ★ | | |
|---|---|---|---|
| **Published By:** | **National Association of Purchasing Management** | | |
| **Availability:** | **First business day of the month** | | |
| **Frequency:** | **Monthly** | | |
| **Volatility:** | **Moderate** | | |

## HOW THE MARKET REACTS

| | | | Stock Market | Bond Market | Dollar |
|---|---|---|---|---|---|
| Fixed-Income: | NAPM | ↑ | | ↓ | |
| | NAPM | ↓ | | ↑ | |
| Equity: | NAPM | ↑ | ↑ | | |
| | NAPM | ↓ | ↓ | | |
| Dollar: | NAPM | ↑ | | | ↑ |
| | NAPM | ↓ | | | ↓ |

### NOTEWORTHY CHARACTERISTICS

✓ First complete look at the manufacturing sector.

✓ Tracks the economy fairly well

THE PURCHASING
MANAGERS' INDEX
CORRELATES WELL
WITH GDP GROWTH

Always on the lookout for more data, analysts and investors have become hooked on the results of a monthly survey arranged by the National Association of Purchasing Management (NAPM). Released on the first working day of the month, the association's *Report on Business* often provides the first comprehensive look at the manufacturing sector via its "diffusion index" (described below). And since it generally arrives shortly before the all-important employment report (covered later in Chapter 6), the NAPM index is used to fine-tune forecasts of the Bureau of Labor Statistics data. As *Figures 5-1* and *5-2* indicate, the NAPM index tracks the economy's ups and downs fairly well. In fact, many consider this series a valuable adjunct to the Commerce Department's index of leading indicators. As we will see in our upcoming discussion, readings above 50 represent an expanding manufacturing sector, whereas figures below 50 indicate declining factory activity. The movement away from 50 indicates the magnitude of the expansion or decline.

*Figure 5-1*
*How the NAPM Survey Tracks the Economy*

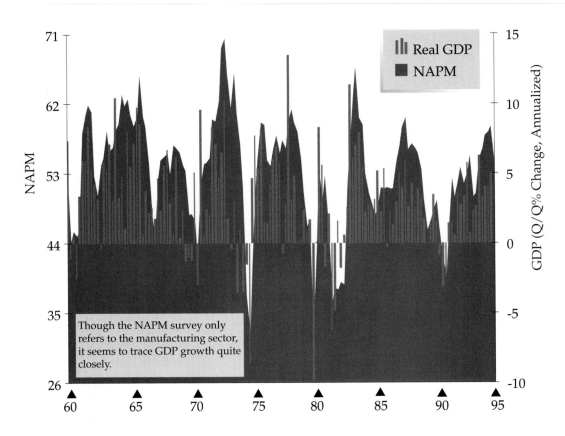

Though the NAPM survey only refers to the manufacturing sector, it seems to trace GDP growth quite closely.

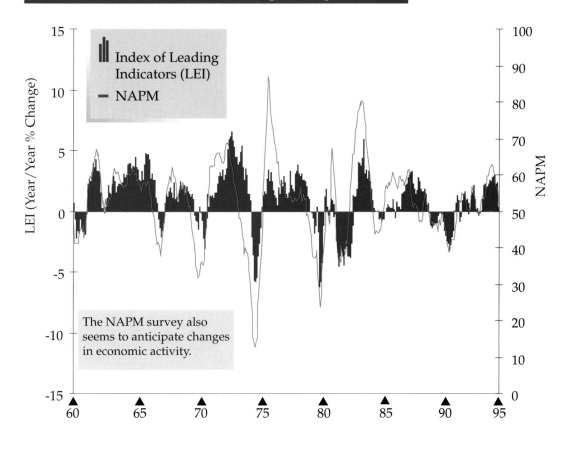

*Figure 5-2 NAPM Versus Leading Indicators*

The NAPM survey is valued not only for its timeliness, but also for its information, which is obtained directly from purchasing executives in over 250 industrial companies. Twenty-one industries in 50 states are represented on the Business Survey Committee. Participants respond to a questionnaire regarding production, orders, commodity prices, inventories, vendor performance, and employment by generally characterizing activity in each category as up, down, or unchanged. For each subgroup a *diffusion index* is formed. The diffusion index is calculated by adding the percentage of positive responses to one-half of those who report conditions as unchanged. Various weights (shown in Figure 5-3) are applied to the individual components to form a composite index. The resulting single-index number is then seasonally adjusted to allow for intra-year variations in the weather, holidays, and any institutional changes.

NAPM INDEX IS DERIVED FROM THE RESPONSES TO SIX QUESTIONS

*Figure 5-3*
*Composition of the NAPM Index*

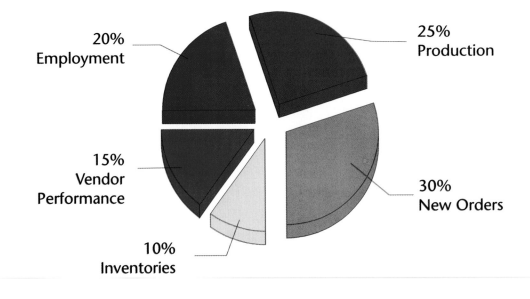

20%
Employment

25%
Production

15%
Vendor
Performance

30%
New Orders

10%
Inventories

A READING ABOVE
50 IMPLIES AN
INCREASE; BELOW
50, A DECLINE

A reading of 50 can be thought of as a "swing point." To understand this, consider the following example. Forget, for the moment, that there are a number of different categories and assume that NAPM asks only one question: "Did orders increase, decrease, or remain the same this month?" Let us also assume that *everybody* — 100% of the respondents — reported that orders were unchanged *(Figure 5-4)*. To calculate the index, we take one-half of the percentage of those who said orders were unchanged (1/2 x 100 = 50) and add the percentage of those who said orders increased (zero). Thus, in this example, the orders index would be 50, which means orders were unchanged in that month. A reading above 50 implies an orders increase; a reading below 50 indicates an orders decline. As a rule of thumb, when the NAPM index approaches 60, you can bet investors will begin to worry about the consequences of an overheated economy — higher inflation, bottlenecks, and a Federal Reserve leaning in the direction of tighter credit. Conversely, a slide towards 40 strongly suggests that a recession is near at hand. Even though NAPM is basically concerned with manufacturing-type firms, we have seen that this sector generally leads the overall economy — despite the high (and rising) proportion of services in the U.S. economy.

*Figure 5-4*
*How NAPM Index is Calculated*

1. If *everybody* agrees that orders were unchanged:

|  |  |  |
|---|---|---|
| Up | = | 0% |
| Same | = | 100% |
| Down | = | 0% |

|  |  |  |  |  |
|---|---|---|---|---|
| NAPM | = | (% Up) | + | ½ (% same) |

or     50     =     0%     +     ½ (100%)

2. If *some* respondents report higher orders:

|  |  |  |
|---|---|---|
| Up | = | 20% |
| Same | = | 80% |
| Down | = | 0% |

|  |  |  |  |  |
|---|---|---|---|---|
| NAPM | = | (% Up) | + | ½ (%same) |

or     60     =     20%     +     ½ (80%)

While most economists now try to estimate the NAPM index, there is little data upon which to base an educated guess. Those of us who attempt a forecast use information from a similar-type survey conducted by the Federal Reserve Bank of Philadelphia — available about two weeks earlier. Also, the Chicago branch of NAPM, one of the association's regional arms, releases the results for the Chicago area one day prior to the national data. These two sources of information provide some clues, but there is still a wide margin for error. Because there is only limited information available on which to base a forecast, there is often a major "surprise factor" attached to a NAPM release. For that reason, it can sometimes prompt a large market reaction.

**NAPM IS DIFFICULT TO FORECAST**

**THE MARKETS REACT TO OVERALL NAPM INDEX AND SEVERAL OF ITS COMPONENTS**

A few years ago market participants paid attention only to the overall NAPM index. But as the markets have become increasingly sophisticated, they have begun to focus on several of its components as well as the overall index. Specifically, the employment category is sometimes viewed as a harbinger of the change in payroll employment for that month. The employment report, of course, is generally released just a few days later and is widely acknowledged to be the most important economic release of the month. Any clue concerning its strength or weakness is most welcome. In addition, the "prices paid" component has become quite important to the market as a leading indicator of inflation. It became the center of attention in February 1994, soon after the Federal Reserve indicated that it deemed this category to be one of its leading indicators of inflation.

**A NUMBER OF REGIONAL FEDERAL RESERVE BANKS PRODUCE NAPM-LIKE INDEXES**

Many of the regional Federal Reserve Banks have begun to release NAPM-like indexes for their own districts. In addition to the Philadelphia Federal Reserve Bank index, which was noted above, the Atlanta Federal Reserve Bank index seems to garner a lot of attention. The New York, Detroit, and Milwaukee Federal Reserve Banks have also gotten into the act. The problem with every one of these indexes — other than the one from Philadelphia — is that they come out long *after* the NAPM report. Hence, they have no value as a forecasting tool.

**IF NAPM RISES, THE BOND MARKET DECLINES**

The bond market views strength in the NAPM index as bearish and weakness in the NAPM index as bullish *(Figure 5-5)*. Of course, one must use some common sense here. If the index rises to 45 in February from 44 in January, the bond market is unlikely to fall apart. Remember, the below-50 reading indicates that the manufacturing sector continued to contract in February, but its *rate* of decline was a bit slower in that month because the February reading of 45 was higher than the January level of 44. Conversely, if interest rates have been trending up along with economic activity, and NAPM rises to 58 from 55, the bond market quickly reprices — downward.

**STOCKS SHOULD IMPROVE**

The same logic applies to the stock market. If recent earnings reports have been favorable, and interest rates have been holding steady at relatively low levels, a NAPM index increase can be construed as bullish. However, if other indicators have been suggesting "end-of-cycle" problems — an overheating economy, accelerating inflation, and rising interest rates — a strong index reading will be taken bearishly by the equity market.

The dollar will take its cue from the Federal Reserve. If the economy is strong, the U.S. currency rallies on news of advancing manufacturing activity, owing to possible future Fed tightening efforts that would push interest rates higher. Conversely, if the economy is sluggish, the dollar drifts lower on a weak NAPM report because the markets may anticipate that interest rate levels will fall.

AND THE DOLLAR
MAY RISE

*Figure 5-5*
*Market Reaction to*
*NAPM*

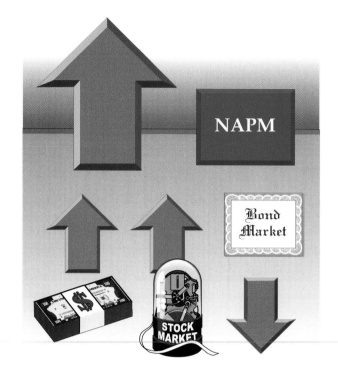

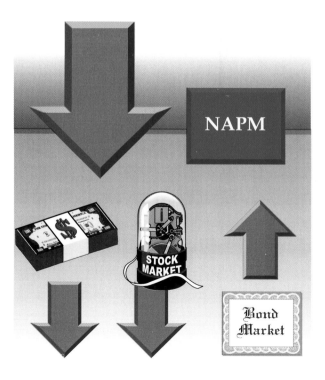

THE KING OF KINGS!

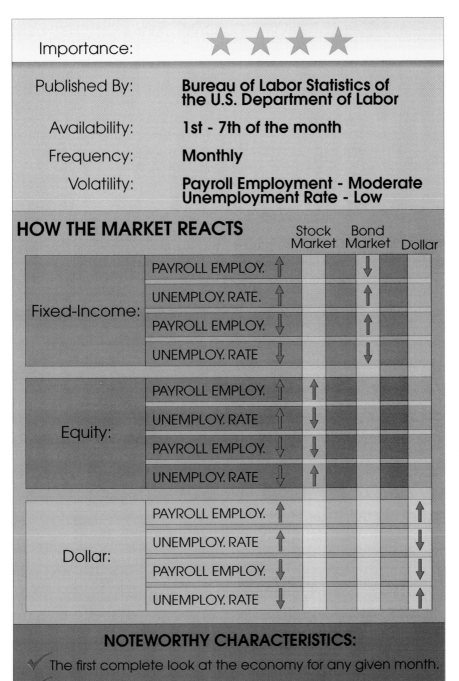

| Importance: | ★ ★ ★ ★ |
|---|---|
| Published By: | **Bureau of Labor Statistics of the U.S. Department of Labor** |
| Availability: | **1st - 7th of the month** |
| Frequency: | **Monthly** |
| Volatility: | **Payroll Employment - Moderate** **Unemployment Rate - Low** |

## HOW THE MARKET REACTS

| | | Stock Market | Bond Market | Dollar |
|---|---|---|---|---|
| **Fixed-Income:** | PAYROLL EMPLOY. ↑ | | ↓ | |
| | UNEMPLOY. RATE. ↑ | | ↑ | |
| | PAYROLL EMPLOY. ↓ | | ↑ | |
| | UNEMPLOY. RATE ↓ | | ↓ | |
| **Equity:** | PAYROLL EMPLOY. ↑ | ↑ | | |
| | UNEMPLOY. RATE ↑ | ↓ | | |
| | PAYROLL EMPLOY. ↓ | ↓ | | |
| | UNEMPLOY. RATE ↓ | ↑ | | |
| **Dollar:** | PAYROLL EMPLOY. ↑ | | | ↑ |
| | UNEMPLOY. RATE ↑ | | | ↓ |
| | PAYROLL EMPLOY. ↓ | | | ↓ |
| | UNEMPLOY. RATE ↓ | | | ↑ |

## NOTEWORTHY CHARACTERISTICS:

✓ The first complete look at the economy for any given month.

✓ Helps to forecast many other economic indicators.

EXCEPT FOR GDP, EMPLOYMENT IS THE MOST IMPORTANT *MONTHLY* ECONOMIC INDICATOR

It's been said that economists never agree on anything. But there may be one exception — the value of the monthly employment report. From our perspective, it represents the single most important report each month. There is no question that the GDP report is the most important economic indicator and, in fact, almost all of the other indicators tell us something about GDP. But GDP is a *quarterly* measure of economic activity (although it is revised monthly). The employment data are monthly and help us refine our GDP estimate for that quarter. Before we view the employment report, we have obtained information on car sales, which tells us a little bit about retail sales and consumption — but car sales represent less than 5% of GDP. We have also received the purchasing managers' index (NAPM), which gives us a vague idea of what is happening in the manufacturing sector. You will recall that this report indicates whether production, employment, orders, etc., are higher or lower than in the previous month. But other than this generalized feeling for activity in the goods-producing sector, there is no concrete evidence to help analysts and investors refine their forecasts of the economy's direction. Even if we agree that the NAPM is portraying an accurate picture of the manufacturing sector, it is important to recognize that it only represents about 42% of GDP. We know nothing about the construction industry or services, which make up over one-half of our economy, until this report is released. Therefore, no other monthly economic indicator is as important as the employment report.

THIS REPORT PROVIDES INFORMATION ON EMPLOYMENT, AVERAGE WORKWEEK, AND HOURLY EARNINGS

The monthly employment report provides a wealth of information about virtually every sector of the economy. In addition to basic employment statistics for nine major sectors of payroll employment shown in *Figure 6-1*, we discover how many hours

| Goods-Producing | Service-Producing |
|---|---|
| •Manufacturing | •Transportation & Public Utilities |
| •Construction | •Wholesale Trade |
| •Mining | •Retail Trade |
| | •Finance, Insurance, & Real Estate |
| | •Services |
| | •Government |

*Figure 6-1 Major Categories of Payroll Employment*

people worked in each of those categories (average workweek) and how much they were paid (average hourly earnings). This information is invaluable.

The employment figures are crucial. If we know how many people were employed in the manufacturing sector in a given month, how long they worked, and how much overtime they accrued, it is not too difficult to predict how much they produced — virtually every economist uses this report as one method of estimating industrial production *(Figure 6-2)*. If, in addition to the above information for all workers, we also know how much these people were paid, we can make a reasonable projection of the change in personal income in that month. The data for the construction industry helps in making a forecast of housing

THIS REPORT HELPS ESTIMATE ALMOST EVERY OTHER ECONOMIC INDICATOR

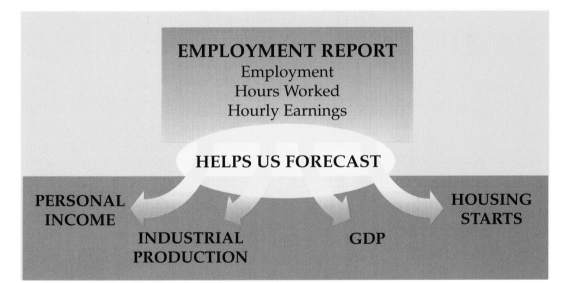

*Figure 6-2*
*Data from the Employment Report Help Us Forecast Several Other Economic Factors*

starts. After all, if construction employment surged in a given month, there is a good chance that housing starts also surged. Admittedly, not all of those employed in the construction industry build houses. Some undoubtedly built roads and schools. But there is at least a reasonable correlation between construction employment and starts. Finally, economists use this report to help refine their GDP forecasts for the quarter. GDP is supposed to measure the aggregate volume of goods and services produced. If we take the number of jobs and multiply it by the average workweek, we can determine the number of aggregate hours worked for that month. If we perform the same calculation for every month and then average the data for the quarter, we should be able to produce a reasonable GDP estimate. This estimate, however, is not a perfect measure, primarily because changes in productivity from one quarter to the next may cause problems. Yet, if productivity is reasonably stable, this method of estimating GDP works well. The point is that the employment report provides a wealth of information that we use in formulating forecasts for many of the other economic indicators released later in the month.

## THE UNEMPLOYMENT RATE IS VERY IMPORTANT TO POLITICIANS

The monthly employment report also contains information about the unemployment rate. Because this rate is so politically sensitive, it tends to generate the most press coverage, although from a market viewpoint it is less valuable than the payroll employment data. From a market perspective, the unemployment rate is important to the degree that the Fed becomes involved. From a political point of view, if the unemployment rate rises to "unacceptable" levels, Congressional pressure on the Federal Reserve to ease monetary policy intensifies dramatically.

## THE UNEMPLOYMENT RATE MAY ALSO BE A HARBINGER OF INFLATION...

A second reason why the unemployment rate is important to the markets is because there is a (loose) link between the unemployment rate and inflation. According to this "natural rate" hypothesis, aggregate demand may push unemployment below this rate, but only at the cost of not merely higher, but *accelerating* inflation. Similarly a shortfall of aggregate demand may push unemployment above the natural rate, but this will lead to decelerating inflation. Economists are not certain of this natural rate of unemployment, but most estimates are somewhere between 5% and 6%. While we clearly believe in this theory, we focus a bit more closely on the unemployment rate for married men. As shown in *Figure 6-3*, we have found that in the 21-year period from 1973-1994, there were 13 years when the unemployment rate for married men was above 4%; the inflation rate fell in 11 of those 13 years. Similarly, there were 8 years when the unemployment rate for married men was below 4%; the inflation rate rose in all but one of them. Thus, the evidence strongly suggests that the U.S. economy will suffer accelerating inflation if the unemployment rate for married men drops below about 4%.

## Unemployment and Inflation 1973 - 1993

| Change in Inflation Rate | Unemployment Rate for Married Men | |
|---|---|---|
| | < 4% | > 4% |
| Increased | 7 Years | 1 Year |
| No Change | 0 Years | 1 Year |
| Declined | 1 Year | 11 Years |

*Figure 6-3*
*Unemployment and Inflation 1973-1993*

There is no question that an increase in the unemployment rate is a clear sign that the economy is weak and vice versa. However, the markets do not pay as much attention to this rate because it is a *lagging* indicator of economic activity, which means that it turns up *after* the economy has peaked and begun to move into a recession and begins to fall *after* a recession has ended and the economy, once again, has begun to expand *(Figure 6-4)*. For example, if firms experience a dropoff in sales activity, the first warning signal is a rise in inventory levels. Firms then try to trim inventories by cutting back on the number of hours their employees work. If sales do not rebound soon and/or inventory levels begin to decline, at some point management would have to consider a cutback in employment. Thus, a rise in the unemployment rate is regarded as a *lagging* indicator of economic activity. This process works equally well in reverse. Companies do not run out and hire additional bodies as their first response to a sales pickup. The sales gain has to be sustained for some period of time. (It should be noted that, in contrast, payroll employment is a *coincident* indicator of economic activity — it changes direction at the *same time* as the economy.)

... BUT IS A LAGGING INDICATOR OF ECONOMIC ACTIVITY

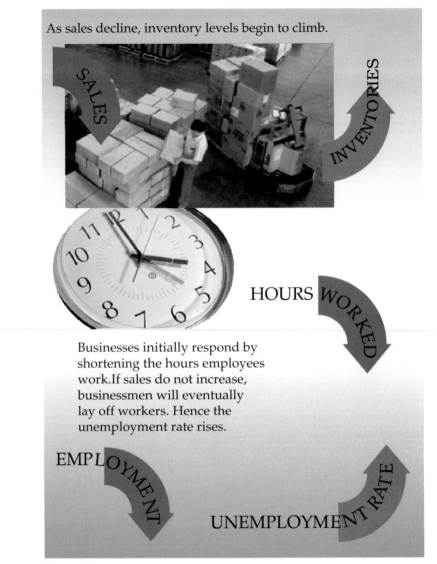

As sales decline, inventory levels begin to climb.

Businesses initially respond by
shortening the hours employees
work.If sales do not increase,
businessmen will eventually
lay off workers. Hence the
unemployment rate rises.

*Figure 6-4*
*Unemployment Rate Is a Lagging Indicator of Economic Activity*

One word of caution: While the payroll employment data are extremely valuable, beware of revisions. In the introduction to this book, we warned that many economic series were subject to sizable revisions and this is one of them. As an example, the May 1990 data indicated that payroll employment rose 164,000 (which was less than expected), and the April data was revised downward from an initial increase of 64,000 to a decline of 23,000. This weaker-than-expected report caused a major bond market rally; yields on that day dropped by 16 basis points. What is interesting is that a month later, the May gain revised from an increase of 164,000 initially to an astonishing increase of 356,000! This rise sent the bond markets into a tailspin, and over the next two days, bond yields rose by 15 basis points. In two successive months, revisions to the employment data caused two major swings in the bond market.

The change in payroll employment is particularly hard to predict because we do not have a great deal of data on which to base a forecast. Most economists look at weekly initial unemployment claims and/or the number of people who are receiving unemployment insurance benefits. Others try to glean some insight from the purchasing managers' report, particularly from the employment category. And still others incorporate information from the previous month's help-wanted advertising index. However, the truth is that none of these data correlate well with payroll employment. The initial claims and benefits data seem to be more helpful in forecasting changes in the unemployment rate. The purchasing managers' index may give us some idea of what is happening to employment in the manufacturing sector. Unfortunately, manufacturing represents only about 16% of total employment. Because we do not have much to go on, our forecast errors tend to be large. Since our projections can be far off the mark — and this report is so important — it frequently is a major market mover.

The monthly report is derived from two surveys of employment (*Figure 6-5*). The labor force, household employment, and the unemployment rate are calculated from what is known as the "household survey." The payroll employment statistics, the average workweek, overtime, average hourly earnings, and the aggregate hours index are derived from the "establishment survey." Both surveys are conducted by the Bureau of Labor Statistics (BLS) — a unit of the Department of Labor — for the calendar week that includes the 12th of the month. The data are generally released the first Friday of the following month.

*Figure 6-5 Payroll Employment and the Unemployment Rate Are Derived from Separate Surveys*

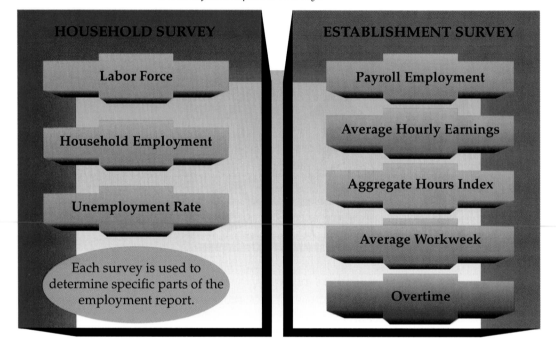

HOUSEHOLD SURVEY

- Labor Force
- Household Employment
- Unemployment Rate

Each survey is used to determine specific parts of the employment report.

ESTABLISHMENT SURVEY

- Payroll Employment
- Average Hourly Earnings
- Aggregate Hours Index
- Average Workweek
- Overtime

HOUSEHOLD SURVEY

The household survey provides the basis for calculating the unemployment rate. Each month the BLS collects information from a sample of 59,500 households. To be included in the ranks of the unemployed, you have to satisfy two criteria. First, you have to be unemployed. Second, you have to be actively seeking employment (*Figure 6-6*). Basically the BLS asks two questions. First, "Are you employed?" If yes, then you are automatically a part of the labor force, and thereby counted as being employed. If you happen to be temporarily laid off or on strike, the BLS still counts you as employed in this particular survey. If you are not employed, then it asks "Are you looking for work?" If you say no, you are not included in the labor force and, therefore, have no impact on the calculation of the unemployment rate. If you say yes, you are officially registered as being both unemployed and a member of the labor force. This means that you now have the somewhat dubious distinction of being incorporated in the unemployment statistics for that month.

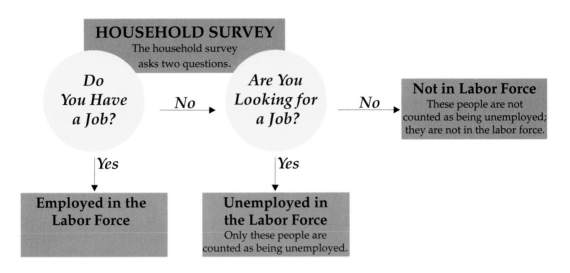

*Figure 6-6 Who Is "Unemployed" and Who Is Not*

In early 1994 the Labor Department changed the way that it conducts the household survey to remove an important bias. Previously, when a woman answered the door, the Labor Department official *assumed* she was a housewife. As a result, she was not counted as part of the labor force, was not counted as being unemployed, and was not included in the calculation of the unemployment rate. Now BLS officials must *specifically ask* that woman if she is actively seeking work. If she says yes, then she is counted as being unemployed and included in the calculation of the unemployment rate. This structural change in the survey caused the unemployment rate to revise upwards by about 0.5%. As a result, there was more slack in the labor market and less upward pressure on the inflation rate — a favorable development for the market. This is a good example of the never-ending search by government agencies, and others, for ways to improve the quality of the data they release. Unfortunately, budget cutbacks are severely hampering this effort, and data quality seems to have deteriorated. This means that both market participants and, more importantly, policymakers must weigh all of the available evidence before deciding the degree of strength or weakness in the economy and the degree of upward or downward pressure on the inflation rate. This is akin to the old "preponderance of evidence" concept that is frequently used in a court of law. For example, if 15 of the 20 indicators discussed in this book are stronger-than-expected and the remaining 5 are weak, the odds are quite high that the economy is growing more quickly than had been anticipated, and one should adjust his or her thinking accordingly.

BLS RECENTLY REVISED THE HOUSEHOLD SURVEY

THERE ARE TWO DIFFERENT MEASURES OF THE UNEMPLOYMENT RATE

To calculate the unemployment rate, the BLS will divide the number of people that are unemployed by the number of people in the labor force and multiply by 100 *(Figure 6-7)*. Most analysts, however, refer to the *civilian* unemployment rate, which excludes the military. By definition, all members of the military have jobs — the unemployment rate among the armed forces is zero. Inclusion of the military essentially biases the unemployment rate slightly downward. Hence, the civilian rate is presumably more sensitive to changes in economic activity.

$$\text{Unemployment Rate} = \frac{\text{Number of People Unemployed}}{\text{Labor Force}} \times 100$$

For March 1995, we had the following:

$$5.5\% = \frac{7{,}237}{132{,}513}\ \text{(thousands)} \times 100$$

*Figure 6-7*
*How the Unemployment Rate Is Calculated*

ESTABLISHMENT SURVEY

ESTABLISHMENT SURVEY DATA ARE GENERALLY REGARDED AS MORE ACCURATE

Payroll employment, the average workweek, average hourly earnings, overtime, and the aggregate hours index are all calculated from the establishment survey. Once again the data are collected from a large survey, but this time the responses come directly from businesses. For this reason, it is generally regarded as more accurate. The problem with the household survey is that, when government representatives ask questions about employment, they often get less than truthful answers for a variety of reasons. Some people may fear that the data will be reported to the immigration authorities. Others may worry that if they truthfully say they are not looking for work they may jeopardize their unemployment benefits. Employers, however, have no reason to avoid the questions and will usually give straightforward answers.

THESE TWO SURVEYS MEASURE EMPLOYMENT IN VERY DIFFERENT WAYS

One problem that occurs regularly is that these two surveys

invariably produce different estimates of employment — some-times startlingly different — which make analysis difficult. Some of the discrepancy results from differences in coverage and definition *(Figure 6-8)*. For example, the household surveys include self-employed workers and domestics. Because these people are not on a payroll, they are obviously not in the estab-lishment survey. Also, in the household survey a person is counted only once even if he or she may have more than one job. In the establishment survey, however, a worker can be counted several times. If he or she has two jobs and is on the payroll of two different employers, the person is counted twice. Finally, recall that if someone is temporarily laid off or on strike, he or she is counted as employed in the household survey. That is not the case with payroll employment. If a person is on strike and therefore off the payroll throughout the entire survey period, he or she is not counted as employed in the establishment survey.

| *Employment as Measured by:* | Household Survey | Establishment Survey |
|---|---|---|
| **Wage Earners** | | |
| First Job | Yes | Yes |
| Second Job | No | Yes |
| **On Strike** | Yes | No |
| **Self-Employed Workers** | Yes | No |
| | | |
| Undercounts People with Two Jobs | Yes | No |
| Doublecounts People with Two Jobs | No | Yes |

Figure 6-8
*The Two Employment Surveys Have Numerous Differences*

WHICH SURVEY
SHOULD WE LOOK
AT? IT IS NOT CLEAR,
BUT PROBABLY
BOTH

The payroll survey is probably more important because the markets react to it, but it is not entirely clear which survey is the better measure of employment. Even the experts are puzzled. As shown in *Figure 6-9*, the ratio of establishment payrolls to household workers rose sharply in the 1980s. In fact, the payroll employment survey recorded two million more jobs than the household survey in the nearly decade-long period of expansion that began in 1982. How can this be? This discrepancy began to appear as early as 1984, but it widened appreciably in mid-1987. An article published in the *Monthly Labor Review* in August 1989

*Figure 6-9*
*The Establishment to Household Employment Ratio*

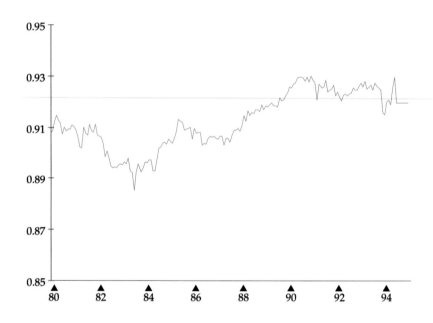

suggests that this gap has widened in large part because of multiple job holding that, of course, boosts the payroll data. In addition, the article suggests that the establishment of new firms plays a role in the discrepancy. Until hard data become available, the Labor Department must estimate the number of jobs originating from new firms based on historical trends. If the actual rate of job creation is not as strong as it was previously in the business cycle, the payroll data will again be overstated. Finally, the article suggests that population estimates and the difficulty of estimating the inflow of aliens into the country are factors. If the number of illegal immigrants has been growing rapidly, the household estimates will be understated. In short, there are a number of valid reasons for differences between these two surveys. But because it is not clear which survey is presenting a more accurate picture of the labor situation at the moment, it is worthwhile to be aware of the employment changes registered by both.

As noted earlier, this report has the potential to be a major market mover. This occurs for two reasons. First of all, since the employment data are very difficult to forecast and market estimates are frequently wide of the mark, the employment report has a significant surprise factor. Second, the data are so comprehensive that they are viewed as reasonably representative of the state of the economy for that particular month — they are almost regarded as gospel. If the employment data are much stronger or weaker than what market participants thought previously, then the initial expectation simply must have been wrong. Yet, if we continue to see sizable revisions to these data, then at some point the markets may become more skeptical. But for now that is not the case.

THE EMPLOYMENT REPORT HAS A MAJOR MARKET IMPACT BECAUSE IT SETS TONE FOR THE ENTIRE MONTH

This sense of whether the employment report is strong or weak depends upon several different elements, the most important of which is payroll employment. However, the markets also take into consideration the length of the workweek, factory employment, and even the unemployment rate. Furthermore, the change in average hourly earnings is viewed as an indicator of wage pressures. If wages are rising rapidly, the cost of production is also climbing — therefore, the inflation rate is likely to rise. A "weak" employment report is viewed positively by the fixed-income market.

MARKET REACTION BASED UPON COMBINATION OF EMPLOYMENT, HOURS, EARNINGS, AND THE UNEMPLOYMENT RATE

A "STRONG" EMPLOYMENT REPORT CAUSES THE BOND MARKET TO NOSE DIVE

If the essence of the employment report suggests that the economy is much stronger than expected, the bond market swoons — prices fall and bond yields rise *(Figure 6-10)*. This occurs because a faster pace of economic activity implies a higher rate of inflation and, presumably, higher interest rates.

STRONG EMPLOYMENT BOLSTERS STOCKS

The stock market generally favors more economic growth than less. Thus, a "strong" employment report indicates a healthier pace of economic activity that, presumably, enhances corporate profits. The stock market should respond positively to that information. In addition, a bit of inflation probably is good for the stock market because it enables corporations to raise prices. This, too, boosts earnings. But there is a major caveat: If the report is so strong that the Federal Reserve responds by raising interest rates, or if there is a sharp rise in inflationary expectations, the stock market will react adversely. Thus, the best report for the equity market is one that shows moderate growth. Too much growth, in this case, is not a good thing.

STRONG EMPLOYMENT PROBABLY HELPS THE DOLLAR

The dollar responds to the likely change in interest rates. If the employment report is indicative of a stronger-than-expected economy, this implies either an increase in interest rates or less of an interest rate drop-off than had been anticipated previously. If interest rates are expected to rise, generally this boosts the value of the dollar. Thus, a strong employment report generally is viewed as a plus for the dollar; a weak one is viewed negatively.

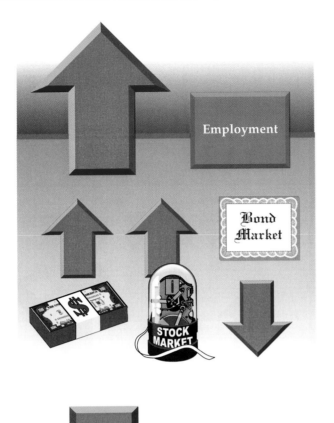

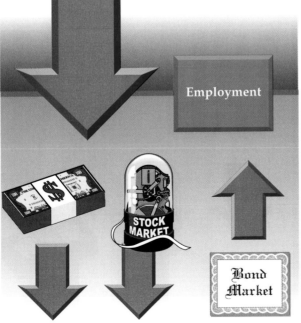

*Figure 6-10*
*Market Reaction to the*
*Employment Data*

SNEAK PREVIEW OF INFLATION

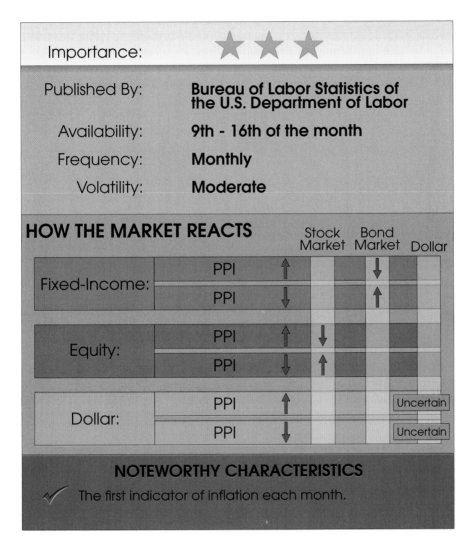

| Importance: | ★ ★ ★ |
| --- | --- |
| Published By: | **Bureau of Labor Statistics of the U.S. Department of Labor** |
| Availability: | **9th - 16th of the month** |
| Frequency: | **Monthly** |
| Volatility: | **Moderate** |

## HOW THE MARKET REACTS

| | | | Stock Market | Bond Market | Dollar |
| --- | --- | --- | --- | --- | --- |
| Fixed-Income: | PPI | ↑ | | ↓ | |
| | PPI | ↓ | | ↑ | |
| Equity: | PPI | ↑ | ↓ | | |
| | PPI | ↓ | ↑ | | |
| Dollar: | PPI | ↑ | | | Uncertain |
| | PPI | ↓ | | | Uncertain |

## NOTEWORTHY CHARACTERISTICS

✓ The first indicator of inflation each month.

**KEEPING TABS ON INFLATION IS OF UTMOST IMPORTANCE**

For every investor, keeping tabs on inflation is of utmost importance. The pace of inflation, whether measured by the PPI, the CPI, or one of the GDP price deflators, influences everything from Federal Reserve policy to choosing the right mutual fund. But it also matters from whence inflation comes — oil shocks, drought, labor settlements, or medical care costs *(Figure 7-1)*. Some of these causes indicate prolonged or widespread problems, whereas others are short-lived or isolated events. One must be careful to sort out the differences. For example, sharply rising compensation levels are more serious than a poor harvest, because the latter only boosts the inflation rate *temporarily*. A drought undoubtedly causes the prices of agricultural products to rise, but once new crops are planted and harvested, price levels should decline. That is not the case with wages — they go up, but they seldom go back down.

*Figure 7-1*
*Inflation Can Stem from Any of Several Causes*

**3% INFLATION GENERALLY IS DEEMED ACCEPTABLE**

Historically, it is safe to characterize overall inflation as tolerable or intolerable. We are quite used to price increases of 3% to 4%, although many thoughtful observers would say these rates are "too high." But from a purely political viewpoint, these increases are not extreme. However, when inflation accelerates into the 6% - 10% area, the ball game changes. The public demands that "something be done."

**THERE ARE SEVERAL WAYS TO COMBAT INFLATION**

In the past, Washington policymakers have responded with wage and price controls, price "guidelines," or severe Federal Reserve restraint *(Figure 7-2)*. In any case, the result is usually the same: As *Figure 7-3* demonstrates, it is no coincidence that the two most severe recessions since 1960 followed double-digit inflation rates. For this reason alone, investors must monitor and

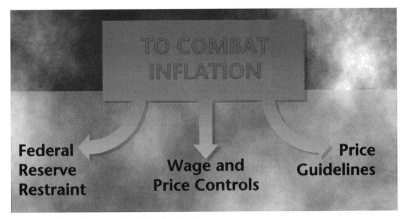

Figure 7-2 Ways to Combat Inflation

— if possible — attempt to predict broad price trends. One important source of information arrives monthly via the producer price index or PPI.

Figure 7-3
Producer Price Index

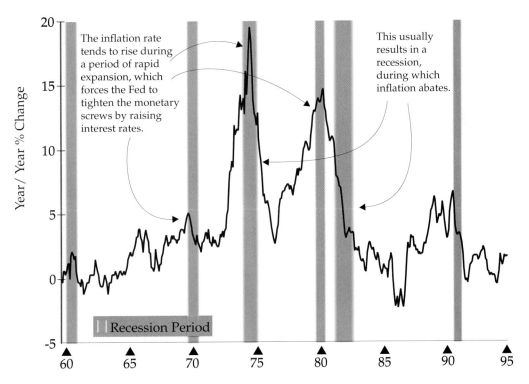

**PPI IS THE FIRST REPORT ON INFLATION**

The PPI is a measure of prices at the *producer* level and is the first inflation report to hit the Street each month. Since the PPI is released prior to its more famous cousin — the Consumer Price Index — some analysts simply look at "wholesale" prices to predict retail prices. But that is not a good strategy. Although *Figure 7-4* indicates a high degree of correlation over time, the two indexes are quite different. Thus, month to month, the PPI may go one way and the CPI another.

**THE PPI IS AN INDEX OF COMMODITY PRICES — NO SERVICES ARE INCLUDED**

As we note elsewhere in the book (Chapter 2 and Chapter 10), there are a variety of inflation measures, each with its own strengths and weaknesses. Regarding the PPI, it should be understood at the onset what is being measured — and what is not *(Figure 7-5)*. The most important concept to remember is that the PPI is an index of *commodity* prices. In contrast, the CPI measures the prices of both commodities and *services* — housing, transportation, medical, and other services have a weighting of almost 57% in the CPI. Another difference between the CPI and PPI (for finished goods) is that the PPI measures, in part, the cost of capital goods purchased by businesses. These, of course, are

*Figure 7-5*
*Coverage of the PPI Versus the CPI*

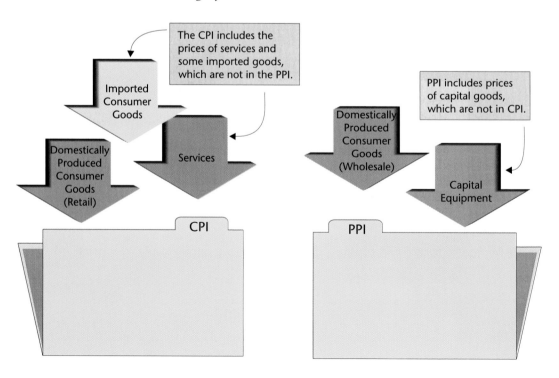

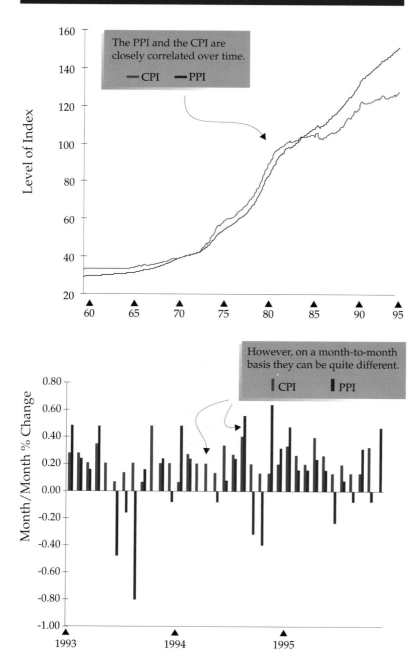

Figure 7-4
Consumer Price Index Versus Producer Price Index

not included in the CPI. Conceptually, the PPI for finished *consumer* goods, with a weighting of about 75%, is similar to the CPI *excluding services*. However, the PPI and CPI can behave differently owing to the differences in composition.

DATA COMPILED BY THE LABOR DEPARTMENT

How are the data put together? Labor Department economists compare prices for a multitude of items — some 3,450 commodities. Prices are sampled monthly and, in most cases, pertain to the Tuesday of the week that contains the 13th of the month. The Department analysts then weight these items in proportion to their contribution to GDP. As with the GDP deflators (see Chapter 2), the PPI is defined as equal to 100 in the base year 1982.

*Figure 7-6*
*Composition of PPI*

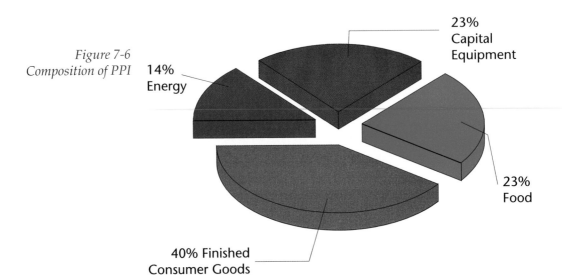

23%
Capital
Equipment

14%
Energy

23%
Food

40% Finished
Consumer Goods

PPI CONTAINS DATA ON BOTH CONSUMER GOODS AND CAPITAL EQUIPMENT

When analysts and reporters refer to the PPI, they generally mean the PPI for finished goods. What are the major items in this report? *Figure 7-6* indicates that consumer-related goods account for 77% of this series. Consumer goods, principally passenger cars, represent 40% of the PPI. Consumer foods provide an additional 23%. Within consumer foods are prices for meat and fish, dairy products, and fruits and vegetables. And the energy category, largely gasoline and fuel oil, represents an additional 14% of this index. Within the capital equipment category, which accounts for the remaining 23% of the PPI, passenger cars and trucks play a major role. You may have noticed that automobiles are included in *two* categories. This is because businesses purchase cars along with consumers. The weighting scheme of passenger vehicles in each major grouping is different and is determined by its contribution to GDP.

Many economists look at the PPI excluding the (often volatile) food and energy groups. This is simply another way of dissecting the data. It is a well-known fact that both food and energy prices tend to be highly volatile. Food prices, for example, can be greatly influenced by the weather and by changes in crop production. In 1980, a severe drought in many areas of the country substantially increased food prices for almost a year. For that reason, it was important to isolate the food price runup from the rest of the PPI to get a handle on inflation's true path. Similarly, energy prices can be extremely volatile. *Figure 7-7* shows how wild these swings have been. Oil prices, for example, exploded in 1979, only to fall apart in 1986. More recently, energy prices surged again in mid-1990 with Iraq's invasion of Kuwait. Thus, when the PPI is released each month, the specialist tries to "see through" the data and determine whether the trend (or core rate) of inflation has fundamentally changed.

MANY ECONOMISTS EXCLUDE THE VOLATILE FOOD AND ENERGY CATEGORIES

*Figure 7-7*
*PPI: Food and Energy*

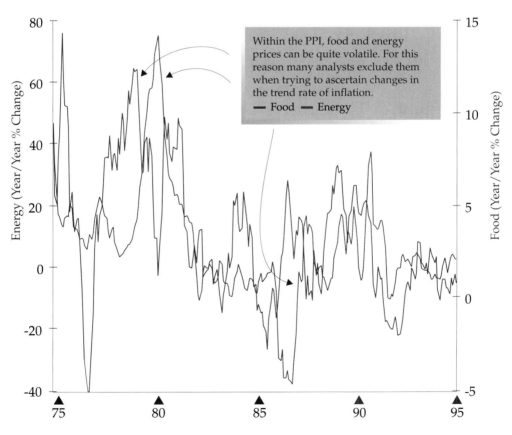

Within the PPI, food and energy prices can be quite volatile. For this reason many analysts exclude them when trying to ascertain changes in the trend rate of inflation.
— Food — Energy

PPI PROVIDES INFORMATION ON PRICES AT THREE STAGES OF PRODUCTION

Note also that the PPI report indicates producer prices by *stage of processing*. In fact, the data contains information on three indexes: finished goods, intermediate goods, and crude materials *(Figure 7-8)*. As noted above, *finished goods* do not undergo any further processing. It is this category that is widely reported in the press. *Intermediate goods* are those that have undergone partial processing, but are not yet completed. *Crude materials* are just that — products entering the market for the first time, which have not been manufactured and which are not sold directly to producers. Why do we care about these other measures of inflation? We care because price changes at these earlier stages of production will frequently foreshadow movements in the PPI for finished goods. Indeed, in recent years there has been increasing attention paid to monthly changes in the so-called "core" rate of inflation at the intermediate stage of production. As shown in *Figure 7-9*, there is a lead time of about one year from the time that prices begin to climb at this intermediate stage of production, until they filter into the finished goods index.

Numerous items, representing many of the materials used by basic industry, are included in the PPI for intermediate goods: electric power, gasoline, steel, fabricated metals, and motor vehicle parts. Food plays a small role in this index. The PPI for crude materials, however, is dominated by foodstuffs. The other important elements in this index subset are energy-related — coal, natural gas, and crude petroleum.

*Figure 7-8*
*The PPI Report Contains Price Information at Three Stages of Production*

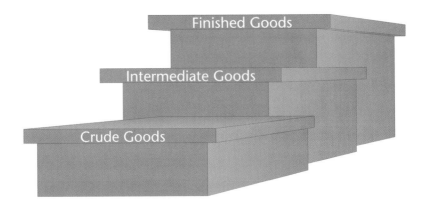

In early 1994 the Federal Reserve indicated that it was using commodity prices as one of a variety of leading indicators of inflation trends. Not surprisingly, the markets then began to focus heavily on the various measures of commodity prices — the Commodity Research Bureau (CRB) indexes of spot and futures commodity prices, the CRB for raw industrial commodities, and the Journal of Commerce index of raw industrial prices. We do not intend to include a lengthy discussion of commodity prices in this book, but there is one important point that the reader must understand: The linkage between commodity prices and inflation is quite loose. As shown in *Figure 7-10*, there is little correlation between the CRB futures price index and subsequent changes in producer prices. There are a variety of reasons for this (*Figure 7-11*). First of all, the CRB index is heavily weighted towards agricultural commodities, grains in particular, which are not included in the PPI *(Figure 7-12)*. As a result, there have been numerous occasions when the CRB rose sharply in the first half of a week because of forecasts of hot, dry weather in the Midwest, but then plunged in the second half of the week because it rained overnight in Chicago. Thus, the CRB index is as much a

**THE LINKAGE BETWEEN COMMODITY PRICE INDEXES AND INFLATION IS QUITE LOOSE**

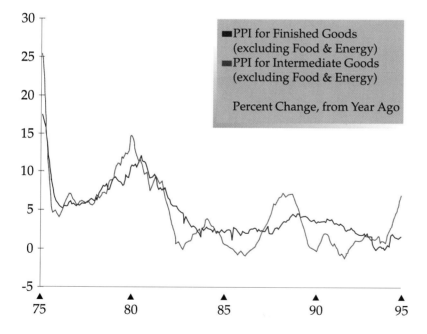

Figure 7-9
*PPI for Finished Goods Versus PPI for Intermediate Goods*

weather report as anything else! If one really wants to look at commodity prices, the Journal of Commerce index and the CRB for raw industrial commodities are far more intellectually appealing since they measure prices of commodities actually used in the production process. In addition, they are marginally more significant from a statistical viewpoint. Second, commodity

*Figure 7-10*
*PPI Inflation and Commodities Inflation*

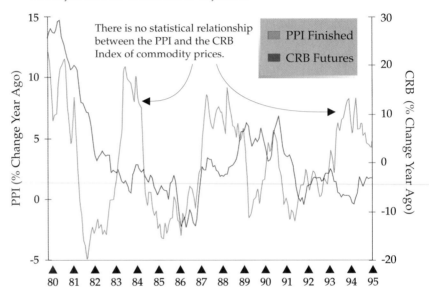

prices are notoriously volatile because they are as much (or more) the result of speculative activity as they are indicators of changes in the underlying supply of and demand for the basic commodity. This makes it virtually impossible to know how long prices must rise (or fall) before one can conclude that the trend has changed. One week? A month? Six months? A year? It is simply not clear. Finally, commodity prices are not seasonally adjusted while the PPI is. This is important because, for example, gasoline prices typically rise 4% to 5% in May as the summer driving season begins, but then fall by a similar amount in September once summer ends and the kids go back to school. The various commodity price indexes are subject to these sharp price swings. But because these price changes occur on a regular basis and are, therefore, "seasonal", the PPI takes them into account and is thus unaffected.

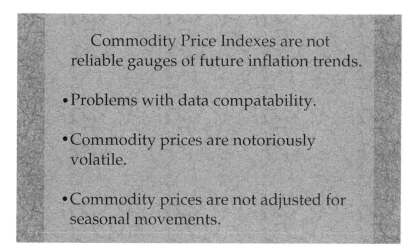

*Figue 7-11*
*Reasons for Loose*
*Correlation Between*
*CRB Index and PPI*

Commodity Price Indexes are not
reliable gauges of future inflation trends.

• Problems with data compatability.

• Commodity prices are notoriously
volatile.

• Commodity prices are not adjusted for
seasonal movements.

*Figure 7-12 Composition of CRB Futures Price Index*

| Composition of CRB Futures Price Index | | |
|---|---|---|
| **Grains** *Not in PPI* | Wheat<br>Corn<br>Soybeans<br>Soybean Oil<br>Soybean Meal | **Industrials** Crude Oil<br>Heating Oil<br>Unleaded Gas<br>Copper<br>Lumber<br>Cotton |
| **Imports** | Coffee<br>Wild Sugar<br>Cocoa | **Metals** Silver<br>Gold<br>Platinum |
| **Meats** | Live Cattle<br>Pork Bellies<br>Live Hogs | **Miscellaneous** Orange Juice |

Recall that the PPI is an *index*, with the 1982 average equal to
100. However, it's the monthly *change* in the index that is widely
reported by the wire services. For example, the index rose to
126.0 in November 1994 from 125.4 in October, which represents
a 0.4785 percent change. (To *annualize* this rate, add a one to the
number (1.004785) and multiply by 12, which equals 5.7%.)

DON'T READ TOO
MUCH INTO ANY
REPORT — PPI CAN
BE VOLATILE

However, it is best not to think in these terms — the slightest variation in a month-to-month change leverages the annualized rate, which occasionally results in wild looking numbers. The "professionals" generally look at the situation in a broader context and will consider a variety of approaches:

> · Compare the most recent month to the prior two to three months;
> · Take a look at a *moving average* of PPI releases for the past six or twelve months;
> · Determine year-over-year inflation rates.

And so forth. The point here is that investors may get burned by reading too much into an isolated report. It's better to identify a *trend* and decide whether or not a new direction is under way.

**SHARP RISE IN PPI IS BAD NEWS FOR BOTH STOCKS AND BONDS**

Having said that, what is a typical short-term market response *(Figure 7-13)?* Given a PPI report — or any other inflation measure — the fixed-income and equity markets tend to move in the same direction. This marks a refreshing change from other economic releases — a higher-than-anticipated rise in the PPI is bearish for both bonds and stocks. Faced with higher inflation, buyers of fixed-income instruments will demand an "inflation premium" since their coupon income is worth less in real terms. The bond's principal — to be paid back at maturity — is also worth less. While some maintain that "a little inflation" is good for stocks, history shows that above a certain inflation threshold, the argument is not valid. Here again, future earnings and dividend income are both subject to the same loss of purchasing power as coupon income is — security prices will adjust downward.

**THE DOLLAR'S REACTION IS LESS CLEAR**

As for the dollar, the situation is tricky and, on many occasions, perverse. The dollar tends to strengthen on rising short-term interest rates. This is especially true if U.S. rates are moving higher relative to foreign rates. Ironically, if a "bad" inflation number is reported — *and if the Federal Reserve is sure to tighten* — the dollar could actually rise. On the other hand, if inflation is a problem, and for whatever reason the Fed *cannot* tighten (e.g., if the economy is weakening), then common sense does indeed prevail — a string of poor inflation reports "devalues" the dollar, causing it to fall in foreign exchange markets.

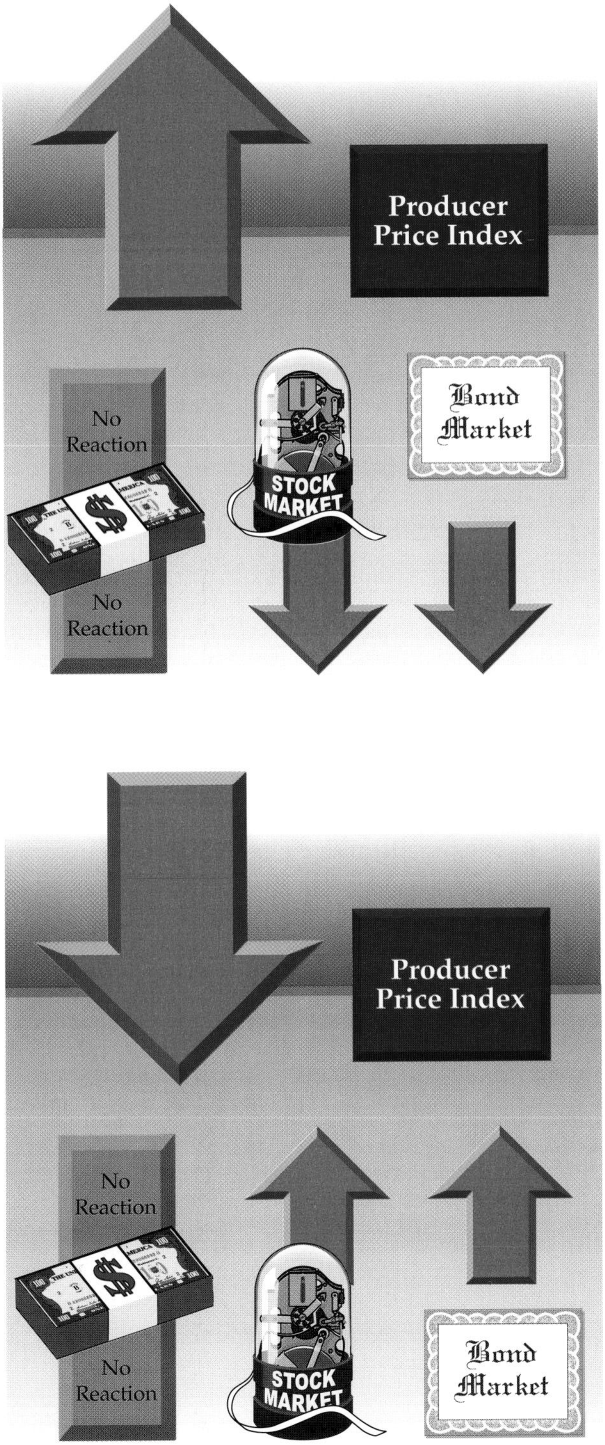

*Figure 7-13*
*Market Reaction to PPI*

## WHAT IS THE CONSUMER UP TO?

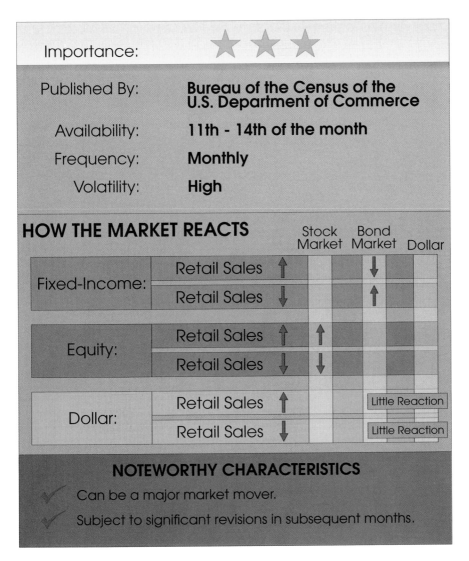

| Importance: | ★ ★ ★ |
|---|---|
| Published By: | **Bureau of the Census of the U.S. Department of Commerce** |
| Availability: | **11th - 14th of the month** |
| Frequency: | **Monthly** |
| Volatility: | **High** |

### HOW THE MARKET REACTS

| | | | Stock Market | Bond Market | Dollar |
|---|---|---|---|---|---|
| Fixed-Income: | Retail Sales ↑ | | | ↓ | |
| | Retail Sales ↓ | | | ↑ | |
| Equity: | Retail Sales ↑ | | ↑ | | |
| | Retail Sales ↓ | | ↓ | | |
| Dollar: | Retail Sales ↑ | | | | Little Reaction |
| | Retail Sales ↓ | | | | Little Reaction |

### NOTEWORTHY CHARACTERISTICS

✓ Can be a major market mover.

✓ Subject to significant revisions in subsequent months.

FIRST SOLID
INDICATION OF
STRENGTH OR
WEAKNESS IN
CONSUMER
SPENDING

The primary reason we are interested in retail sales is because they provide the first solid indication of consumer spending for a given month. What we *really* want to know is what happened to personal consumption expenditures (PCE), in real terms, for a given month. Why? Because that is the "C " (consumption) part of our familiar GDP = C + I + G + X - M equation. The reason this is so important is that consumption spending represents over one-half of GDP. Because retail sales provide us with some information about consumption, they allow us to refine our estimates of both PCE and GDP.

RETAIL SALES
EXCLUDING AUTOS,
MOST IMPORTANT
PART OF THIS
REPORT

Probably the most important part of the retail sales report is the percentage change in sales, excluding the automobile component. The reason is that the Commerce Department actually uses this growth rate to estimate the non-auto, non-service portion of personal consumption expenditures. Basically, it estimates spending on services and automobiles separately, but then uses the retail sales report to determine spending on everything else — which represents about 40% of the total. Thus, it is quite clear that the retail sales report supplies useful information to market participants about a significant portion of this critical GDP category.

THE REPORT HAS
SEVERAL
DRAWBACKS

CONTAINS DATA ON PURCHASES OF GOODS ONLY — NO SERVICES

The retail sales report has a number of significant drawbacks (*Figure 8-1*). First of all, it only provides information about what the consumer spends on purchases of goods. Consumption spending — which is what goes into GDP — includes purchases of both goods and services. The retail sales report tells us nothing about what the consumer may be spending on health insurance, legal fees, education, airfares, and other services.

DATA REPORTED IN NOMINAL TERMS — NOT ADJUSTED FOR INFLATION

A second problem is that retail sales are reported in *nominal* terms rather than real, i.e., adjusted for inflation. For example, retail sales in a given month could register an increase of 0.9%. Part of that rise probably reflects a larger volume of sales, but some part of the gain undoubtedly represents higher prices. Because the data that go into GDP and consumption are inflation-adjusted, it would be particularly helpful if we could split apart the 0.9% increase and say definitively that inflation-adjusted or "real" retail sales rose 0.6%, and that price increases accounted for the remaining 0.3% of the gain. Regrettably, the Census Bureau does not provide this type of breakdown. Therefore, each month economists have to examine the nominal increase and make an estimate of how much of that rise may be attributable to inflation.

### DATA ARE EXTREMELY VOLATILE

Third, and probably most important, retail sales are an extremely volatile number. Not only are they difficult to forecast, but they are frequently subject to massive revisions. For this reason, the preliminary retail sales data must be viewed with a considerable amount of caution. The retail sales report released January 13, 1995, highlighted both of these problems. On that day, the Census Bureau reported that retail sales for December declined 0.1% when the street was expecting a 0.7% increase. In addition, the Census Bureau reported a huge downward revision to retail sales for November. Previously, the Bureau indicated that November sales had risen 1.2%; after the revision they showed a gain of only 0.2%. These data completely altered the outlook for consumption spending in the fourth quarter of 1994. Previously, most economists had expected growth in personal consumption expenditures for the quarter of about 6.0%; following this report, it became apparent that consumption would climb by only about 4.5%. Thus, the PCE outlook was essentially revised downward

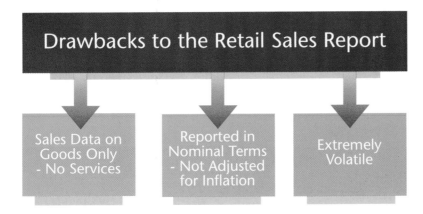

Figure 8-1
*The Retail Sales Report Has a Few Problems*

by 1.5%. Because consumption spending accounts for over half of GDP, this implied that GDP forecasts for the fourth quarter had to be trimmed by 1.0% from what they had been just one day earlier.

**RETAIL SALES ARE QUITE DIFFICULT TO FORECAST**

The retail sales report is difficult to forecast primarily because there is little information on which to base a projection *(Figure 8-2)*.

*Figure 8-2*
*How to Forecast Retail Sales*

**WE MUST RELY ON UNIT CAR SALES...**

Almost all economists track the car and truck sales data that are released at the end of each month (see Chapter 4). However, these data tell us only the *number* of new cars and trucks that were sold each month. The monthly retail sales report reflects the *dollar value* of those sales. In addition, the motor vehicle component of retail sales includes sales of used cars and trucks and sales of auto parts. As a result, the unit car sales data do not provide a great deal of information about the motor vehicle component of retail sales. And, even if one could accurately forecast this category, it only represents about 25% of the total.

Many economists also track chain store sales data to evaluate the general merchandise and apparel categories, which together account for about 17% of retail sales. But here the relationship between the data that are reported and what we actually see on the retail sales release is even more tenuous. Theoretically, the analyst can simply add up the data reported for the various stores each month, divide by the seasonal factor (because the raw data are not adjusted for normal seasonal movements), and arrive at a reasonable estimate of general merchandise and apparel store sales. Yet this does not work very well. Part of the problem may be data comparability — some chains will open new outlets, others may go out of business, and still others have merged with stores that did not report in the previous month. If the data from one month to the next are not comparable, their value as a forecasting tool is greatly diminished. A further complication is that the percentage increases that are reported by the stores are on a year-to-year basis, e.g., January of one year versus January of the previous year. But when economists analyze the retail sales data, they are interested in the change from one month to the next, e.g., December to January.

**AND CHAIN STORE SALES**

The Johnson Redbook is "the bible" of the retail trade industry. It contains considerable detail on various aspects of consumer spending, but it is widely followed for its weekly estimate of chain/department store sales. The Redbook surveys about 30 department, chain, and discount stores each week that have total sales of about $19 billion. This is roughly 57% of the $33 billion of general merchandise and apparel store sales reported in the retail sales report. Retailers are asked to report the percent change in sales for a given week from the comparable week one year earlier. The Redbook then applies these changes to the year ago data, to determine sales for that week. The monthly figure is simply the average percent change for however many weeks are available. For example, if sales in the first two weeks of a month are 12.4% and 9.2% higher than in the comparable weeks one year earlier, the Johnson Redbook will indicate that sales for that month are 10.8% or (12.4% + 9.2%)/2 higher than in the comparable month one year earlier. It then takes this average percent change for the month, compares it to the sales figure twelve months earlier, and determines sales for the current month. Finally, it compares the dollar volume of sales in the current month to the previous month to calculate a percent change. This is a rather convoluted method and does not produce very good results. First of all, the estimates vary widely

**THE JOHNSON REDBOOK DATA ARE NOT VERY HELPFUL**

The Johnson Redbook is not a good indicator of chain/department store sales.

|  | Johnson Redbook | General Merchandise and Apparel Store Sales |
|---|---|---|
| **1994** | | |
| July | 1.2% | 0.2% |
| August | -1.1% | 0.3% |
| September | 2.3% | 0.4% |
| October | -0.4% | 0.9% |
| November | -0.7% | 0.1% |
| December | 3.0% | -0.3% |

*Figure 8-3*
*Changes in the Johnson Redbook Versus Chain Store Sales*

as each additional week of data is received. If, for example, the first week of the month is very strong, the Redbook will indicate a huge increase for the month because it basically assumes that same strength will apply to every other week in the month, which is unlikely to be the case. Second, the final percent change for the month does not track the percent change for the general merchandise and apparel store categories very well. *Figure 8-3* shows the percent changes for these two series for the last six months of 1994. The data go in different *directions* in four of those six months! Given all the problems, we don't believe the JRB is worth the effort. And even if we could get it right, it's only 17% of retail sales.

**40% OF RETAIL SALES ARE DURABLE GOODS; 60% NONDURABLES**

The retail sales data are collected monthly by the Census Bureau of the Department of Commerce from a monthly survey of retail establishments of all sizes and types throughout the country. The survey is supposed to be a statistically valid random sample that provides information on a wide variety of retail establishments. For example, as shown in *Figure 8-4*, retail sales are broken down into two major categories, durables and nondurables, with the former accounting for about 40% and the latter, 60%. *Durables* are dominated — not surprisingly — by autos and trucks. Automobile, truck, and auto-related sales represent about 3/5 of durable goods sales. The remaining 2/5 of durables are accounted for by building materials, hardware, furniture, home furnishing and household appliance sales. *Nondurable* goods sales are made by general merchandise (primarily department) stores, grocery stores, gas stations, apparel shops, restaurants, drug and mail-order houses. Keep in mind that the reported data are supposed to represent sales of *merchandise* for cash or credit by establishments primarily engaged in *retail trade*. Sales of manufacturers and wholesalers are not included. Similarly, sales of service establishments are not a part of this report.

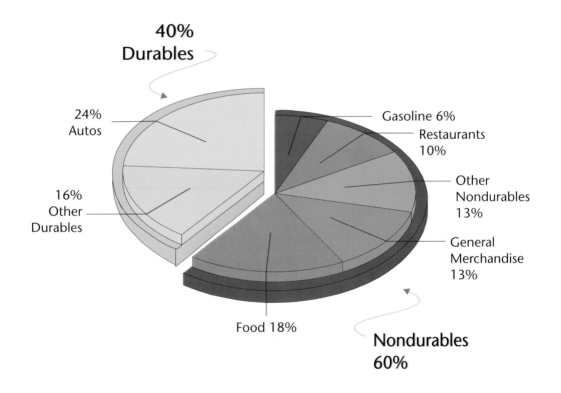

*Figure 8-4*
*Composition of Retail Sales*

RETAIL SALES CAN BE
A MAJOR MARKET
MOVER —A STRONG
REPORT IS NEGATIVE
FOR BONDS

Because retail sales are rather difficult to forecast and the revisions are frequently large, the retail sales report has the potential to provide major surprises *(Figure 8-5)*. As a result, market reactions can be quite pronounced. Again, the sales report released on January 13, 1995, prompted economists to lower their estimates of personal consumption spending in the fourth quarter of 1994 by about 1.5% and their GDP forecasts by about 1.0%. Because market participants now anticipated much less GDP growth in the fourth quarter, inflationary expectations were reduced and many thought a Federal Reserve tightening move was less imminent. On that day bond yields fell by 9 basis points (or .09%) to 7.79%. Thus, a lower-than-expected figure for retail sales implied less GDP growth, slower inflation, and lower interest rates, suggesting that the fixed-income markets should react positively. Stronger-than-expected sales would have been viewed negatively by the fixed-income markets.

POSITIVE FOR
STOCKS

For the equity market, a solid pace for sales is generally viewed as beneficial *unless* interest rates move substantially higher.

AND NEUTRAL FOR
THE DOLLAR

For the dollar, retail sales news is not generally very important. Exceptions occur if there is concern about sharply rising imports. In that situation, a sizable gain for retail sales can imply strong imports, which would be a negative for the U.S. currency.

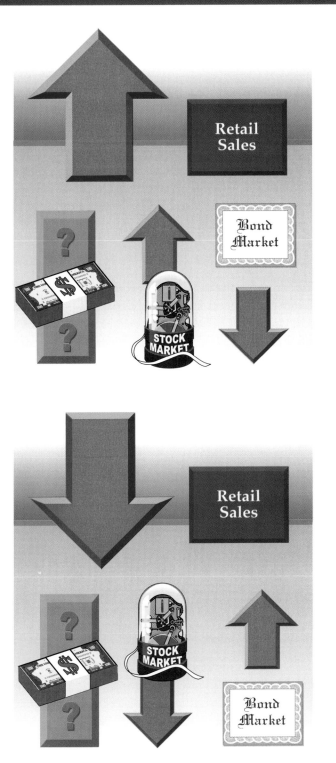

*Figure 8-5*
*Market Reaction to*
*Retail Sales*

### THE FED TAKES THE ECONOMY'S TEMPERATURE

| Importance: | ★ ★ ★ |
|---|---|
| Published By: | **Board of Governors of the Federal Reserve System** |
| Availability: | **14th - 17th of the month** |
| Frequency: | **Monthly** |
| Volatility: | **Low** |

## HOW THE MARKET REACTS

| | | Stock Market | Bond Market | Dollar |
|---|---|---|---|---|
| **Fixed-Income:** | INDUSTRIAL PROD. ↑ | | ↓ | |
| | CAPACITY UTILIZ. ↑ | | ↓ | |
| | INDUSTRIAL PROD. ↓ | | ↑ | |
| | CAPACITY UTILIZ. ↓ | | ↑ | |
| **Equity:** | INDUSTRIAL PROD. ↑ | ↑ | | |
| | CAPACITY UTILIZ. ↑ | ↑ | | |
| | INDUSTRIAL PROD. ↓ | ↓ | | |
| | CAPACITY UTILIZ. ↓ | ↓ | | |
| **Dollar:** | INDUSTRIAL PROD. ↑ | | | Little Reaction |
| | CAPACITY UTILIZ. ↑ | | | Little Reaction |
| | INDUSTRIAL PROD. ↓ | | | Little Reaction |
| | CAPACITY UTILIZ. ↓ | | | Little Reaction |

### NOTEWORTHY CHARACTERISTICS:

✓ Tells us what is happening in the manufacturing sector.

✓ Easily predictable: little market impact.

INDUSTRIAL
PRODUCTION
REPORT TELLS US
SOMETHING ABOUT
GOODS
PRODUCTION

Each month the Federal Reserve Board simultaneously publishes data on industrial production and capacity utilization. The index of industrial production measures the physical output (by volume) of the nation's factories, mines, and utilities. Taken together, these goods-producing industry groups account for about 42% of the economy *(Figure 9-1)*. But this report tells us nothing about the pace of expansion in the service sector or in the construction industry, which, combined, represent the remaining 58% of GDP. Nevertheless, we are interested in industrial production because the manufacturing sector is quite responsive to changes in economic activity. As shown in *Figure 9-2*, there is a reasonably strong correlation between production and GDP.

*Figure 9-1*
*GDP: Goods Versus Services*

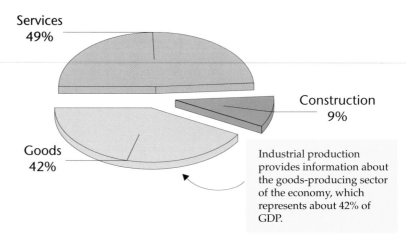

Services
49%

Construction
9%

Goods
42%

Industrial production provides information about the goods-producing sector of the economy, which represents about 42% of GDP.

INFORMATION IS IN
"REAL" (INFLATION-
ADJUSTED) TERMS

One advantage of the production data over many other series is that they measure changes in the *quantity* of output as opposed to the *dollar volume* of that production. This corresponds closely to the concept of real GDP, which attempts to measure changes in the physical output of all the goods and services produced in the economy. Many series calculate the dollar amount that was spent, but we cannot determine with certainty how much of that increase was attributable to a pickup in "real" spending and how much was caused by inflation. Yet, with the production data, we are seeing a "real" increase or decrease — they measure the change in the quantity of output produced. We do not have to worry about the extent to which inflation may be distorting the data.

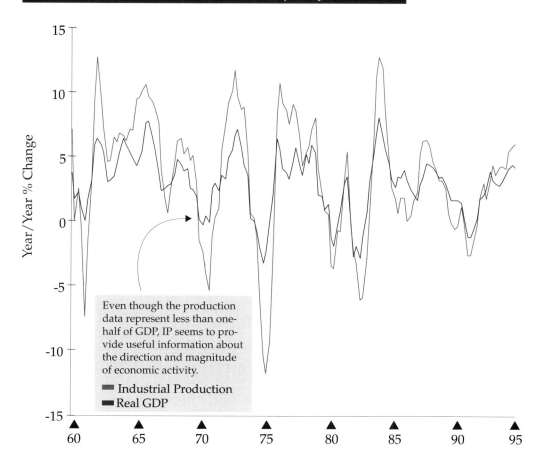

Figure 9-2
Real GDP Versus Industrial Production

Many economists utilize this report to achieve a more accurate GDP estimate for the quarter. After all, GDP measures the inflation-adjusted dollar value of all the goods and services produced by the United States on a quarterly basis. Knowing what is happening to 42% of the economy each month gives analysts a leg up in determining the overall pace of economic activity. GDP estimates formulated on this basis are known as "production-based" estimates of GDP. In these forecasts, most economists gather the industrial production statistics and then utilize data from the employment report and whatever else they can find to determine services. Most of us also formulate a second GDP equation based on demand. That is, we add up the available data on consumption, capital spending, trade, and so forth (the familiar C + I + G + X - M equation). If both estimates

INDUSTRIAL
PRODUCTION HELPS
ECONOMISTS
ESTIMATE GDP

converge, we are happy! If they do not, we try to reconcile the difference and attribute it to changes in productivity, an inventory buildup, or change in overseas demand. The important point is that the industrial production data enhance our ability to project GDP growth for that quarter.

CAPACITY UTILIZATION MEASURES EXTENT TO WHICH CAPITAL STOCK IS BEING USED

At the same time that it releases the production data, the Federal Reserve provides an estimate of capacity utilization that measures the extent to which the capital stock of the nation is being employed in the production of goods. Like production, the utilization rate rises and falls in synch with the business cycle. As the economy lifts out of recession, production accelerates and the utilization rate rises. Just beyond the peak of the cycle, production falls off and the utilization rate declines.

HIGH UTILIZATION RATES CAN BE INFLATIONARY

The reason we monitor the capacity utilization rate is because there is a threshold beyond which any further pickup in production is inflationary. Any further demand for manufactured goods outstrips the ability of manufacturers to boost production. As demand increases relative to supply, there is a tendency for prices to rise. Indeed, the importance of this series was enhanced when, in early 1994, the Federal Reserve indicated that it was using capacity utilization as one of its leading indicators of inflation. For the most part, the general public focuses on the overall utilization rate, and there is a common perception that when the utilization rate rises above some magic level, producer prices inevitably rise. *Figure 9-3* suggests that there *is* a relationship between utilization rates and the PPI, but the level at which prices begin to climb is somewhat variable — it seems to occur somewhere between 82-85%. But specialists have focused often on the utilization rate for primary-processing industries like raw steel, paper, textiles, chemicals, rubber, and plastics because late in the business cycle the combination of inventory shortages and rising demand for consumer and capital goods conspire to create price pressures in many of these industries. For this series, the so-called magic number appears to be about 85%.

Not only is the inflation threshold difficult to determine, it may also change over time — it seems to depend upon the combination of labor compensation, productivity, and competitive pressures. For example, specialists were surprised that inflation remained well-behaved in 1994 despite a high level of capacity utilization. Possibly labor costs in the manufacturing sector played a significant role in keeping those inflationary pressures in check. By the end of 1994 capacity utilization had surpassed the 85% mark. But *Figure 9-4* indicates that, in recent years, unit labor costs in the manufacturing sector were falling, presumably the result of high productivity and intense competitive pressures — in 1994, unit labor costs in manufacturing *fell* by about 2.0%. The last two times that capacity utilization was around the 85% mark, in the late 1970s and again in 1989, unit labor costs were rising. Thus, the 1994 experience is quite different and may explain why the inflation rate in that period remained well in check. After all, labor costs represent about two-thirds of a manufacturer's total cost. If they are falling, there is little pressure on that producer to raise prices.

*Figure 9-3*
*Producer Price Index Versus Capacity Utilization*

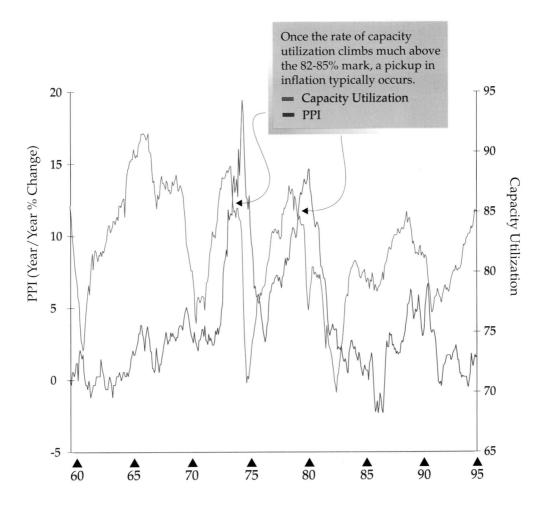

Once the rate of capacity utilization climbs much above the 82-85% mark, a pickup in inflation typically occurs.
━ Capacity Utilization
━ PPI

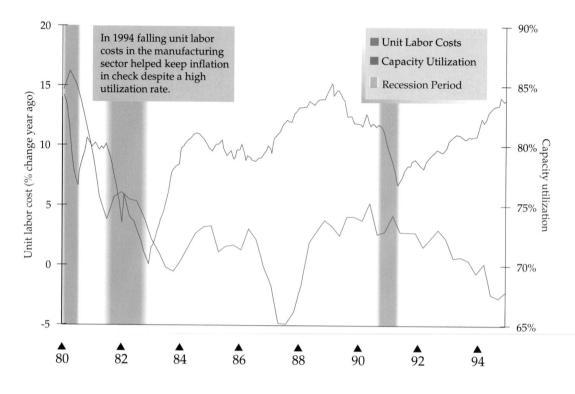

In 1994 falling unit labor costs in the manufacturing sector helped keep inflation in check despite a high utilization rate.

- Unit Labor Costs
- Capacity Utilization
- Recession Period

*Figure 9-4*
*Unit Labor Costs in Manufacturing Versus Capacity Utilization*

**INDUSTRIAL PRODUCTION IS A MEASURE OF THE PHYSICAL VOLUME OF OUTPUT**

The index of industrial production measures the physical volume of output for manufacturing, mining, and utilities. The series is prepared by the Board of Governors of the Federal Reserve System and is available close to the 15th of the month. Since it is an index number, output is expressed as a percentage of production in some base year, currently 1987. As shown in *Figure 9-5*, this index stood at 122.6 in February 1995, which means that production in that month was 22.1% higher than it was on average in 1987. The data are usually expressed as percent increases or declines relative to the prior month. For example, in January 1995 the index stood at 122.0. Thus, between January and February the series rose 0.05% or (122.6-122.0)/122.0 (This calculation can sometimes differ from the published percent change because the Federal Reserve uses unrounded data.)

INDUSTRIAL PRODUCTION AND CAPACITY UTILIZATION SUMMARY

## INDUSTRIAL PRODUCTION

| | Proportion in Total IP | Index, 1987 = 100 | | | | Percent Change | | | |
|---|---|---|---|---|---|---|---|---|---|
| | | Nov | Dec | Jan | Feb | Nov | Dec | Jan | Feb |
| Total Index | 100.0 | 120.3 | 121.7 | 122.0 | 122.6 | +0.7 | +1.1 | +0.2 | +0.5 |
| Manufacturing | 85.5 | 122.6 | 124.1 | 124.3 | 124.8 | +0.9 | +1.2 | +0.2 | +0.4 |
| Motor Vehicles & Parts | 4.8 | 141.4 | 144.6 | 146.1 | 147.4 | +2.2 | +2.2 | +1.1 | +0.9 |
| Mining | 6.8 | 98.3 | 100.1 | 100.0 | 100.2 | -0.9 | +1.9 | -0.1 | +0.1 |
| Utilities | 7.7 | 116.5 | 115.8 | 117.3 | 120.3 | -0.6 | -0.6 | +1.3 | +2.6 |

The rise in IP from 122.0 to 122.6 represents an increase of 0.5%.

## CAPACITY UTILIZATION

| | Percent of Capacity | | | |
|---|---|---|---|---|
| | Nov | Dec | Jan | Feb |
| Total Index | 84.8 | 85.5 | 85.5 | 85.7 |
| Manufacturing | 84.4 | 85.2 | 85.1 | 85.1 |
| Motor Vehicles & Parts | 87.2 | 88.8 | 89.4 | 89.7 |
| Mining | 88.2 | 89.8 | 89.7 | 89.9 |
| Utilities | 85.8 | 85.2 | 86.2 | 88.3 |

Because automobile production represents 4.8% of total IP, the 0.9% rise from 146.1 to 147.4 means that auto production accounted for 0.4% of the 0.5% increase in IP for February.
(0.9% x .048 = 0.4%)

Figure 9-5
Industrial Production and Capacity Utilization Summary

To construct the index, the Board uses two types of data. In some areas of production, the Federal Reserve can obtain a direct measure of the physical amount of goods produced. In other cases, where direct measurement is impossible, the Federal Reserve estimates output by using a combination of hours worked by production workers (from the monthly employment report) and industrial electric power consumption. For that reason, it is not surprising that the data on employment and hours worked by manufacturing workers released by the Bureau of Labor Statistics each month are *extremely* helpful in forecasting

THE FEDERAL RESERVE USES SOME HARD DATA, BUT A GREAT DEAL MUST BE ESTIMATED the change in industrial production. Of the various economic indicators, industrial production is probably the easiest to predict.

**WE CAN DETERMINE ANY PARTICULAR CATEGORY'S CONTRIBUTION TO THE TOTAL CHANGE**

Once the Fed has deduced the volume of production for about 250 individual series, it multiplies each series by the weight that particular component had in the base year. It then adds up the contribution from each of these separate categories to determine the overall index. This method has the advantage of allowing us to determine the contribution stemming from any one particular category. For example, in *Figure 9-5* we can see that the index for utilities rose from 117.3 to 120.3 in February 1995, a gain of 2.6%. That same table reveals that the utilities category represents 7.7% of the series. Thus, one can conclude that the utilities category accounted for slightly more than 0.2% of the overall increase of 0.5% (2.6% x .077).

**CAPACITY UTILIZATION MEASURES THE PERCENT OF MAXIMUM *SUSTAINABLE* OUTPUT BEING USED**

Capacity utilization is the ratio of the index of industrial production to a related index of capacity. The production measure, discussed in detail previously, is rather straightforward, but the capacity part of the equation is a bit ambiguous. What is "capacity" supposed to represent? The maximum amount of output that can be generated in the event of war? The maximum amount of output that can be produced without giving rise to inflation? The Fed has decided that it does not want to measure peak output. Rather, it attempts to define a realistically *sustainable* maximum level of output. It defines capacity as the maximum level of production that can be obtained using a normal employee work schedule, with existing equipment, and allowing normal downtime for maintenance, repair, and cleanup. This means that two companies, with identical equipment but with different work schedules, can have different capacities. (It also means that in times of peak production, utilization rates can sometimes exceed 100.0% which, at first blush, seems impossible.)

**ONCE INDUSTRIAL PRODUCTION HAS BEEN PROJECTED, CAPACITY UTILIZATION IS EASY TO ESTIMATE**

Once economists have made their forecast of industrial production, by definition they have also made their projection of capacity utilization because capacity is estimated to grow at a steady pace of about 3.0% per year, or 0.25% per month. Thus, the monthly increase in capacity utilization is about 0.25% less than the rise in production.

The Industrial Production report tells us something about the pace of economic activity. Presumably, a faster pace of production indicates a more rapid rate of economic activity, which leads to either increases in interest rates or smaller declines than were predicted previously. Thus, an unanticipated rise in industrial production usually prompts a sell-off in the bond market *(Figure 9-6)*. However, economists generally have been able to deduce the change in this series far in advance of its release. As a result, the outcome is usually well-anticipated and the market reaction is small.

**A FASTER PACE OF PRODUCTION LEADS TO A BOND MARKET SELL-OFF**

The equity markets also view a rise in production as indicative of a faster pace of economic activity which, for them, is positive. But, as is the case for bonds, production is not usually much of a market mover.

**FASTER PRODUCTION CAN TRIGGER A STOCK MARKET RALLY**

The dollar typically does not respond much to changes in production. In theory, however, a faster rate of growth in the economy leads to higher short-term interest rates. Thus, an unanticipated increase in industrial production boosts the dollar to some extent.

**A FASTER PACE OF PRODUCTION INCREASES THE VALUE OF THE DOLLAR**

Changes in capacity utilization are not generally very important to the markets because they are directly related to production. If economists miss their forecast of production, they also, by definition, will be off target on their estimate of capacity utilization. The only time the utilization rate seems to be important is when it has neared the 85% area. Then market participants pay more attention and begin to worry about bottlenecks and a possible rise in inflation — bad news for both bonds and stocks.

**CHANGES IN UTILIZATION RATES GENERALLY ARE NOT IMPORTANT TO THE MARKETS**

*Figure 9-6*
*Market Reaction to*
*Industrial Production*

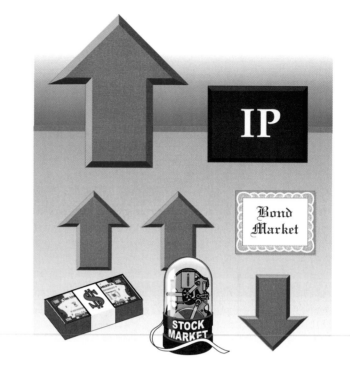

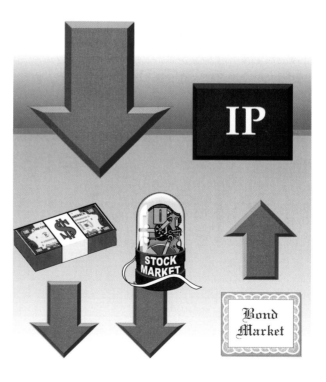

I FEEL GOOD!

| Importance: | ★ ★ |
| --- | --- |
| Published By: | **Survey Research Center of the University of Michigan** |
| Availability: | **Preliminary: 13th -20th for previous month (2nd or 3rd Friday) Final: 2 weeks later (last Friday)** |
| Frequency: | **Monthly** |
| Volatility: | **Moderate** |

## HOW THE MARKET REACTS

| | | Stock Market | Bond Market | Dollar |
| --- | --- | --- | --- | --- |
| Fixed-Income: | CONSUMER SENTIMENT ↑ | | ↓ | |
| | CONSUMER SENTIMENT ↓ | | ↑ | |
| Equity: | CONSUMER SENTIMENT ↑ | ↑ | | |
| | CONSUMER SENTIMENT ↓ | ↓ | | |
| Dollar: | CONSUMER SENTIMENT ↑ | | | ↑ |
| | CONSUMER SENTIMENT ↓ | | | ↓ |

## NOTEWORTHY CHARACTERISTICS

✓ Consumer sentiment is a leading indicator of economic activity.

✓ There are three different measures of consumer confidence.

CONSUMER SENTIMENT SURVEYS ARE RELATIVELY IMPORTANT INDICATORS OF THE FUTURE COURSE OF THE ECONOMY

If a meaningful number of consumers become concerned about job security, they most certainly will begin to feel less confident about the future — and less prone to spend. In this situation the most likely category of expenditures to be affected is consumer durables — houses, cars, furniture, and appliances. If you are worried about your job, you are probably not going to rush out to buy a new house or car and take on the monthly payments typically associated with such purchases. Furthermore, once you have made the decision to cut back on these expenditures — and postponed them for some time — it makes sense that when your degree of confidence picks up, these will be the first items you buy.

THERE ARE THREE DIFFERENT MEASURES OF CONSUMER CONFIDENCE — WE ARE PRIMARILY INTERESTED IN THE ONE CONDUCTED BY THE UNIVERSITY OF MICHIGAN

This chapter will focus upon the consumer sentiment survey conducted by the University of Michigan, primarily because the expectations component of this report is one of the eleven components of the index of leading indicators. Recently the Commerce Department did extensive statistical work and decided that of all the available measures of confidence, this one seemed to be most closely correlated with the future pace of economic activity. *Figure 10-1* indicates that consumer confidence does, indeed, seem to turn up and down just prior to changes in the business cycle. It is, therefore, a leading economic indicator. The series is derived from a monthly telephone survey of about 500 consumers. Preliminary results are released about two weeks after the end of the month, with final results available generally on the last Friday of the month. The Michigan index of "consumer sentiment" combines responses to five questions about the survey participants' personal financial situation and their view of both current and future general business conditions *(see Figure 10-2)*. Two of the questions (#1 and #5) refer solely to the present. Responses to these questions form the basis for the "current economic conditions" component of the survey. Thus, the U of M's current conditions category focuses directly on the risk of near-term financial distress and its implications for current purchases of consumer durable goods. The other three questions (#2, #3, and #4) are forward-looking questions that ask about expected conditions over the next one to five years. They are combined to form the "index of consumer expectations." As a rule of thumb, the expectations categories combined receive roughly a 60% weighting in the calculation of the sentiment index, while current conditions comprise about 40%. Thus, the overall index of consumer sentiment is heavily weighted towards the respondents' assessment of economic conditions 1-5 years into the future.

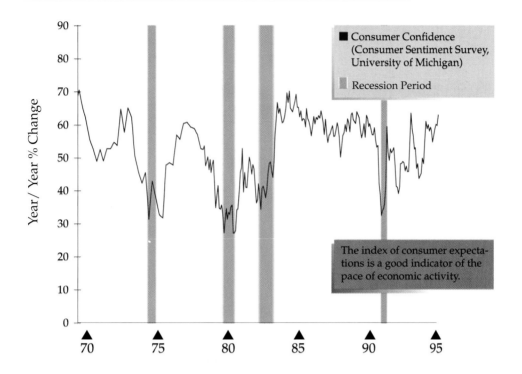

*Figure 10-1*
*Consumer Expectations Index*

There is another survey of consumer confidence conducted monthly by the Conference Board. This is a much broader survey of some 5,000 respondents, but it is done by mail. Hence, its results are less timely. The data are generally released a few days prior to the end of the month. They come almost two weeks after the University of Michigan's *preliminary* report, but will typically beat the *final* Michigan data by a couple of days. Like its University of Michigan counterpart, the Conference Board survey asks for the consumers' assessment of both current and future economic conditions. But in evaluating current conditions, the Conference Board explicitly asks about the respondents' job and income prospects rather than the Michigan survey's somewhat vague notion of their "financial situation." Furthermore, the Conference Board asks survey participants about expectations over the next six months, a much shorter time period than in the Michigan survey. The results of the two surveys are then combined to form the overall index of "consumer confidence." Specifically, the Conference Board gives the expectations compo-

THE CONFERENCE BOARD PUBLISHES ANOTHER MONTHLY SERIES ON CONSUMER CONFIDENCE nent a 60% weighting, while the current conditions weighting is 40% — roughly the same as in the Michigan survey. But because the expectations category refers to six months in the future in this survey as opposed to 1-5 years in the Michigan report, the Conference Board index of consumer confidence has a decidedly shorter time horizon than its U of M counterpart.

*Figure 10-2*
*Questions Asked by the*
*University of*
*Michigan's*
*Consumer Sentiment*
*Survey*

**University of Michigan's Consumer Sentiment Survey**

*1. We are interested in how people are getting along financially these days. Would you say that you (and your family living there) are better off or worse off financially than you were a year ago?*

*2. Now looking ahead—do you think that a year from now you (and your family living there) will be better off financially, or worse off, or just about the same as now?*

*3. Now turning to business conditions in the country as a whole—do you think that during the next twelve months we'll have good times financially, or bad times, or what?*

*4. Looking ahead, which would you say is more likely—that in the country as a whole we'll have continuous good times during the next five years or so, or that we will have periods of widespread unemployment or depression, or what?*

*5. About the big things people buy for their homes—such as furniture, a refrigerator, stove, television, and things like that, generally speaking, do you think now is a good time for people to buy major household items?*

**THERE IS ALSO A WEEKLY SURVEY OF "CONSUMER COMFORT"**

The ABC News/Money Magazine people have joined forces to produce a *weekly* consumer confidence measure, which they call the "index of consumer comfort." Every week they conduct a telephone survey of about 1,000 respondents. The survey week ends on a Monday, and the results are published late in the day on Wednesday. Unlike the other two series, however, this survey only captures *current conditions*. While the survey is done weekly, the markets do not pay much attention to it. Economists will frequently use these weekly data to formulate their forecasts of the University of Michigan and Conference Board series. But this is risky because the other two series are heavily weighted towards future rather than current economic conditions. This "consumer comfort" measure, with its exclusive focus on current conditions, is a fundamentally different concept. Despite differences in the way the three consumer yardsticks are constructed, the trend movements in these series are quite similar *(see Figure 10-3)*. On a month-to-month basis, however, they can tell quite different stories. As noted earlier, we tend to focus more heavily on the University of Michigan's survey of consumer sentiment. In part this is because its expectations component is one of the eleven components of the index of leading indicators but also, due to differences in construction, it seems to be less volatile despite its smaller sample size.

*Figure 10-3*
*Consumer Confidence Measures*

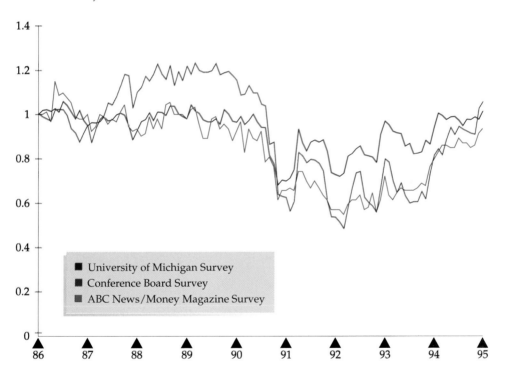

As shown in *Figure 10-4*, the University of Michigan will take the percent of respondents that report better conditions, subtract the percent that say conditions are worse, and add 100. The Conference Board, however, takes the percent of better responses, divides by the sum of better and worse, and seasonally adjusts the results. We have found that monthly changes in the

OVER TIME ALL THREE OF THESE MEASURES OF CONFIDENCE WILL MOVE TOGETHER

Conference Board series on consumer confidence are about double that of the University of Michigan's series on consumer sentiment. Thus, it gives the appearance of being far more volatile, with higher highs and lower lows. The ABC/Money Magazine series simply reflects the percent of better responses less the percent that say conditions are worse. When consumers are worried about the future, this series can obviously be negative, which is a somewhat annoying feature. It can easily be converted to a more normal-looking series, however, by simply adding 100 to the result.

**THE TWO UNIVERSITY OF MICHIGAN SERIES SEEM TO PERFORM BETTER THAN THEIR CONFERENCE BOARD COUNTERPARTS**

We have found that the *current conditions* component from the Michigan survey is a fairly good indicator of the future pace of spending on consumer durables. You will recall that one of the two questions that is used to derive this series asks specifically about whether this is a good time to purchase consumer durables. The *expectations component* from the University of Michigan seems to be helpful in forecasting housing expenditures where longer term decisions are involved. The Conference Board survey provides similar results, but in both cases the results were somewhat less favorable.

**A RISE IN CONFIDENCE CAN SPOOK THE BOND MARKET**

A rise in consumer confidence can give the bond market the jitters because it is indicative of a faster pace of economic activity in the months ahead *(see Figure 10-5)*. If GDP growth accelerates, the odds are that interest rates will rise, which causes bond prices to fall. A drop in confidence will trigger the opposite bond market response. Because the confidence numbers are hard to predict, the reaction can be quite sizable. Furthermore, bond market participants will sometimes draw a distinction between the "current economic conditions" and the "index of consumer expectations" categories, with greater weight being attached to the latter. This is because the expectations component is presumably more indicative of future economic activity, but also because it is incorporated directly into the index of leading indicators. Large changes in confidence will push that series significantly higher or lower.

If a jump in confidence is indicative of a faster pace of economic activity, it should generally be viewed favorably by the stock market because of its positive impact on corporate profits. At some point, however, when the economy is at or close to full employment, equity participants may worry that a rise in confidence may be inflationary. In that case, the Fed will tighten, interest rates will rise, and the economy may well dip into recession — obviously not a desirable outcome for stocks. In general, however, a rise in confidence is good for stocks, particularly for consumer durable-goods-producing companies.

**THE STOCK MARKET RESPONDS FAVORABLY TO A JUMP IN CONFIDENCE**

A faster pace of economic activity is usually somewhat supportive of the dollar because of the presumed impact on interest rates. But, as is frequently the case with these economic indicators, a faster pace of economic activity implies a faster growth rate for imports and a larger trade deficit — not what the foreign exchange markets would like to see. While the situation is frequently confusing, on balance a rise in confidence is usually dollar positive.

**A RISE IN CONFIDENCE MAY HELP THE DOLLAR**

*Figure 10-4  Comparison of Consumer Sentiment, Consumer Confidence, and Consumer Comfort*

| Method of Calculation | Number of Respondents |
|---|---|
| 1. Consumer Sentiment (University of Michigan) | 500 |
| Sentiment = % Better - % Worse + 100 | |
| 2. Consumer Confidence (Conference Board) | 5,000 |
| $\text{Confidence} = \dfrac{\% \text{ Better}}{\% \text{ Better} + \% \text{ Worse}} \times \text{Seasonal Factor}$ | |
| 3. Consumer Comfort (ABC/Money Magazine ) | 1,000 |
| Comfort = % Better - % Worse | |

*Figure 10-5*
*Market Reaction to*
*Consumer Sentiment*

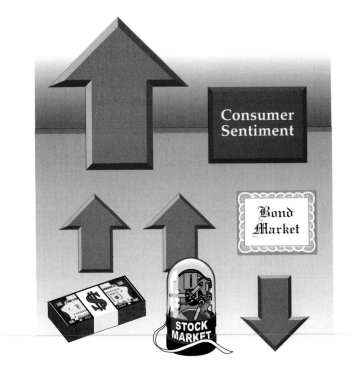

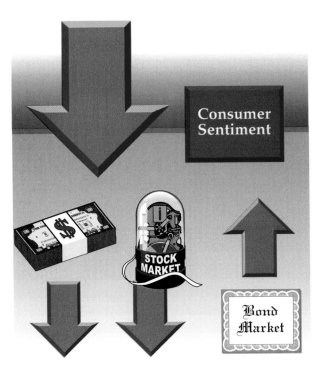

HELTER SHELTER

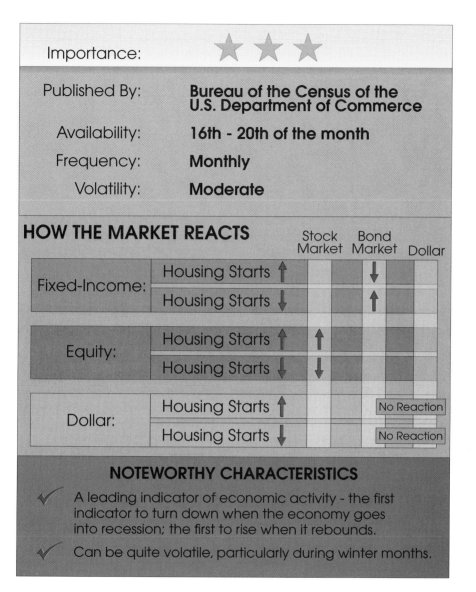

| Importance: | ★ ★ ★ |
| --- | --- |
| Published By: | **Bureau of the Census of the U.S. Department of Commerce** |
| Availability: | **16th - 20th of the month** |
| Frequency: | **Monthly** |
| Volatility: | **Moderate** |

## HOW THE MARKET REACTS

| | | Stock Market | Bond Market | Dollar |
| --- | --- | --- | --- | --- |
| Fixed-Income: | Housing Starts ↑ | | ↓ | |
| | Housing Starts ↓ | | ↑ | |
| Equity: | Housing Starts ↑ | ↑ | | |
| | Housing Starts ↓ | ↓ | | |
| Dollar: | Housing Starts ↑ | | | No Reaction |
| | Housing Starts ↓ | | | No Reaction |

## NOTEWORTHY CHARACTERISTICS

✓ A leading indicator of economic activity - the first indicator to turn down when the economy goes into recession; the first to rise when it rebounds.

✓ Can be quite volatile, particularly during winter months.

**THE HOUSING SECTOR TENDS TO LEAD THE REST OF THE ECONOMY**

Housing starts are an extremely important indicator when forecasting the economy because most economic turnarounds in the post-World War II period have been precipitated by changes in household spending habits. Invariably, these changes become apparent first in the housing and automobile sectors of the economy *(Figure 11-1)*. This occurs partly because these types of

*Figure 11-1*
*Housing Starts*

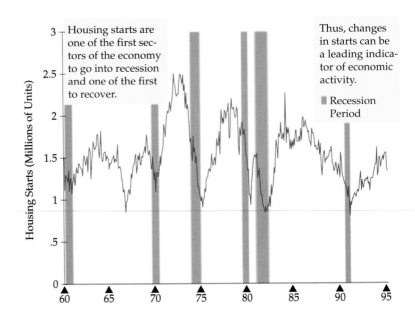

Housing starts are one of the first sectors of the economy to go into recession and one of the first to recover.

Thus, changes in starts can be a leading indicator of economic activity.

■ Recession Period

expenditures account for such a large portion of consumer spending *(Figure 11-2)*. It is fairly obvious that if the consumer is concerned about the outlook for the economy and his or her job six months from now, or worried about the level of interest rates and the ability to repay debts, he or she is probably going to postpone plans to buy a new house or new car as both represent "big ticket" items in the family budget.

*Figure 11-2*
*United States*
*Household Budget*

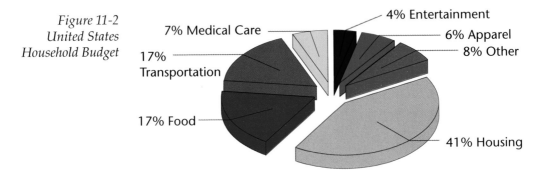

4% Entertainment
7% Medical Care
6% Apparel
8% Other
17% Transportation
17% Food
41% Housing

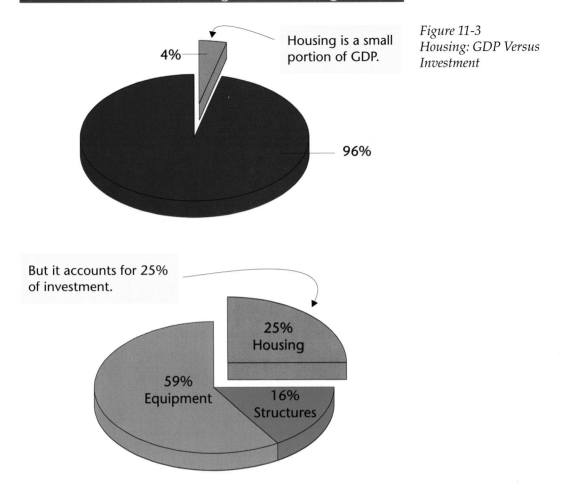

*Figure 11-3*
*Housing: GDP Versus*
*Investment*

Since the housing sector accounts for 25% of investment spending and 4% of the overall U.S. economy *(Figure 11-3)*, a sustained decline in housing starts causes the economy to slow down and possibly head into recession. Likewise, a sharp rise in starts accomplishes the opposite — it boosts economic activity, which helps pull the economy out of recession. Keep in mind that these figures only represent the *direct* effect of housing on the economy. It is also important to recognize that there is a multiplier effect that takes place, as the demand for housing-related durables, like furniture and appliances, is tied closely to housing market activity.

HOUSING IS A VERY
IMPORTANT SECTOR
OF THE ECONOMY

**CHANGES IN HOUSING ARE TRIGGERED BY CHANGES IN MORTGAGE RATES**

Changes in housing starts generally are triggered by changes in interest rates, especially mortgage rates *(Figure 11-4)*. High rates ultimately result in a decline for home sales which, in turn, produces a drop-off in starts. Conversely, low mortgage rates tend to spur both housing sales and starts.

*Figure 11-4 Mortgage Rates Versus New Home Sales*

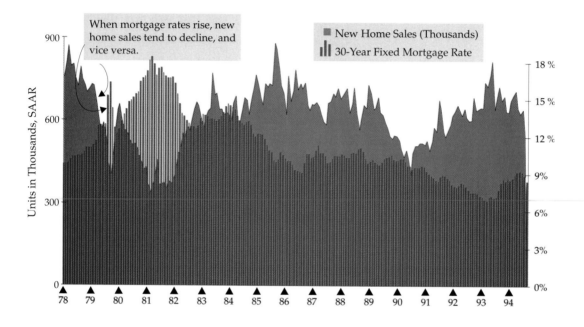

**REPORT PROVIDES DATA ON BOTH SINGLE- AND MULTI-FAMILY DWELLINGS**

Data on privately owned housing starts are collected by the Bureau of the Census, a unit of the Department of Commerce.

*Figure 11-5 New Privately Owned Housing Units Started*

| | | Single-Family | Multi-Family | | Geographic Area | | | |
|---|---|---|---|---|---|---|---|---|
| | | | 2-4 | 5 units | North- | Mid- | | |
| | Total | 1 unit | units | or more | east | west | South | West |
| **1994** | | | | | | | | |
| Sept. | 1,511 | 1,235 | 42 | 234 | 136 | 337 | 659 | 379 |
| Oct. | 1,451 | 1,164 | 39 | 248 | 130 | 313 | 648 | 360 |
| Nov. | 1,536 | 1,186 | 62 | 288 | 159 | 380 | 661 | 336 |
| Dec. | 1,545 | 1,250 | 33 | 262 | 139 | 341 | 714 | 351 |
| **1995** | | | | | | | | |
| Jan. | 1,359 | 1,059 | 37 | 263 | 115 | 292 | 623 | 329 |
| Feb. | 1,323 | 1,053 | 38 | 232 | 130 | 296 | 553 | 344 |

New Privately Owned Housing Units Started (Thousands, SAAR) 1994/1995

Starts are divided into single-family and multi-family categories *(Figure 11-5)*. In both cases, a housing unit is considered "started" when excavation actually begins. A single-family home counts as one start; a 100-unit apartment building counts as 100 starts. In general, construction of single-family houses is regarded as a better indicator of future economic trends, mainly because it is less volatile. Multi-family starts tend to fluctuate, as construction of apartment buildings may add large multiple units in any given month. The weather is another factor one should monitor when analyzing a single month's data. Particularly adverse weather conditions may temporarily reduce the level of starts for a month or two, but as the weather improves, starts typically surge and compensate for losses in prior months.

Building permits are released along with housing starts. Collected monthly from some 19,000 permit issuers, the number of permits frequently provides clues to the upcoming month's level of starts *(Figure 11-6)*. One should expect starts to be about 10% higher than permits, as a general rule, simply because some localities do not require permit issuance. Since permits are such a good indicator of future economic activity, the Commerce Department includes this series in its index of leading economic indicators (see Chapter 15).

**CHANGES IN BUILDING PERMITS LEAD STARTS BY ABOUT ONE MONTH**

*Figure 11-6 Housing Starts and Building Permits*

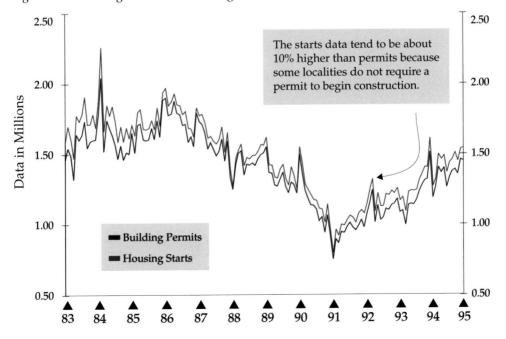

The starts data tend to be about 10% higher than permits because some localities do not require a permit to begin construction.

Building Permits
Housing Starts

**FORECASTING STARTS AND PERMITS IS TRICKY BUSINESS**

As noted previously, adverse weather conditions can cause sharp fluctuations in the level of both starts and permits, which makes forecasting difficult. Economists use a variety of techniques to estimate these two series. First, they may use the employment and hours worked data for the construction industry from the employment report that is issued two weeks earlier. After all, if one knows how many people were working in the construction industry and how long they worked, one should have some indication of how many houses were started in that month. Also, the level of single-family permits in the previous month can provide some sense of what single-family starts will be in the current month since these permits tend to lead starts by about one month. Finally, as described in more detail in the chapter on new home sales (Chapter 16), the National Association of Home Builders provides a monthly survey of conditions in the housing sector that is released one day prior to the housing starts release. The "traffic" data, in particular, have tracked new home sales fairly well in recent years. If home sales rise or fall by any significant amount, it makes sense that builders will quickly alter their construction plans. We should see a response first in single-family permits, followed by a change in single-family starts one month later.

**RISE IN STARTS PROMPTS A BOND MARKET SELL-OFF**

Starts and permits typically presage changes in the level of economic activity and GDP. Therefore, a larger-than-expected increase in either series is viewed negatively by the fixed-income market *(Figure 11-7)*. A weaker-than-expected report is taken bullishly, since a soft housing sector ultimately leads to lower interest rates.

**STOCKS' RESPONSE DEPENDS UPON WHERE WE ARE IN THE BUSINESS CYCLE**

The stock market's response to housing starts and permits is usually tied to the outlook for the economy. However, the reaction may be positive or negative depending upon where we are in the business cycle. If inflation is a concern (usually late in the cycle), a lower-than-expected starts figure could be construed bullishly. Conversely, early in the cycle, equity players prefer strength in the housing sector, especially if interest rates are not particularly bothersome.

**THE DOLLAR SHOULD NOT BE AFFECTED**

The U.S. dollar is generally not affected by housing reports unless the Federal Reserve is trigger-happy to ease or tighten credit.

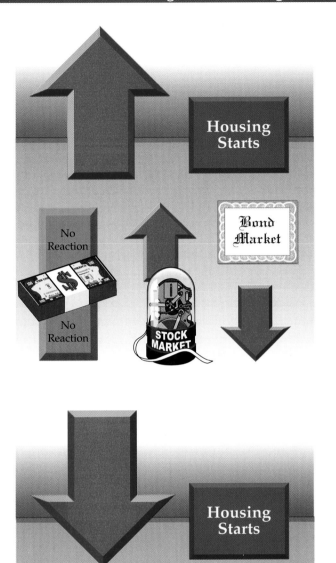

*Figure 11-7
Market Reaction to
Housing Starts*

## WHAT IS YOUR WALLET REALLY WORTH?

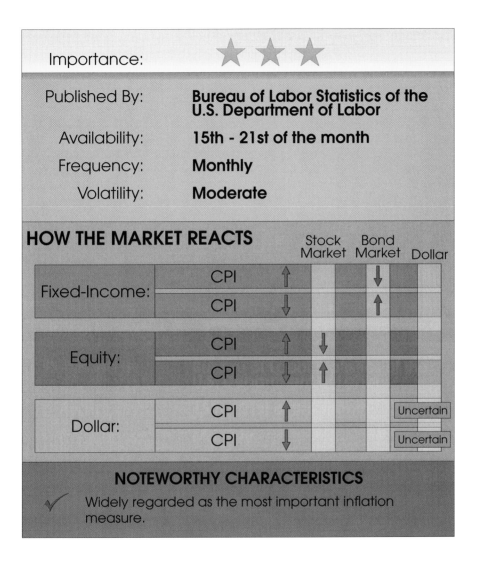

| Importance: | ★ ★ ★ |
|---|---|
| Published By: | **Bureau of Labor Statistics of the U.S. Department of Labor** |
| Availability: | **15th - 21st of the month** |
| Frequency: | **Monthly** |
| Volatility: | **Moderate** |

**HOW THE MARKET REACTS**

| | | | Stock Market | Bond Market | Dollar |
|---|---|---|---|---|---|
| **Fixed-Income:** | CPI | ↑ | | ↓ | |
| | CPI | ↓ | | ↑ | |
| **Equity:** | CPI | ↑ | ↓ | | |
| | CPI | ↓ | ↑ | | |
| **Dollar:** | CPI | ↑ | | | Uncertain |
| | CPI | ↓ | | | Uncertain |

**NOTEWORTHY CHARACTERISTICS**

✓ Widely regarded as the most important inflation measure.

CPI IS THE MOST WIDELY UTILIZED MEASURE OF INFLATION

The consumer price index (CPI) is widely regarded as *the* measure of inflation although, as we will see later, it does have some drawbacks. The CPI is a measure of prices at the consumer level for a fixed basket of goods and services. Because it is an index number, it compares the level of prices to some base period. Currently, the base period is the average level of prices that existed between 1982 and 1984, which is set to equal 100. For example, in December 1994, the index stood at 150.2, which means that prices for that fixed basket of goods and services were 50.2% higher than they were in the base period. By comparing the level of the index at two different points in time, one can make a statement about how prices have moved in the interim. In December 1993 the CPI was 146.3; by December of 1994 it had climbed to 150.2. Dividing the latter by the former, subtracting 1, and multiplying by 100, we learn that consumer prices rose 2.7% during 1994.

THERE ARE REALLY TWO CONSUMER PRICE INDEXES — THE CPI-U AND THE CPI-W

The CPI-U relates to all urban workers who cover about 80% of the civilian population. The CPI-W, which relates to wage earners and clerical workers, is much smaller and covers only about 40% of the population. The CPI-U is the most popular version and the one that receives all the press attention. When those of us in the market talk about the CPI, we are really talking about the CPI-U. But, curiously, the CPI-W is used to adjust private sector collective bargaining agreements and payments to Social Security recipients and government/military retirees. For example, Social Security cost-of-living adjustments (COLAs) which become effective on January 1 of each year, are equal to the change in the average level of the CPI-W for the third quarter of the current year from the third period of the previous year. (Income tax brackets, however, are indexed to the third quarter over third quarter change in the CPI-U.)

THE LABOR DEPARTMENT CONDUCTS A PERIODIC SURVEY TO DETERMINE WHAT CONSTITUTES THE CPI

To determine what items should go into the CPI, the Bureau of Labor Statistics (BLS) conducts a survey of consumer expenditures about every 10 years. That survey estimates the loaves of bread purchased per month by the consumer, the quarts of milk consumed, and so forth. The most recent extensive survey covered the period from 1982 to 1984. As consumer buying patterns change over the years, the items that are included in the CPI also change. From that survey of consumer expenditures, the BLS is able to determine the appropriate weights to attach to every one of the 364 items that go into the index. Each month the Bureau combines those individual items into seven major

expenditure categories that, together with the relative importance of each, are shown in *Figure 12-1*.

*Figure 12-1*
*CPI Weightings*

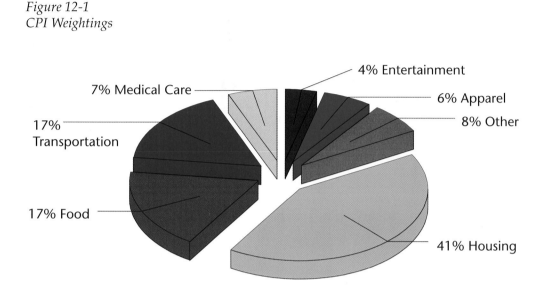

The CPI includes imports, which is obviously very important
during periods when the value of the dollar is changing rapidly.
But the CPI also has some flaws. The biggest problem is that the
coverage of the CPI is not nearly as extensive as some other
measures of inflation *(Figure 12-2)*.

THE PRIMARY
ADVANTAGE OF THE
CPI IS THAT IT
INCLUDES PRICES
OF IMPORTED
GOODS

As noted in the chapter on GDP, the *fixed-weight deflator* — the
nearest competitor to the CPI in terms of importance — includes
over 5,000 items. This compares to 364 items in the CPI (see also
Chapter 2 and *Figure 2-16*). In addition to prices of consumer
goods and services, the fixed-weight deflator includes prices of
capital goods, inventories, and housing. Thus, it is a much
broader measure of inflation but it, too, has deficiencies — it is
strictly a domestic measure of inflation. This happens because
GDP is a measure of the value of goods and services produced in
the U.S. The fixed-weight deflator, therefore, tells us nothing
about what is happening to the prices of imported goods. Given
the increasing importance of the trade sector in our economy, this
is a serious drawback.

The *implicit deflator* is also important, but because the weights attached to goods and services are based on their relative importance to GDP, it is not really a measure of pure inflation.

Finally, the PPI is a measure of the prices that producers pay for the goods that they buy (see Chapter 7). The PPI tells us quite a

*Figure 12-2 Coverage of the Various Measures*

| | CPI | Fixed-Weight Deflator | Implicit Deflator | PPI |
|---|---|---|---|---|
| Domestically Produced Consumer Goods | Yes (retail) | Yes | Yes | Yes (wholesale) |
| Imported Consumer Goods | Yes | No | No | No |
| Housing | Yes | Yes | Yes | No |
| Capital Equipment | No | Yes | Yes | Yes |
| Services | Yes | Yes | Yes | No |
| Biggest Drawbacks | ✓Smallest sample size | ✓No imported goods | ✓No imported goods ✓Weights shift | ✓No services ✓No housing |
| Biggest Advantages | ✓Includes imported goods | ✓Large sample size | ✓Large sample size | ✓Hints of future inflation |

bit about what is happening to commodity prices, but it tells us nothing about the construction industry or services. Since services and construction represent over one-half of the economy (49% and 9%, respectively), the PPI is, in a sense, incomplete. Nevertheless, it provides some hints about upcoming changes in many of the goods categories included in the CPI.

All things considered, many economists regard the CPI as the most relevant measure of inflation, although every one of these four inflation indexes provides a part of the story.

The CPI is a "fixed-weight" price index, and it is the nature of such an index to overestimate inflation to the extent that the base period is increasingly far in the past. Estimates of this overstatement vary, but they are generally in a range from ½% to 1½%. The problem arises primarily because the current CPI is based on spending patterns that existed between 1982 and 1984. But the consumer has changed considerably in the decade since the last survey was taken. For example, shoppers are far more inclined to avoid a name brand product today and seek its far less expensive generic equivalent. If the CPI accurately reflected these changes in spending patterns, it would be rising more slowly. A similar type of distortion occurs in the health care industry where the BLS uses list prices in determining price movements. But almost all providers of medical services have contracts with private insurance companies, Medicare, and Medicaid that limit the fees for almost all services. These discounted prices are what the providers of care actually receive for their services and are, therefore, a more accurate indicator of what health care actually costs. Indeed, the Health Care Financing Administration developed an index of these so-called "transactions" prices for hospital services and found that it is growing only about 70% as fast as the comparable BLS series!

A second overstatement of the CPI stems from inadequate adjustment for improvements in quality. These changes are being made at an incredibly rapid rate, and the BLS price indexes have not kept pace. For example, in the health care industry the CPI uses per day hospital charges as its unit of measurement. But today, patients tend to leave earlier than they did ten years ago and, once home, recuperate faster. This comes about because of improved surgical techniques and high-tech machinery that allows faster diagnosis. So even though the *per day* charge for a hospital stay has risen, the *total* cost of the operation has fallen because of these technological advancements. Also, many operations are now being done on an outpatient basis. A particular type of knee surgery, for example, has fallen from $13,500 ten years ago to $3,500 at one West Coast hospital when it began performing the procedure on an outpatient basis. This is a 75% decline in the cost of that operation. But once an outpatient procedure replaces the conventional one, the procedure drops out of the BLS hospital price index. In a sense, the price decrease is lost.

THE CPI IS GENERALLY BELIEVED TO OVERSTATE THE TRUE INFLATION RATE BY ABOUT 1%

THIS OVERSTATEMENT OF THE CPI CAN BE VERY COSTLY FOR THE TAXPAYER

With income taxes and all government entitlements programs indexed to the CPI, any overstatement can be very costly for the American taxpayer. Federal Reserve Chairman Greenspan recently testified that a 1% reduction to indexed programs would lower the annual level of the deficit by about $55 billion after five years. These days, as Congress attempts to find budget savings under every rock, that represents a sizable drop.

ECONOMISTS CONCENTRATE ON THE CPI EXCLUDING FOOD AND ENERGY — THE CORE RATE OF INFLATION

As was the case with the PPI, economists will invariably exclude the volatile food and energy components and focus on the CPI excluding food and energy, the so-called "core" rate of inflation. They do this because food prices can be quite volatile depending upon weather conditions. You may recall that there was a severe drought in 1988, which temporarily boosted food prices. However, when supplies increased later in that year, food prices fell sharply. Similarly, oil prices can, upon occasion, fluctuate wildly. If oil prices surge in one month only to plummet two months later, it makes sense to exclude their impact on the overall CPI. But economists are often accused of "ex-ing" too many items — ex food, ex energy, ex tobacco, ex autos — and perhaps some of that criticism is valid. But the reason we exclude certain items is because we want to determine changes in the *trend* rate of inflation and not be distracted by aberrations. If oil prices rise and it seems likely to be a temporary phenomenon, we rightfully should look at the CPI excluding the impact of the higher oil prices. But if oil prices rise and remain high for three to six months, that is a different story. In that situation we should not be so quick to delete the effect of the oil price runup.

CPI INCLUDES PRICES FOR A BROAD RANGE OF CONSUMER-RELATED GOODS AND SERVICES

The consumer price index is released monthly by the Bureau of Labor Statistics of the Department of Labor. It reflects prices of food, clothing, shelter, fuels, transportation fares, charges for doctors' and dentists' services, drugs, and all sorts of other goods and services that people buy for day-to-day living. Prices are collected in 85 cities across the country on 364 different products from 18,000 tenants, 18,000 housing units, and 24,000 establishments of all kinds. The data are then weighted by their relative degree of importance and combined into the seven broad categories that were shown earlier. The CPI is released between the 15th and 21st of the month.

The markets respond to the CPI exactly the same way they react to the PPI *(Figure 12-3)*. A higher-than-expected figure is bearish for both stocks and bonds, while lower-than-anticipated gains are bullish. A pickup in inflation implies higher bond yields, which prompts bond price declines. But keep in mind that the reaction in the fixed-income market is more closely tied to the CPI *excluding* the frequently volatile food and energy components, because that series is believed to be a better approximation of the underlying rate of inflation. Analysts are also somewhat forgiving of a one-month blip. They are not going to get too excited until they see higher-than-expected data for two or three consecutive months, because it takes that much time to determine whether the trend rate of inflation has changed.

**IF CPI RISES, THE BOND MARKET WILL FALL**

A higher-than-expected inflation rate is also likely to trigger a stock market decline. Remember, stock prices reflect the value of a stream of future earnings. To the extent that inflation accelerates, those future earnings are clearly worth less. It is also reasonable to assume that higher inflation may prompt higher wage demands — a cost that firms and shareholders would have to bear.

**IF THE CPI RISES, THE STOCK MARKET WILL FALL**

The impact on the dollar is less clear. In some theoretical sense, higher inflation should be viewed negatively by overseas investors because the return on their dollar-denominated investments will be eroded by inflation. And, in fact, a higher-than-anticipated rate of inflation can sometimes be dollar bearish. But if foreign investors believe that the Federal Reserve will tighten and push short-term interest rates in the United States higher relative to those in other countries, the dollar can actually strengthen. This may seem a little perverse, but it has happened on any number of occasions.

**THE DOLLAR'S REACTION IS LESS CLEAR**

*Figure 12-3*
*Market Reaction to CPI*

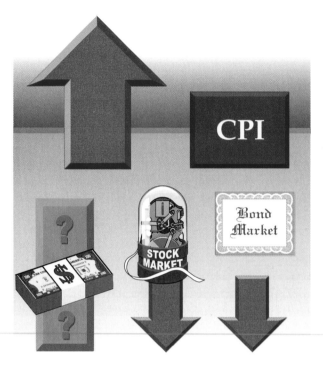

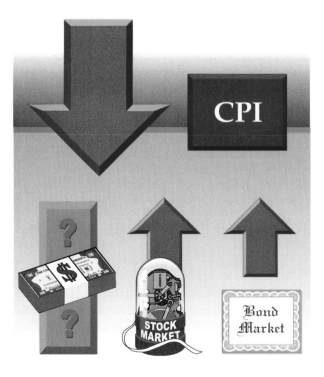

THE PRINCE OF VOLATILITY

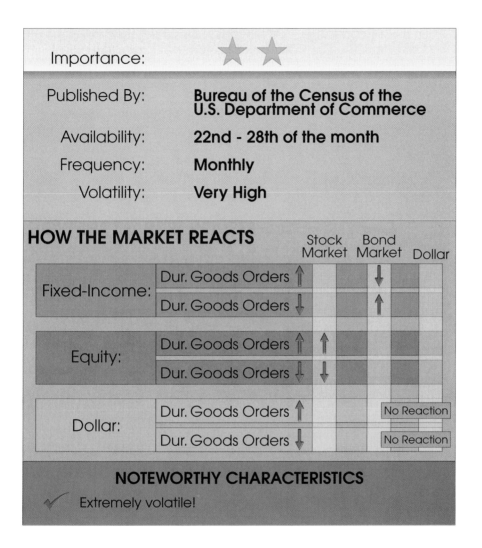

| Importance: | ★ ★ | | | |
|---|---|---|---|---|
| Published By: | **Bureau of the Census of the U.S. Department of Commerce** | | | |
| Availability: | **22nd - 28th of the month** | | | |
| Frequency: | **Monthly** | | | |
| Volatility: | **Very High** | | | |

### HOW THE MARKET REACTS

| | | Stock Market | Bond Market | Dollar |
|---|---|---|---|---|
| **Fixed-Income:** | Dur. Goods Orders ↑ | | ↓ | |
| | Dur. Goods Orders ↓ | | ↑ | |
| **Equity:** | Dur. Goods Orders ↑ | ↑ | | |
| | Dur. Goods Orders ↓ | ↓ | | |
| **Dollar:** | Dur. Goods Orders ↑ | | | No Reaction |
| | Dur. Goods Orders ↓ | | | No Reaction |

### NOTEWORTHY CHARACTERISTICS

✓ Extremely volatile!

ORDERS ARE A
LEADING INDICATOR
OF ACTIVITY IN THE
MANUFACTURING
SECTOR

Durable goods orders have the *potential* to provide market participants with much information. Orders are generally believed to be a harbinger of activity in the manufacturing sector because a manufacturer must have an order before contemplating a step-up in production. Conversely, a drop-off in orders eventually causes production to be scaled back; otherwise the manufacturer accumulates inventories that must be financed. It should be noted that 3 of the 11 components of the Commerce Department's index of leading indicators represent various types of orders — new orders for consumer goods, plant and equipment orders, and the change in the backlog of orders for durable goods industries. Clearly, orders are important in anticipating changes in production; they tend to decline 8 to 12 months ahead of a cyclical downturn, and begin to rise about one month ahead of a recession trough.

THE ORDERS DATA
ARE EXTREMELY
VOLATILE

Unfortunately, the orders data have two major drawbacks. The first problem is that they are *extremely* volatile *(Figure 13-1)*. There is no question that this is the most volatile of all the indicators described in this book, although its monthly fluctuations seem to have moderated somewhat in the past couple of years. In 1994, for example, the average monthly change (without regard to sign) was 2.2%, and those changes ranged in size from -3.9% to +6.5%. Durable goods orders are quite volatile primarily because they include civilian aircraft and defense orders. If Boeing lands a big order for one of its jumbo jets, the civilian aircraft category can change by $3-4 billion. Given that the current level of durable goods orders is about $160 billion, fluctuation in this civilian aircraft category alone can easily give rise to changes of 2%. Defense orders can do the same thing — toss in an order for a B-1 bomber or an aircraft carrier, and we will see surges in the defense category as well.

THEY ARE
NOTORIOUS FOR
SIZABLE REVISIONS

The second problem is that orders are notorious for sizable revisions once more complete data become available one week later. There have been times in the past when the advance report on durables showed an increase of, say, 2.0%, but a week later it turned into a similar-sized decline. These revised data are contained in the report on manufacturing orders, shipments, and inventories, which is discussed in Chapter 18. Essentially, the Census Bureau releases these data on durable goods orders and shipments sooner than they probably should. It would not be surprising if, at some point, they decide to dispose of this early report. The Commerce Department went through a similar

*Figure 13-1 Durable Goods Orders*

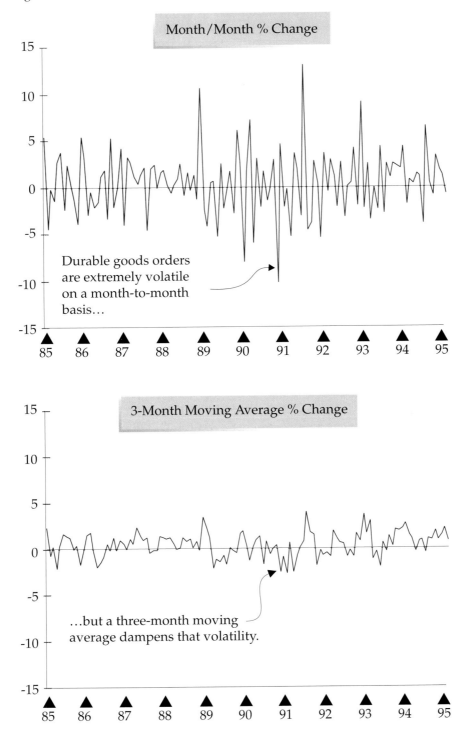

Month/Month % Change

Durable goods orders are extremely volatile on a month-to-month basis…

3-Month Moving Average % Change

…but a three-month moving average dampens that volatility.

problem with its so-called "flash" GDP report, which was released in the final month of a quarter for that same quarter. The revisions tended to be so large that eventually they decided to do away with it.

THIS VOLATILITY FORCES ECONOMISTS TO MAKE A NUMBER OF ADJUSTMENTS

Any series that is extremely volatile forces analysts to make a number of adjustments in order to interpret the data *(Figure 13-2)*. The first adjustment is looking at the data excluding the transportation category, knowing that swings in aircraft orders can be overwhelming. Analysts do the same thing with defense orders because they too can be subject to wild gyrations. By examining durable goods orders excluding transportation and excluding defense, specialists get a sense for whether the monthly change is attributable to one of the extremely volatile components. If it is, they tend to dismiss its significance. If not, then the change is probably more meaningful. Finally, analysts look at a three-month moving average, or the year-over-year percentage change, in an attempt to smooth the data and more readily determine changes in trend growth.

*Figure 13-2  How to Use the Durable Goods Data*

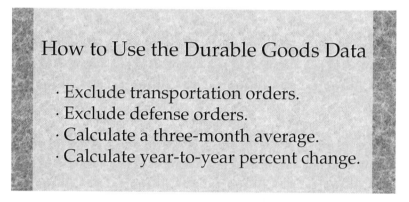

How to Use the Durable Goods Data

· Exclude transportation orders.
· Exclude defense orders.
· Calculate a three-month average.
· Calculate year-to-year percent change.

DURABLES ARE DIFFICULT TO FORECAST

The final point about the durable goods report is that it is particularly difficult to forecast. Indeed, many economists simply do not bother because there is very little data on which to base a forecast. The automobile and truck production data can help us get a handle on motor vehicle orders and shipments, but this represents only about 25% of the total. Some analysts will also track aircraft orders that are reported in the paper. But, unfortunately, there is little correlation between the time an order is reported in the paper and when that order eventually shows up on the company's books — when it is included in the Census Bureau's data. About the most we can do for many of these categories is to look at the change in the prior month. If it surged in that previous month, we will generally anticipate an offsetting decline in the current month and vice versa. This approach is not very sophisticated, but it is about all we can do when forecasting durables.

In addition to the data on durable goods *orders*, this report provides information on durable goods *shipments*. For purposes of this report, the terms "shipments" and "sales" are basically synonymous. Since manufacturing and trade sales are generally a coincident indicator of the economy, they are useful in confirming the peak or trough of a business cycle. To the extent that factory sales represent about 45% of total business sales, and shipments of durables account for the volatility in the factory portion, these data can help us get an early indication of an economic turning point.

**THIS REPORT ALSO CONTAINS DATA ON SHIPMENTS OF DURABLES**

In particular, one should pay some attention to the shipments and orders of *non-defense capital goods* — these two series provide some indication of current and future capital spending by businesses. Specifically, there is a reasonable correlation between shipments of non-defense capital goods and the producers' durable equipment category of GDP. This is an important part of the investment component, the "I" part of the familiar GDP = C + I + G + X - M equation. Equipment spending accounts for nearly 10% of GDP and about 60% of fixed investment. Thus, it is worth monitoring the data on the shipments of non-defense capital goods to get an idea about equipment spending in the current quarter, and to the comparable orders data to determine what is likely to happen in the months ahead.

**NON-DEFENSE CAPITAL GOODS CATEGORY PROVIDES INFORMATION ABOUT CAPITAL SPENDING PATTERNS**

To some extent the backlog measures the stack of orders on a businessman's desk. Each month new orders are added to the pile. Those orders that have been filled and shipped during the course of the previous month will be removed. If this pile of orders (or backlog) is growing, it makes sense that, at some point, the company will begin to step up production.

**THE BACKLOG OF ORDERS IS ALSO IMPORTANT**

THE CENSUS BUREAU CONDUCTS AN EXTENSIVE SURVEY TO COLLECT DATA

The data on durable goods orders, shipments, and the order backlog are compiled by the Census Bureau of the Department of Commerce from a monthly survey of approximately 5,000 manufacturers. But these sample data are used to estimate a universe of some 70,000 establishments. Thus, the Census Bureau is sampling less than 10% of the existing manufacturing firms. The reported data are supposed to represent firm orders for immediate or future delivery. These orders must be legally binding — supported by a signed contract, a letter of intent, or some similar type of document. Options to place additional orders at some future date are *not* included. In the aircraft industry, for example, an airline could place an order to purchase 10 aircraft for delivery over the next five years, and take an option to purchase 10 additional aircraft at some point in the future. Those additional aircraft would not be included in the durable goods report until a firm order is actually submitted. The shipments data represent the sum total of sales for that month whether for domestic use or for export.

BECAUSE DURABLES ARE HARD TO PREDICT, SURPRISES ARE FREQUENT

Because this series is both very volatile and difficult to forecast, street projections are frequently wide of the mark. Thus, there is room for shifts in the general perception of what is happening in the manufacturing sector. In the past, this series rarely generated much market excitement; but more recently there have been several occasions when the durable goods report was a market mover.

IF DURABLES SURGE, THE BOND MARKET WILL DECLINE

If the fixed-income market is surprised by a particularly strong durable goods report, i.e., a much larger-than-expected increase for a particular month (perhaps in conjunction with an upward revision), the fixed-income markets react negatively *(Figure 13-3)*. Such a report indicates more strength in the manufacturing sector and, therefore, more rapid GDP growth. If the economy is expanding more rapidly than anticipated, the markets worry about a pickup in the rate of inflation. If all of this transpires, the odds are that interest rates will rise — the prices of fixed-income securities will decline.

The reaction in the equity market is always tough to gauge. In general, a larger-than-expected rise in durables is greeted favorably. When orders rise, presumably profits are enhanced, which is a plus. But there is a caveat. If the bond market sells off sharply owing to fears of higher interest rates, then the equity markets will probably also decline — higher interest rates are always unwelcome in the equity market.

STOCKS COULD GO UP OR DOWN DEPENDING ON THE BUSINESS CYCLE...

In theory, a faster pace of economic activity is good for the dollar. Yet, in practice, this report is ignored in the foreign exchange market.

THE DOLLAR SELDOM REACTS TO THIS REPORT

*Figure 13-3
Market Reaction to
Durables*

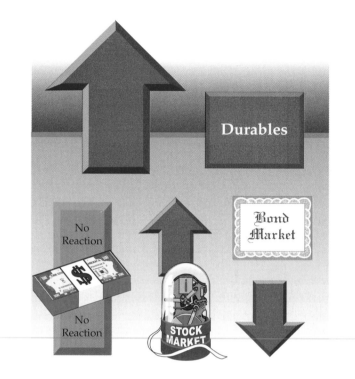

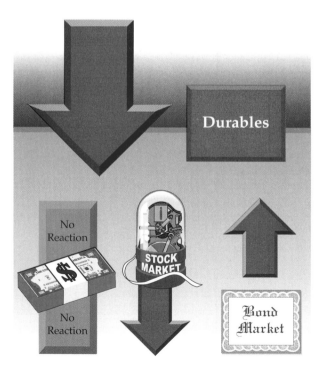

YOU MUST HAVE IT TO SPEND IT!

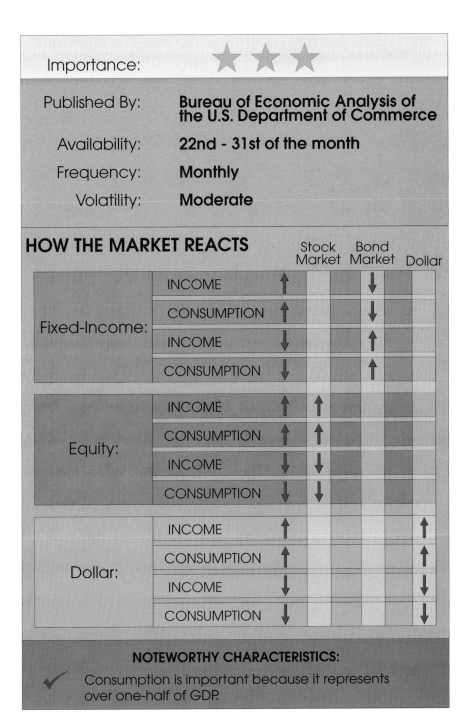

| Importance: | ★ ★ ★ |
| --- | --- |
| Published By: | **Bureau of Economic Analysis of the U.S. Department of Commerce** |
| Availability: | **22nd - 31st of the month** |
| Frequency: | **Monthly** |
| Volatility: | **Moderate** |

## HOW THE MARKET REACTS

| | | | Stock Market | Bond Market | Dollar |
| --- | --- | --- | --- | --- | --- |
| **Fixed-Income:** | INCOME | ↑ | | ↓ | |
| | CONSUMPTION | ↑ | | ↓ | |
| | INCOME | ↓ | | ↑ | |
| | CONSUMPTION | ↓ | | ↑ | |
| **Equity:** | INCOME | ↑ | ↑ | | |
| | CONSUMPTION | ↑ | ↑ | | |
| | INCOME | ↓ | ↓ | | |
| | CONSUMPTION | ↓ | ↓ | | |
| **Dollar:** | INCOME | ↑ | | | ↑ |
| | CONSUMPTION | ↑ | | | ↑ |
| | INCOME | ↓ | | | ↓ |
| | CONSUMPTION | ↓ | | | ↓ |

### NOTEWORTHY CHARACTERISTICS:

✓ Consumption is important because it represents over one-half of GDP.

PERSONAL CONSUMPTION EXPENDITURES REPRESENT OVER ONE-HALF OF GDP

Probably the most important part of this report is the information on personal consumption expenditures (PCE) because this is by far the largest component of GDP — it represents over one-half of the total (*Figure 14-1*). Consumption expenditures represent the market value of all goods and services purchased by individuals. Each month we receive additional information on consumption spending, which allows us to refine our GDP estimates. It is clearly not the *only* item factored into GDP, and occasionally, errors in our forecasts of trade, inventories, or government spending can throw our GDP estimates way off target. But if we know what happens to more than one-half of the pie, there is no doubt that we have a strong hint about what is going to happen to GDP growth for that quarter!

*Figure 14-1*
*Composition of GDP: Consumption*

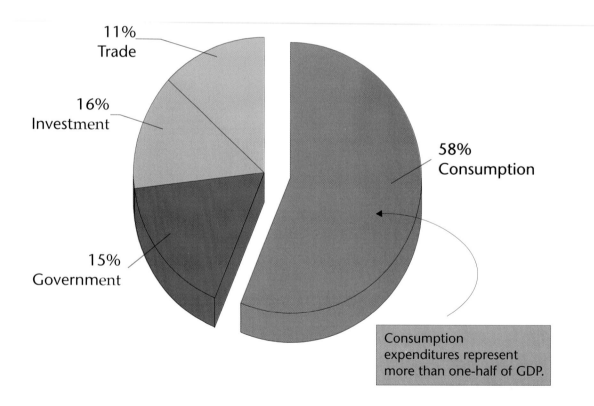

11%
Trade

16%
Investment

58%
Consumption

15%
Government

Consumption expenditures represent more than one-half of GDP.

Figure 14-2
Sources of Personal Income

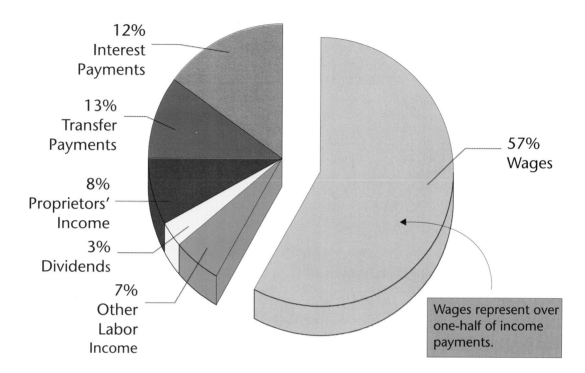

12%
Interest
Payments

13%
Transfer
Payments

8%
Proprietors'
Income

3%
Dividends

7%
Other
Labor
Income

57%
Wages

Wages represent over
one-half of income
payments.

Personal income represents the compensation that individuals receive from all sources *(Figure 14-2)*. That includes wages and salaries, proprietors' income, income from rents, dividends and interest, and transfer payments, such as Social Security, unemployment, and welfare benefits. We are interested in income because it provides the fuel for further spending. If we do not have it, we eventually are forced to cut back. We can always borrow money, allowing us to spend for a while longer. But by doing so, we increase our monthly payments — and have just that much less to spend on other things. Pay me now, or pay me later!

A related item that is not known until approximately a week later is "real" income, or income after adjustment for inflation. If personal income is expanding, but the increase merely reflects a rise in inflation, then the consumer's welfare or "real" purchasing power has not changed. These two measures of income, nominal and real, are considered to be good barometers of the current strength of the economy.

INCOME PROVIDES
THE FUEL FOR
FURTHER SPENDING

**THE SAVINGS RATE IS A GOOD INDICATION OF CONSUMERS' WILLINGNESS TO SPEND**

The personal income release also contains data on the savings rate, which reflects consumers' desire to save *(Figure 14-3)*. The savings rate is defined as the difference between disposable income and consumption (which represents savings), divided by disposable income (where disposable income equals personal income less tax payments). In the early 1970s the savings rate was generally 8% or higher. As inflation picked up in the mid-70s and consumers began to fear higher inflation rates in the future, the savings rate fell to about 6%. This rate, more recently, has dipped to about the 4% mark. Monthly changes in this rate are not particularly significant, but it is worthwhile to keep an eye on the savings rate trend as an indicator of shifts in consumer spending patterns. A sharp drop in the savings rate, for example, indicates that the consumer is dipping into savings to finance purchases. This is not a sustainable situation, and one should expect to see slower consumption and GDP growth in the months ahead.

**INCOME ESTIMATES RELY ON DATA FROM A WIDE VARIETY OF SOURCES**

The income and consumption data are prepared monthly by the Commerce Department's Bureau of Economic Analysis. Given the many different types of income, there is a wide variety of source data. For example, wage estimates are prepared primarily from the payroll employment data that is submitted by the Bureau of Labor Statistics. Data on transfer payments come from information collected by the Social Security Administration, the Veterans Administration, and the monthly statement of receipts and outlays published by the Treasury Department. Dividend income is estimated from a sample of corporate dividend payments. Interest income is derived by applying interest rates to household asset data that is collected by the Federal Reserve Board. You get the idea.

**THE CONSUMPTION DATA RELY HEAVILY ON THE RETAIL SALES REPORT AND ON CAR AND TRUCK SALES**

Similarly, the monthly estimates of consumption expenditures involve data collection from many different sources. As we will see, the Commerce Department relies heavily upon trends in the Census Bureau's retail sales report. In addition, the Commerce Department uses the unit car and truck sales data that are reported by each of the manufacturers. They also have some *price* data for cars and trucks, gasoline, and tobacco because prices of these items tend to be quite volatile. After all, if the price of a commodity rises sharply, the dollar amount spent also increases. It should be noted that the personal consumption data are presented in both nominal and "real" or inflation-adjusted terms. This latter series *is* the consumption portion of the GDP estimate.

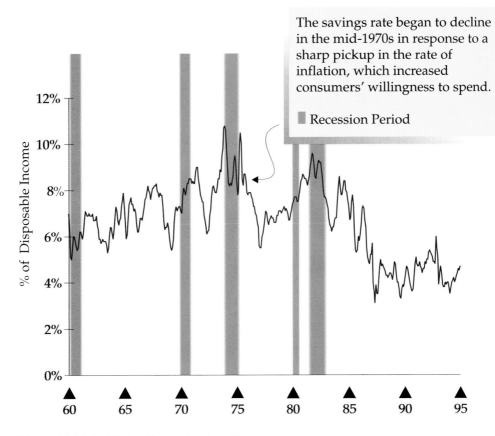

The savings rate began to decline in the mid-1970s in response to a sharp pickup in the rate of inflation, which increased consumers' willingness to spend.

■ Recession Period

*Figure 14-3 The United States Savings Rate*

Simply average the figures for the three months of the quarter and you will have the PCE component of the gross domestic product.

Because PCE is such an important part of GDP, it is important for investors to understand how economists formulate their forecast *(Figure 14-4)*. The first information we receive about the pace of consumer spending for any given month stems from the data on car and truck sales. However, these are unit data. That means we know the *number* of cars and trucks sold during the course of the month. Yet, what we really want to know is the *dollar value* of those sales. Thus, the car and truck sales data are not perfect, but they help us forecast about 6% of the PCE figure for any given month. The next tidbit of information arrives via the retail sales report, which suggests consumer spending on *goods* during the course of the month — cars and trucks, as well as food, clothing, gasoline, and furniture. In fact, the Commerce

Department bases its estimate of consumer spending on goods (except for autos and trucks) on this report. With these data in hand, we now have some idea of what is happening to another 40% of consumer spending. We still have to estimate expenditures on services, which represent the remaining 54% of the series. Fortunately, spending on services tends to be relatively stable and somewhat easier to predict.

| Consumption Component | Source Data | Percent of Total |
|---|---|---|
| Automobiles | Unit car sales | 6% |
| Other Durables | Retail sales | 9% |
| Nondurables | Retail sales | 31% |
| Services | None, rely on trends | 54% |

*Figure 14-4*
*How to Forecast Consumption*

These income and consumption data are compiled, edited, and eventually released one day after the publication of the GDP report, which generally appears in the third week of the month.

**STRONG GAINS IN INCOME AND CONSUMPTION PRODUCE A BOND MARKET SELL-OFF**

Gains in personal income indicate that the economy is growing, and increases in personal consumption expenditures show that the consumer is spending. Therefore, larger-than-expected gains in either personal income or consumption are viewed negatively by the fixed-income markets *(Figure 14-5)*. These markets begin to fear that the Federal Reserve will tighten monetary policy by increasing interest rates. On the other hand, sluggish income growth or a reduced pace of spending is greeted favorably.

**THE STOCK MARKET WILL USUALLY RALLY**

For the stock market, strong income growth is generally a plus because a rapidly expanding economy usually is associated with profit growth. But, as is frequently the case with the equity markets, there is a major caveat. If the robust pace of economic activity causes market participants to believe that the Federal

Reserve is going to boost interest rates, then there truly can be too much of a good thing — growth. In such a situation the stock market will decline.

THE DOLLAR WILL
ALSO RALLY

The reaction of the dollar usually is tied to the expected direction of interest rates. If the bond market frets about strong income and/or consumption growth and pushes interest rates higher, and market participants worry about a Federal Reserve tightening move, the dollar climbs in value. A weaker-than-expected report on income and consumption is dollar bearish.

*Figure 14-5*
*Market Reaction to*
*Personal Income and/or*
*Consumption*

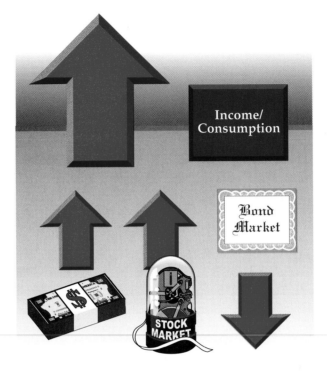

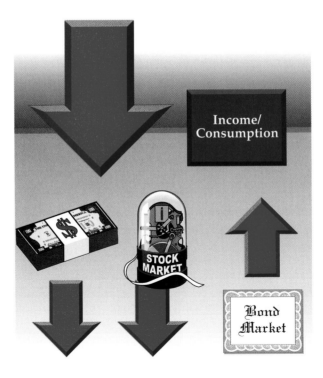

## AN EARLY WARNING SYSTEM

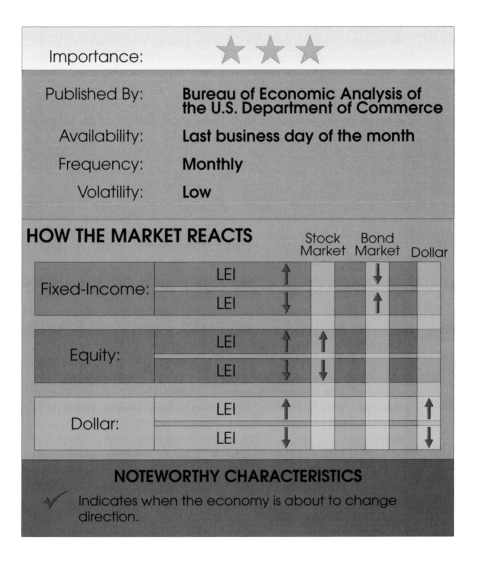

| Importance: | ★ ★ ★ |
|---|---|
| **Published By:** | **Bureau of Economic Analysis of the U.S. Department of Commerce** |
| **Availability:** | **Last business day of the month** |
| **Frequency:** | **Monthly** |
| **Volatility:** | **Low** |

### HOW THE MARKET REACTS

| | | Stock Market | Bond Market | Dollar |
|---|---|---|---|---|
| **Fixed-Income:** | LEI ↑ | | ↓ | |
| | LEI ↓ | | ↑ | |
| **Equity:** | LEI ↑ | ↑ | | |
| | LEI ↓ | ↓ | | |
| **Dollar:** | LEI ↑ | | | ↑ |
| | LEI ↓ | | | ↓ |

### NOTEWORTHY CHARACTERISTICS

✓ Indicates when the economy is about to change direction.

THE INDEX OF LEADING INDICATORS IS DESIGNED TO PREDICT FUTURE ECONOMIC ACTIVITY

The index of leading economic indicators (LEI), a composite of several different indicators, is designed to predict future aggregate economic activity. Historically, the LEI reaches peaks and troughs earlier than the underlying turns in the economy and is, therefore, an important tool for forecasting and planning *(Figure 15-1)*. The index is composed of 11 series, which have varying lead times at cyclical tops and bottoms. As a rule of thumb, turning points in the economy are thought to be signaled by three consecutive monthly LEI changes in the same direction. For example, consecutive readings of -0.5%, -1.1%, and -0.7% would signal a possible recession. However, even though a recession has always been preceded by three straight LEI declines, the converse is not true — since 1952, the LEI has "predicted" ten recessions, but only seven actually occurred. In other words, pronounced weakness in the index is a necessary, but not a sufficient, condition for an economic downturn. *Figure 15-1* demonstrates the historical usefulness of the LEI. While the forecasting record is fairly good, it should be noted that the LEI has performed better at business cycle peaks than troughs. On

*Figure 15-1*
*Index of Leading Indicators*

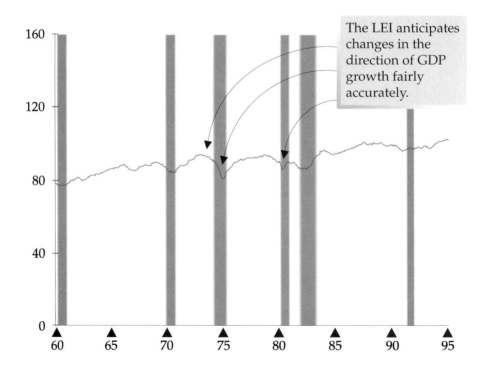

The LEI anticipates changes in the direction of GDP growth fairly accurately.

average, the index has turned down ten months ahead of economic tops, although with high variability. The index seems to give less notice regarding cyclical bottoms. On average, the LEI turns up only one or two months ahead of these economic upswings.

The LEI's individual components were chosen because of their economic significance, statistical adequacy, consistency of timing at cycle peaks and troughs, conformity to expansions and contractions, smoothness, and prompt availability *(Figure 15-2)*. These components are weighted equally to provide a net contribution to the composite index. The specific leading indicators — selected from various sectors of the economy — include the following: the average workweek, weekly jobless claims, new orders for consumer goods, vendor performance, contracts and orders for new plant and equipment, building permits, changes in unfilled durable goods orders, sensitive materials prices, stock prices, money supply, and consumer expectations.

**EACH COMPONENT IS A LEADING INDICATOR**

*Figure 15-2*
*Components of the Index of Leading Indicators*

| | |
|---|---|
| 1 | Average workweek-manufacturing |
| 2 | Initial unemployment claims |
| 3 | New orders for consumer goods |
| 4 | Vendor performance |
| 5 | Plant and equipment orders |
| 6 | Building permits |
| 7 | Change in unfilled orders-durables |
| 8 | Sensitive material prices |
| 9 | Stock prices, S&P 500 |
| 10 | Real M2 |
| 11 | Index of consumer expectations |

**THE TOTAL INDEX PERFORMS BETTER THAN ANY OF ITS PARTS**

How do the individual components relate to the overall economy? The average workweek and jobless claims provide insight into labor market conditions. Employers frequently increase (or decrease) hours worked before hiring (or dismissing) personnel. Jobless claims indicate the amount of slack in the labor market. Consumer goods orders provide clues about future consumer spending. Vendor performance reflects the percentage of companies reporting slower deliveries, which is often a sign of bottlenecks and shortages associated with a strong economy. Unfilled durable goods orders and sensitive materials prices also offer hints regarding economic strength or weakness. Contracts for new plant and equipment reflect business investment spending plans and, by extension, business views on economic conditions. Building permits lead residential construction activity, a highly cyclical sector that has ramifications for other "big ticket" spending. Stock prices, as measured by the S&P 500, reflect consensus expectations about future earnings and overall business conditions. Changes in the money supply (M2) measure banking system liquidity, with higher liquidity associated with increased economic activity. Finally, consumer expectations, monitored by the University of Michigan's Survey of Consumer Sentiment, provide insight into consumer spending plans. Because these 11 series cover so many different sectors of the economy, they perform better as a group than any isolated series.

**A VARIETY OF GOVERNMENT AGENCIES AND PRIVATE SOURCES PROVIDE THE BASIC DATA**

The LEI is compiled by the Bureau of Economic Analysis (BEA) of the Department of Commerce, using data from a variety of private sources and government agencies. A partial list includes the departments of Commerce, Labor, Treasury, Defense, the Federal Reserve, NAPM, the Conference Board, the National Bureau of Economic Research, and many others. The BEA releases the index on the last business day of the month, based on the prior month's information. At the time of publication, all 11 LEI components are available to the BEA. Of these, nine are known in advance and the remaining two can be estimated fairly accurately. As a result, the index is forecasted with an error of less than 0.2%.

## COINCIDENT INDICATORS

The Bureau of Economic Analysis also publishes an index of coincident indicators, designed to turn up or down "coincident" with changes in the economy. Thus, a rise or fall in this index suggests economic expansion or contraction in a given month. The index consists of four components:

· Employees on nonagricultural payrolls
· Personal income less transfer payments
· Index of industrial production
· Business sales

## LAGGING INDICATORS

The Bureau releases an index of lagging indicators that turns up or down four to nine months *after* the economy begins to emerge from or enter into a recession. Essentially, this index is used to confirm whether or not a turning point has occurred. This index has six components:

· Average duration of unemployment
· Ratio of business inventories to sales
· Index of unit labor costs for manufacturing
· Average prime rate charged by banks
· Commercial and industrial loans
· Ratio of consumer installment debt to personal income

Separately, the coincident and lagging indicators series are of little market significance. But the *ratio* of coincident to lagging indicators provides clues to economic turnarounds *sooner* than the leading indicators series itself *(Figure 15-3)*. Why is this so? The answer lies in the business cycle: In the early stages of an economic upswing, coincident indicators rise, while the lagging series — which depicts the economy several months earlier — remains essentially unchanged. Thus, the ratio (coincident/lagging) is rising. Near the peak of an expansion, the rate of increase in the coincident index is less than the rate of increase in the lagging series. Consequently, the ratio begins to fall — possibly signaling a major turning point. Near the trough of a recession, the rate of decline in the coincident series is smaller than the rate of decline in the lagging index — the ratio rises. As *Figure 15-3* suggests, this ratio tends to signal economic turnarounds about two months ahead of the LEI itself.

THE COMMERCE DEPARTMENT PUBLISHES TWO OTHER INDEXES OF ECONOMIC ACTIVITY

THE RATIO OF COINCIDENT TO LAGGING INDICATORS MAY BE THE BEST LEADING INDICATOR OF ALL

*Figure 15-3*
*Ratio of Coincident to Lagging Economic Indicators*

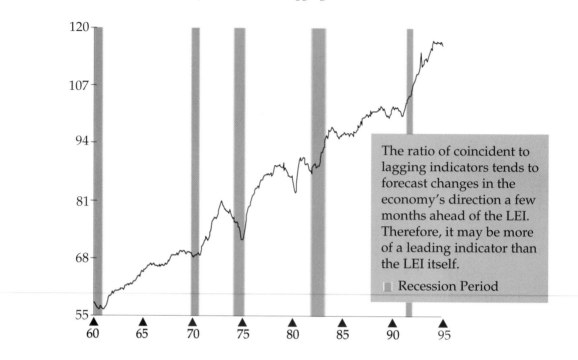

The ratio of coincident to lagging indicators tends to forecast changes in the economy's direction a few months ahead of the LEI. Therefore, it may be more of a leading indicator than the LEI itself.

■ Recession Period

**THE MARKETS SELDOM REACT TO THIS REPORT**

A leading index report seldom shocks the markets, despite its usefulness as a forecasting tool *(Figure 15-4)*. Since most of the 11 components are known through prior releases, forecasts of the LEI's performance are generally accurate. Even so, surprises occasionally occur. The markets usually respond to surprises as they do toward any other macroeconomic indicator. For example, a higher-than-expected (more positive) reading triggers speculation that growth will be strong in coming months. The dollar moves higher on anticipated Federal Reserve tightening moves, whereas the bond market sells off. The reaction from stocks depends upon the current point in the economic cycle. As a general rule, early cycle signs of improvement in business activity are welcome by the equity markets, which begin to factor in a more profitable economic environment. Late in the cycle, further strength is likely to be unwelcome, as fears mount about inflation and Federal Reserve restraint.

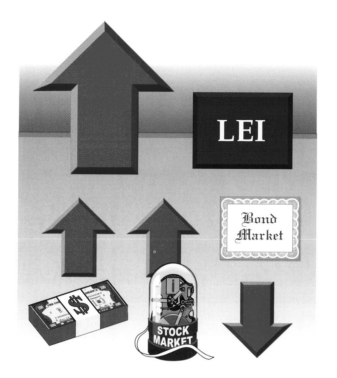

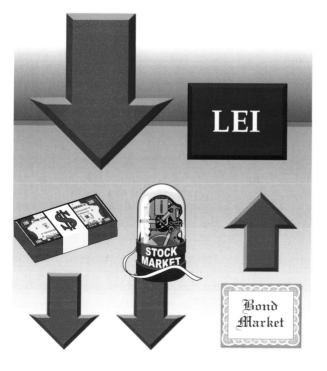

*Figure 15-4*
*Market Reaction to the*
*Index of Leading*
*Indicators*

## HOME SALES ARE A LEADING INDICATOR OF ECONOMIC ACTIVITY

New home sales are an important indicator of strength or weakness in the key housing sector of the economy. Housing is a crucial segment of the economy because, historically, changes in consumer spending patterns have shown up first in autos and housing *(Figure 16-1)*. Therefore, if the selling pace of new homes begins to slacken, eventually housing starts begin to slow, and employment in the construction industry declines. Once the housing sector begins to slide, numerous related industries — like lumber and home furnishings — also begin to suffer. Thus, a drop-off in home sales can be a leading indicator of an impending recession. Similarly, when the economy begins to rebound, the housing and automobile sectors are usually the first to experience recovery.

## DATA ARE PROVIDED FOR FOUR GEOGRAPHICAL AREAS

The Census Bureau provides monthly data on new home sales nationally and for four geographical areas — the Northeast, the Midwest, the South, and the West. The data are collected from realtors throughout the country and represent signed contracts — even though some contracts could fall through prior to closing. It should be noted that there is a similar series on existing home sales that is gathered by the National Association of Realtors. It, too, provides a selling rate for the country as a whole and for the same four regions. However, it is less useful than the new home sales report because the existing home sales data are reported at the time of *closing*, and *not* at the time the contract is signed. Because there is roughly a two-month lag between the time a home buyer signs a contract and settlement, the existing homes sales data tend to lag the new home sales series. In some sense, the existing home sales report simply confirms what was revealed by the new home sales data two months earlier.

## THIS REPORT ALSO CONTAINS DATA ON HOUSE PRICES AND UNSOLD HOMES

In addition to the data on home sales, there is information regarding the average and median sales prices, the number of houses for sale, and the supply of unsold homes (expressed as the number of months it would take at the current selling rate to eliminate all of the unsold homes). The unsold homes series can be viewed as the inventory level of the housing market. As it climbs, builders are forced to finance an ever-growing backlog of unsold homes, which is expensive. Thus, an increase in the supply of unsold homes implies a drop-off in building activity in the months ahead.

*Figure 16-1  New Home Sales*

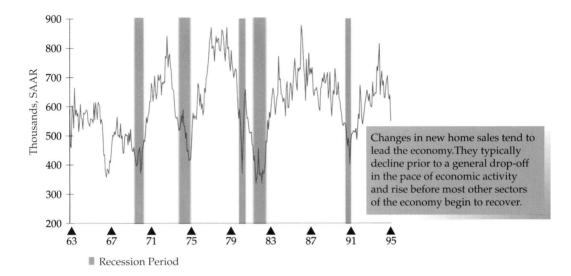

Changes in new home sales tend to lead the economy. They typically decline prior to a general drop-off in the pace of economic activity and rise before most other sectors of the economy begin to recover.

■ Recession Period

**THESE DATA ARE VOLATILE**

The problem with the home sales data is that they tend to be quite volatile. Abnormal weather conditions are a frequent cause of wild gyrations in this series. For example, in January 1994, when bitter cold weather gripped most of the nation, the Census Bureau reported that new home sales fell 21.5%. Another difficulty is that new home sales are subject to substantial revisions. A classic example of this problem arose in November 1994. Initially, Census indicated that home sales in that month were relatively robust at a 696T pace. This was rather puzzling because the Federal Reserve had been raising interest rates, and other indicators of activity in the housing sector were showing signs of a slowdown. But one month later, on the basis of more complete data, the Census Bureau revealed that the selling rate was not 696T, but 641T — a downward revision of about 8% two months after the fact! Given these difficulties in the national data, one can imagine the problems in trying to analyze statistics for the various regions of the country that are based on a sample size that is basically one-fourth as large. These regional home sales data are, in our opinion, virtually useless. Revision problems obviously limit the data's usefulness. As a result, it is usually best to look at a three-month moving average when trying to decipher changes in the growth-rate trend of this series. The data are usually released near month-end for the prior month.

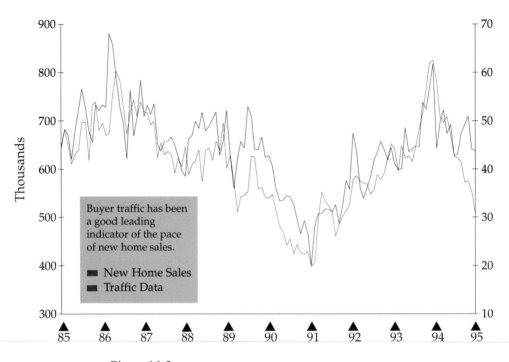

*Figure 16-2*
*New Home Sales and Buyer Traffic*

**THESE DATA ARE VOLATILE—IT IS HARD TO PREDICT HOME SALES**

One piece of information that has helped to anticipate the monthly pace of new home sales is the so-called "traffic" data released by the National Association of Home Builders. These data are derived from a monthly survey of 375 builders — called the Builders Economic Council Survey — and are released one day prior to the housing starts report. Thus, they are available about two weeks prior to the release of the new home sales data. There is a good deal of information in this report from the home builders including builders' assessment of current sales conditions, their expectations for sales six months hence, and their reading of the "traffic" of prospective new home buyers. This last series attempts to measure the number of people that are actively looking for new homes. The builders rate traffic in a given month as high, average, or low. Thus, these data are presented in the same way as the Purchasing Managers' Index (Chapter 5). Similarly, one can construct a *diffusion index* by adding the percentage of "high" responses to one-half of those who report conditions as "unchanged". You will recall that with a diffusion index, a reading of 50 is essentially a "break-even" point, or the point at which home sales did not change in a given month. For example, if *all* participants in the survey indicated that traffic was "average," the diffusion index would be 50: the number reporting "high" traffic (zero), plus one-half of 100 (50). If so, one would conclude that the pace of home sales was unchanged in that month. A reading above 50 indicates that home sales rose in that month; below 50 suggests that sales declined. As shown in *Figure 16-2*, the series has done an excellent job of anticipating new home sales since 1988.

A second piece of information helpful in forecasting new home sales is the series on mortgage applications that is published weekly by the Mortgage Bankers Association. These data are released very early, generally about 7 a.m., every Thursday morning. One can then construct a 4-week moving average to smooth out some of the volatility and compare that to the pace of new home sales. *Figure 16-3* indicates that this series, too, has a reasonable correlation with home sales.

While these bits of information are helpful, the important point is that there is no foolproof way of forecasting the pace of new home sales for any given month. The best one can do is antici- pate changes in the trend rate. Nevertheless, new home sales are

*Figure 16-3*
*New Home Sales and MBA Purchase Index*

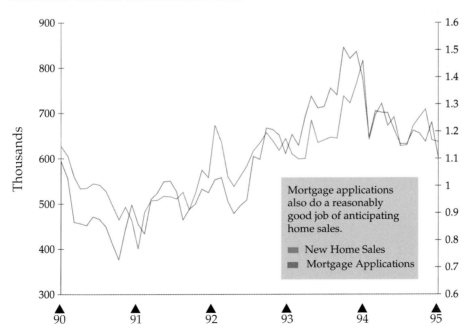

important because, as we have noted on several occasions previously, housing and autos are the two most interest rate sensitive sectors of the economy. They represent "big ticket" items — changes in the direction of which foreshadow similar changes in the rest of the economy.

**A RISE IN SALES MAY PUSH THE BOND MARKET LOWER**

Because new home sales are difficult to predict, there is always the potential for surprise. When surprises occur, the home sales data may have a moderate impact on the fixed-income markets *(Figure 16-4)*. However, traders and salespeople are aware of the volatility and tend to view these data cautiously. Nevertheless, if home sales rise unexpectedly and market participants conclude that this is the beginning of a new trend, fixed-income partici-pants react adversely and push interest rates higher. An antici-pated decline prompts the opposite response.

**THE STOCK MARKET AND THE DOLLAR PROBABLY DO NOT REACT**

The stock market and the foreign exchange markets do not appear to attach a great deal of importance to this report and, as a result, it is rare to decipher a reaction in either market.

*Figure 16-4*
*Market Reaction to*
*New Home Sales*

20% OF THE PIE!

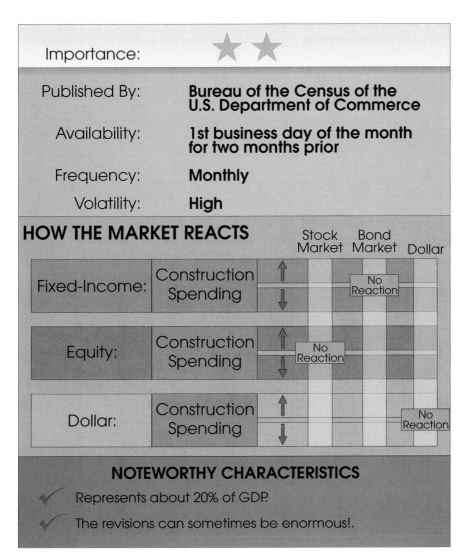

Importance: ★ ★

| Published By: | **Bureau of the Census of the U.S. Department of Commerce** |
| Availability: | **1st business day of the month for two months prior** |
| Frequency: | **Monthly** |
| Volatility: | **High** |

## HOW THE MARKET REACTS

|  |  | Stock Market | Bond Market | Dollar |
|---|---|---|---|---|
| Fixed-Income: | Construction Spending ↑↓ |  | No Reaction |  |
| Equity: | Construction Spending ↑↓ | No Reaction |  |  |
| Dollar: | Construction Spending ↑↓ |  |  | No Reaction |

## NOTEWORTHY CHARACTERISTICS

✓ Represents about 20% of GDP.

✓ The revisions can sometimes be enormous!.

CONSTRUCTION SPENDING PROVIDES INFORMATION ABOUT THREE SEPARATE GDP CATEGORIES

Construction spending measures the value of construction put in place during the course of that particular month. We are interested for two reasons. First, this report supplies us with information about three separate GDP categories that, combined, represent almost 20% of GDP *(Figure 17-1)*. For example, the *nonresidential* construction spending part of this report roughly approximates the nonresidential structures portion of the investment, or "I," component of GDP. Similarly, *residential* construction provides information about the residential component of investment. These two categories combined represent about 41% of "I," and about 7% of overall GDP. In addition, the public construction category supplies information about state and local government spending — another 11% of GDP — which, together with expenditures of the Federal government, make up the "G" part of GDP. Thus, this report provides clues to the behavior of nearly 20% of GDP. That's quite sizable!

*Figure 17-1 Construction Spending Versus GDP*

| Construction Category | Percentage of GDP |
|---|---|
| 1. Nonresidential Spending | 3% |
| 2. Residential Spending | 4% |
| 3. State and Local Government Spending | 11% |
| | 18% |

The construction spending report provides us with information concerning nearly 20% of GDP.

CHANGES IN THE CONSTRUCTION INDUSTRY TEND TO LEAD THE ECONOMY

Second, economists frequently note that the automobile and construction industries are typically the first two sectors to go into recession when the bad times hit and, pleasantly, the first two to recover when conditions improve. Analysts faithfully track home and automobile sales for *hints* about when these changes are beginning to occur, and they revise their GDP forecasts accordingly. This report on construction spending provides an update.

*Figure 17-2* summarizes the construction spending report for January 1995. We have included it to give you an idea of the types of construction incorporated in this report. As the name suggests, the residential category includes single-family homes as well as apartment buildings. Nonresidential construction includes factories, offices, hotels and motels, churches, hospitals, and private schools. Public construction reflects expenditures on highways and streets, military bases, water supply facilities, public school buildings, housing projects, and sewer systems.

RESIDENTIAL, NONRESIDENTIAL, AND PUBLIC CONSTRUCTION ARE THE MOST IMPORTANT CATEGORIES

The Census Bureau derives data on residential spending from its own surveys of housing starts and new home sales. Census looks to the F.W. Dodge Division of the McGraw Hill Information Systems Company to identify high-value nonresidential projects. The Bureau then selects a sample of these projects and requests monthly progress reports from the owners, builders, or architects responsible for these buildings. Similarly, by sampling monthly progress reports of state and local projects, the Census Bureau derives the public construction data.

CENSUS BUREAU TAPS A NUMBER OF DIFFERENT SOURCES FOR THE DATA IT NEEDS

Unfortunately, there are two problems with the monthly construction spending report. First, it is not very timely. It is released on the first business day of the month for two months prior. That makes it one of the *last* pieces of information we receive about the state of the economy for any given month. Since we have already seen 14 reports on various sectors of the economy, we basically *know* what happened during that month. The incremental value of the 15th report is quite small. Second, the report tends to be quite volatile and revisions can be sizable. With any of these volatile reports, economists are forced to work with year-over-year statistics, or 3-month moving averages, in order to detect trend changes. Thus, it takes three or four months before one can conclude that a trend rate of growth has been broken.

THERE ARE TWO PROBLEMS WITH THE CONSTRUCTION SPENDING DATA

## Value of New Construction Put in Place in the United States, Seasonally Adjusted Annual Rate

The construction spending report has information separated into three major categories.

| Type of Construction | Jan 1995 | Dec 1994 | Nov 1994 | Oct 1994 |
|---|---|---|---|---|
| Total New Construction | 529.7 | 530.9 | 525.1 | 521.4 |
| **Private Construction** | 393.1 | 395.2 | 393.5 | 384.9 |
| Residential Buildings | 242.8 | 243.9 | 242.3 | 239.3 |
| New Housing Units | 169.2 | 170.4 | 169.2 | 167.8 |
| One-Unit Structures | 152.1 | 153.4 | 153.0 | 152.8 |
| Two-or More Unit Structures | 17.1 | 17.0 | 16.3 | 15.0 |
| Nonresidential Buildings | 109.4 | 106.2 | 105.6 | 100.8 |
| Industrial | 23.9 | 23.1 | 25.0 | 22.3 |
| Office | 19.1 | 18.6 | 18.6 | 17.7 |
| Hotels and Motels | 5.5 | 4.7 | 4.3 | 3.8 |
| Other Commercial | 35.4 | 34.7 | 33.4 | 32.8 |
| Religious | 3.9 | 3.9 | 3.6 | 3.8 |
| Educational | 5.0 | 4.8 | 4.8 | 4.6 |
| Hospital and Institutional | 11.0 | 11.0 | 10.6 | 10.6 |
| Miscellaneous Buildings | 5.6 | 5.4 | 5.5 | 5.3 |
| Telephone and Telegraph | (NA) | 11.1 | 10.8 | 11.0 |
| All Other Private | 2.8 | 2.8 | 2.8 | 2.9 |
| **Public Construction** | **136.7** | 135.7 | 131.6 | 136.5 |
| Housing and Redevelopment | 5.5 | 5.1 | 4.4 | 5.1 |
| Industrial | 1.7 | 1.5 | 1.4 | 1.5 |
| Educational | 24.2 | 23.6 | 23.9 | 25.2 |
| Hospital | 3.9 | 4.3 | 3.8 | 3.7 |
| Other Public Buildings | 21.3 | 21.6 | 20.5 | 19.0 |
| Highways and Streets | 40.9 | 39.5 | 40.1 | 41.7 |
| Military Facilities | 2.7 | 2.5 | 2.3 | 2.6 |
| Conservation and Development | 7.3 | 7.9 | 6.9 | 7.2 |
| Sewer Systems | 10.8 | 12.1 | 11.3 | 11.0 |
| Water Supply Facilities | 6.3 | 6.4 | 5.8 | 7.3 |
| Miscellaneous Public | 12.0 | 11.3 | 11.1 | 12.3 |

Source: U.S. Department of Commerce, Release for: Jan 1995
Data in billions of current dollars

*Figure 17-2 U.S. Construction Spending Levels, Current Dollars*

From a market point of view, this report is useless! The markets — all of them — essentially ignore it *(Figure 17-3)*. This is probably because, as noted above, it is not very timely. Moreover, even when the data have been released, construction spending can be revised significantly a month later. You might legitimately ask why we bother to include this report in our book if the markets do not react to it. The answer is that the construction report helps the *specialists* achieve a better reading on GDP growth for the current quarter and, perhaps, for the quarter ahead. We noted earlier that the construction categories provide information on about 20% of GDP. That is too large a percentage to ignore, because *ultimately* market movements are going to be heavily influenced by GDP growth.

THE MARKETS
IGNORE THIS REPORT

*Figure 17-3*
*Market Reaction to*
*Construction Spending*

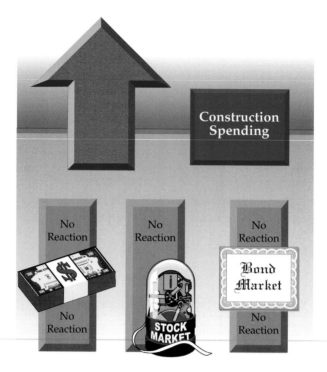

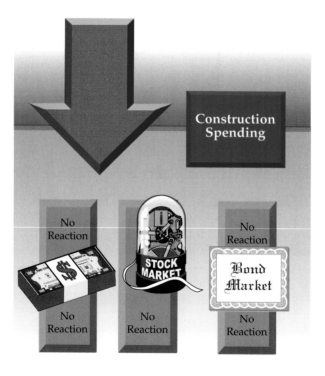

DURABLES REVISITED

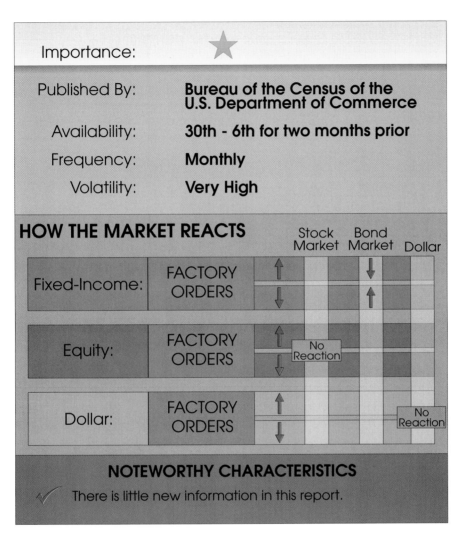

Importance: ★

| | |
|---|---|
| Published By: | **Bureau of the Census of the U.S. Department of Commerce** |
| Availability: | **30th - 6th for two months prior** |
| Frequency: | **Monthly** |
| Volatility: | **Very High** |

**HOW THE MARKET REACTS**

| | | Stock Market | Bond Market | Dollar |
|---|---|---|---|---|
| Fixed-Income: | FACTORY ORDERS | ↑ | ↓ | |
| | | ↓ | ↑ | |
| Equity: | FACTORY ORDERS | ↑ ↓ No Reaction | | |
| Dollar: | FACTORY ORDERS | ↑ | | No Reaction |
| | | ↓ | | |

**NOTEWORTHY CHARACTERISTICS**

✓ There is little new information in this report.

THIS REPORT
CONTAINS MORE
DATA THAN THE
PREVIOUSLY
RELEASED REPORT
ON DURABLES

In many respects, this report is a rehash of the durable goods release that became available a week earlier. (The discussion of durables was contained in Chapter 13. We suggest that if you have not read that chapter yet, you do so now, as we only highlight the points made earlier.) However, the factory orders report merits review because it also contains data on orders and shipments of nondurable goods, manufacturing inventories, and the inventory/sales ratio. Furthermore, this report frequently contains significant revisions to the durable goods data. There have been instances when even the direction of change in orders has been revised from one week to the next — an initially reported increase of sizable dimensions has turned into a decline, and vice versa.

*Figure 18-1*
*Change in Business Inventories*

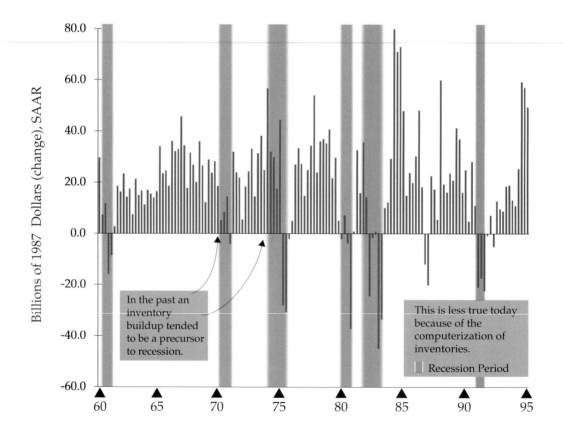

The most important points made earlier are the following:
- Orders data are useful because they tell us something about the likely pace of production in the months ahead.
- They are extremely volatile and can fluctuate by three or four percentage points in any given month.
- They are subject to sizable revisions; and
- They are very difficult to forecast.

This report on factory orders, shipments, and inventories becomes available about one week after the durable goods release. In addition to data on orders for durable goods — those products that have a useful life of more than three years such as aircraft, automobiles, and refrigerators — this report calibrates orders for nondurable goods. Many nondurables are essential commodities that we buy every month — food, clothing, and gasoline — and orders of such tend to be rather stable. Thus, the fluctuation in this series on factory orders stems from its durable goods component.

**IN ADDITION TO ORDERS FOR DURABLE GOODS, WE LEARN ABOUT ORDERS FOR NONDURABLES**

In addition to the revised data on orders and shipments of durables and the inclusion of information on orders and shipments of nondurables, the most important new information is the data on manufacturing inventories. Inventories are important because they suggest the pace of the economy in the months and quarters ahead.

**WE ALSO RECEIVE DATA ON MANUFACTURING INVENTORIES**

Historically, the way the U.S. economy goes into recession is as follows:
- Sales begin to slump;
- Inventory levels start to climb; and
- Businesses sharply scale back production to trim unwanted inventories.

INVENTORIES ARE IMPORTANT BECAUSE A BUILDUP MAY CAUSE A RECESSION

This relationship between the change in business inventories and GDP growth is shown in *Figure 18-1*. The Commerce Department previously included the change in business inventories as one of the components of its leading indicators series. But when it revised this series in March 1989, Commerce dropped the change in business inventories and replaced it with other indicators. The reason was *not* that the inventories data are any less valuable as an indicator of future economic activity, but simply that they were not available in a timely enough fashion to be incorporated in the initial release. When inventories were subsequently included one month later, the leading indicators series became subject to sizable revisions. It is worth noting that we no longer see the same kinds of wild swings in business inventories that we saw in the 1950s, 1960s, and 1970s. Presumably this is because of the computerization of inventories. Businesses are now able to determine instantly what their inventory levels are. As soon as a firm sees a slight rise, it quickly trims production to realign inventory levels with sales. Thus, in the years ahead, changes in business inventories may not be as reliable a guide to future GDP growth as they were previously because changes will be less pronounced.

MANUFACTURING INVENTORIES REPRESENT NEARLY ONE-HALF OF THE TOTAL

This report details manufacturing inventories, which represent nearly one-half of total business inventories *(Figure 18-2)*. To this manufacturing inventory figure one must add inventories at the wholesale and retail levels to obtain overall business inventories — available about two weeks later. Factory inventories represent a large portion of the total and can give us a good idea of what will happen to overall business inventories.

INVENTORIES ARE ALSO AN IMPORTANT (AND VOLATILE) PART OF GDP

Inventory levels are monitored primarily because the annualized *change* in business inventories is included in the quarterly GDP estimate as part of the investment component. As described in the GDP portion of this book (Chapter 2), gross private domestic investment represents the sum of producers' durable equipment, residential and nonresidential construction, and the change in business inventories. Therefore, knowledge of manufacturing inventories provides a clue to the overall change in business inventories, which is an integral part of the investment component of GDP.

*Figure 18-2*
*Who Is Holding the Inventories*

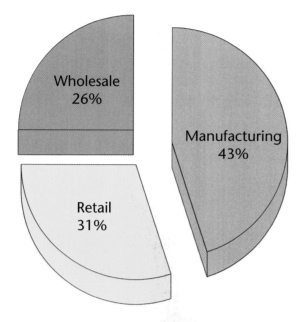

Given data on both manufacturing inventories and sales, economists can calculate the inventory/sales ratio. This ratio is a
lagging indicator of the economy because, historically, inventory
levels continue to rise long after sales growth comes to a halt.
However, most analysts will use this ratio to anticipate changes
in the rate of inventory accumulation. For example, at some
point after a recession trough, this ratio reaches an extremely low
level. At this juncture one can expect manufacturers to accelerate
their rate of inventory accumulation simply to keep pace with a
growing volume of sales. Similarly, when the economy begins to
contract, the inventory/sales ratio rises for several more months.
But at some point companies will become uncomfortable with
the relationship between inventories and sales. As firms cut back
production, inventory levels are reduced and the ratio begins to
fall.

THE INVENTORY/
SALES RATIO IS A
LAGGING
INDICATOR

**DATA ARE COMPILED FROM AN EXTENSIVE SURVEY OF MANUFACTURERS**

These data on orders, shipments and inventories are compiled by the Census Bureau of the Department of Commerce from a monthly survey of approximately 5,000 manufacturers out of a universe of some 70,000 establishments. Most manufacturers with 1,000 or more employees are included, plus a selected sample of smaller companies. The survey respondents are categorized by industry; totals are then expanded to represent the universe of manufacturers. The orders data represent firm orders for immediate or future delivery that are documented by a signed contract or a letter of intent. The shipments data represent the sum total of sales for that month, whether for domestic use or for export. Inventories reflect book values of merchandise on hand at the end of the month according to the valuation method used by each respondent. The data are released by the Census Bureau either just before the end of the month for the month prior, or just after the start of the following month.

**THE MARKETS GENERALLY DO NOT REACT TO THIS REPORT — THE MYSTERY WAS REMOVED ONE WEEK EARLIER**

For the most part the fixed-income markets do not respond to this particular report *(Figure 18-3)*. The reason is simple — the mystery surrounding the data was largely removed with the release of the durable goods report the previous week. Nondurable goods orders and shipments are quite steady and easy to predict. Thus, the only time the markets react is on those occasions when durable goods orders revise significantly, *or* when there is a surprising change in inventories. In that event, stronger-than-expected GDP growth will cause interest rates to rise as market participants worry about higher inflation and/or a Federal Reserve tightening move.

Because the changes in this report are generally well-anticipated, the stock market and the dollar are rarely affected in any significant way.

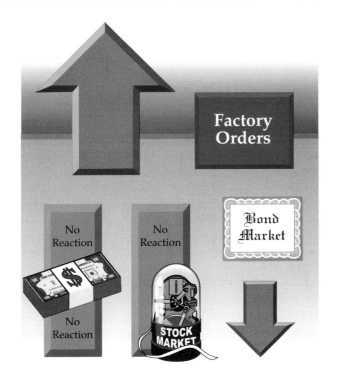

*Figure 18-3*
*Market Reaction to*
*Factory Orders*

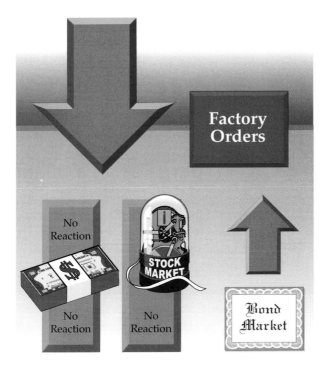

YOU HAVE HEARD IT ALL BEFORE!

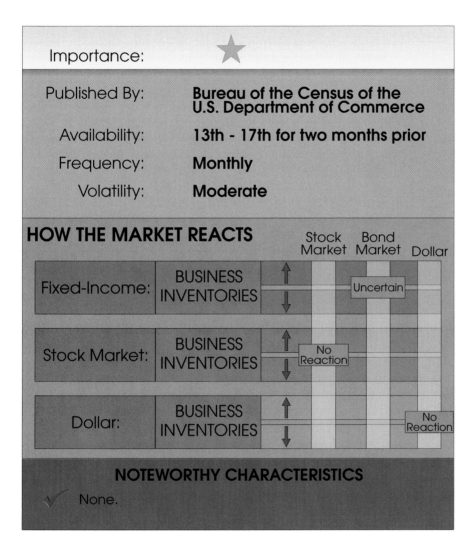

Importance: ★

| | |
|---|---|
| Published By: | **Bureau of the Census of the U.S. Department of Commerce** |
| Availability: | **13th - 17th for two months prior** |
| Frequency: | **Monthly** |
| Volatility: | **Moderate** |

## HOW THE MARKET REACTS

| | | Stock Market | Bond Market | Dollar |
|---|---|---|---|---|
| Fixed-Income: | BUSINESS INVENTORIES | ↑ ↓ | Uncertain | |
| Stock Market: | BUSINESS INVENTORIES | ↑ ↓ No Reaction | | |
| Dollar: | BUSINESS INVENTORIES | ↑ ↓ | | No Reaction |

## NOTEWORTHY CHARACTERISTICS

✓ None.

MOST OF THE DATA
IN THIS REPORT
HAVE ALREADY BEEN
RELEASED

This report on business inventories and sales is a logical extension of several previously released reports — the durable goods data (which contains information on the sales of durable goods by manufacturers), the report on factory orders, shipments, and inventories, the retail sales report, and the wholesale inventories and sales data. (Durables, factory orders, and retail sales are detailed in Chapters 8, 13, and 18. We suggest that if you have not done so already, read those sections now, because our comments in this chapter will be relatively brief.) The data on wholesale inventories and sales are not discussed in this book because they are never mentioned by the press and, therefore, generate no market response. However, they are available about one week prior to the publication date of the business inventories report. From these earlier releases, we know what happened to inventories and sales at both the factory and wholesale stages of production. We also know what happened to retail sales. The only new item in this report is retail inventories.

INVENTORIES ARE
AN IMPORTANT
PART OF THE "I"
COMPONENT OF
GDP

We are interested in inventories for two reasons. First, they are an important part of the investment component of GDP. Second, they provide further clues regarding the likely direction of the economy in the months ahead.

Gross private domestic investment, the "I" component in GDP, includes both residential and nonresidential construction spending, expenditures on producers' durable equipment, and the change in business inventories. Recall that GDP is a measure of *production*. And since we calculate GDP by adding up various types of *sales* data, it is necessary to add the change in business inventories to determine the actual level of production. For example, if a firm produces 100 toasters but sells only 90, the remaining 10 show up as an increase in inventories *(Figure 19-1)*. If we attempt to measure GDP by adding up the *sales* data, we will calculate GDP as 90 *unless* we make some allowance for the increase in inventories. Similarly, if a company continues to sell 90 toasters the following year, but only produces 80 in an effort to bring inventory levels into closer alignment with sales, we will not arrive at the correct figure for GDP and production (80) unless we adjust the sales data (90) for the change in toaster inventories (-10).

*Figure 19-1*
*The Change in*
*Business Inventories*
*and the GDP*

## To estimate GDP from sales data, we must add the change in inventories.

**1** All goods that are produced must either be sold or added to inventories.

**2** GDP measures the dollar amount of goods produced.

**3** But if we simply add up several types of spending (or sales) data, we will not estimate GDP correctly.

**4** To get the correct answer for GDP, we must add the change in business inventories to the sales data.

|  | Change in |  |  |
|---|---|---|---|
| Sales | + Inventories | = | GDP |
| 90 | +10 | = | 100 |
| 90 | -10 | = | 80 |

We noted, in the chapter on factory orders, shipments, and inventories, that one reason the U.S. economy slides into recession is because business inventories rise in response to slumping sales — eventually forcing businesses to cut production to trim unwanted stocks. Aside from the GDP accounting aspect, businesses seem slow to recognize that inventories are reaching dangerous levels until well after the fact. Thus, inventory *levels* tend to be a *lagging* indicator of economic activity. They do not begin to decline (or rise) until well after the peak (or trough) of the business cycle has been attained. The *change* in business inventories, however, begins to slow as the economy approaches a peak and starts to climb as the economy nears the trough of a recession. For this reason, the *change* in business inventories is a *leading* indicator of GDP growth. In fact, until March 1989 the Commerce Department incorporated the change in its index of

BUSINESS INVENTORIES ARE ALSO AN IMPORTANT BAROMETER OF FUTURE ECONOMIC ACTIVITY leading indicators. But because it was never available in a timely manner and gave rise to substantial revisions when it was included a month later, Commerce decided to drop the change in business inventories in favor of other series. Nevertheless, it continues to be a reasonably good leading indicator. *Figure 19-2* shows how the change in business inventories has foreshadowed GDP growth over the course of the past 35 years. It should be noted that the widespread implementation of inventory control procedures (e.g., "just-in-time" inventories) during the 1980s significantly reduced the volume of inventories that firms were required to hold for any given amount of sales. Furthermore, it dampened considerably the volatility of inventories. Throughout that period, we did not witness the dramatic swings in inventories that we had become accustomed to seeing in other decades. Thus, it is likely that, in the years ahead, inventory changes will not be as important a harbinger of business cycle changes.

*Figure 19-2*
*Change in Business Inventories*

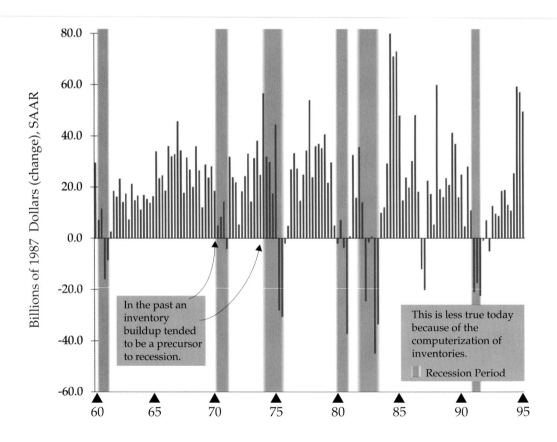

Figure 19-3
Ratio of Business Inventories to Business Final Sales (Quarterly)

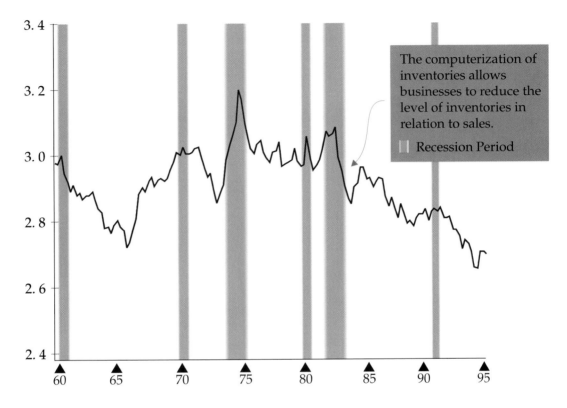

The Commerce Department includes business sales in its monthly index of coincident indicators — they begin to turn up and decline roughly in synch with business cycle troughs and peaks. If we suspect that the economy is about to enter a recession, for example, we can use this series to confirm or refute that notion.

**BUSINESS SALES ARE MORE OR LESS A CONTEMPORANEOUS INDICATOR OF THE ECONOMY**

In our earlier discussion, we noted that companies adjust inventory levels to keep them in close alignment with sales. The way that economists determine whether inventories are consistent with sales is by calculating the inventory/sales ratio. *Figure 19-3* gives you some idea of how this ratio fluctuates throughout the course of the business cycle. You can see quite clearly that the computerization of inventories during the 1980s allowed firms to reduce inventory levels in relationship to sales, and we expect this process to continue.

**FROM THIS REPORT WE CAN CALCULATE THE RATIO OF INVENTORIES TO SALES**

THE DATA ARE COMPILED FROM A MONTHLY SURVEY

The data on business inventories and sales are published by the Census Bureau of the Department of Commerce from a monthly survey of manufacturers' shipments, inventories, and orders and from the merchant wholesalers and retail trade surveys. They are published around the middle of the month for two months earlier. Thus, these data only become available after a considerable lag.

THIS IS ANOTHER REPORT THAT DOES NOT GENERATE ANY SIGNIFICANT MARKET REACTION

The markets do not pay much attention to this report because so much of the underlying data is already available and, as a result, surprises are rare *(Figure 19-4)*. For example, *all* of the sales data have been published previously. Retail sales data for that month were released almost a month earlier; factory sales are published two weeks prior as a part of the report on factory orders; and wholesale sales are released the preceding week. Similarly, manufacturing and wholesale inventories levels are already known. Thus, the only piece of information that is new in this report is retail inventories — but occasionally this can be different from what we expect.

When that occurs, the market's reaction is sometimes difficult to gauge. As noted above, inventories account for a portion of GDP. Therefore, an unanticipated rise in inventory levels boosts GDP growth for that quarter. For the fixed-income markets, faster GDP growth is a negative and, typically, prices fall. But if that inventory gain also boosts the inventory/sales ratio to a high level, then the markets may conclude that the inventory buildup was *unintentional* — in which case businesses have to scale back production in the months ahead, thereby producing slower GDP growth. Viewed in this manner, a rise in inventory levels can be construed as a positive event for the fixed-income markets. For the stock market and the foreign exchange markets, this report is usually a nonevent.

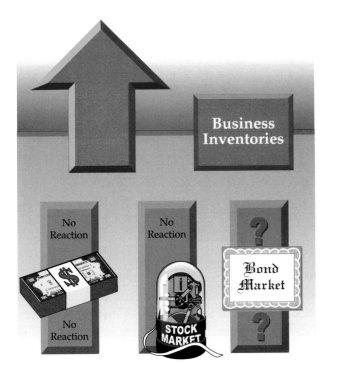

*Figure 19-4
Market Reaction to
Business Inventories*

WHEAT FOR CAVIAR

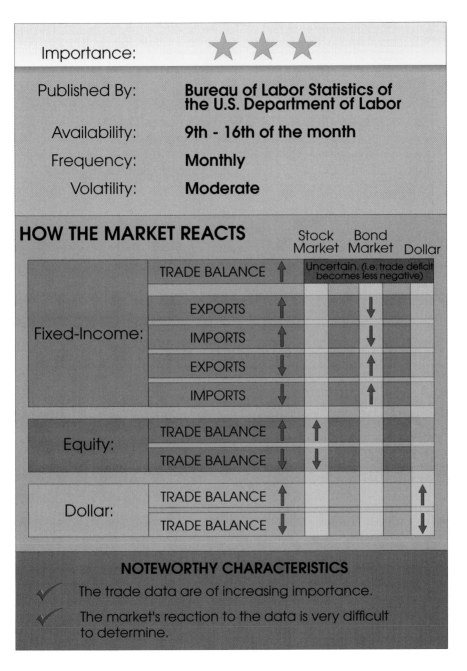

**Importance:** ★ ★ ★

| | |
|---|---|
| Published By: | **Bureau of Labor Statistics of the U.S. Department of Labor** |
| Availability: | **9th - 16th of the month** |
| Frequency: | **Monthly** |
| Volatility: | **Moderate** |

## HOW THE MARKET REACTS

| | | | Stock Market | Bond Market | Dollar |
|---|---|---|:---:|:---:|:---:|
| **Fixed-Income:** | TRADE BALANCE ↑ | | Uncertain. (i.e. trade deficit becomes less negative) | | |
| | EXPORTS ↑ | | | ↓ | |
| | IMPORTS ↑ | | | ↓ | |
| | EXPORTS ↓ | | | ↑ | |
| | IMPORTS ↓ | | | ↑ | |
| **Equity:** | TRADE BALANCE ↑ | | ↑ | | |
| | TRADE BALANCE ↓ | | ↓ | | |
| **Dollar:** | TRADE BALANCE ↑ | | | | ↑ |
| | TRADE BALANCE ↓ | | | | ↓ |

## NOTEWORTHY CHARACTERISTICS

✓ The trade data are of increasing importance.

✓ The market's reaction to the data is very difficult to determine.

**THE TRADE SECTOR HAS GROWN, BUT IT IS STILL RELATIVELY SMALL**

Prior to 1980s, the U.S. economy tended to be viewed as "closed" since the trade sector accounted for a rather small portion of overall production and demand — around 7% of GDP in 1970. But, large swings in exchange rates — following the breakup of Bretton Woods in the early 1970s — and steady growth in world trade have forced the United States to deal with a sector largely ignored. Moreover, heightened competition for global markets, symbolized by Japan's race for market share, has generated a new awareness of trade-related issues. As shown in *Figure 20-1*, the trade sector currently accounts for roughly 11% of GDP — and this percentage will move higher in the years ahead as trade with eastern Europe, the former Soviet republics, China, southern Asia, and Latin America all expand.

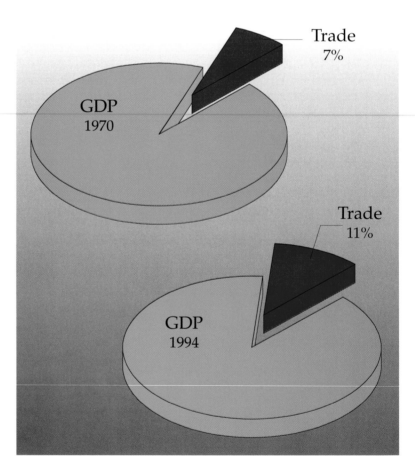

*Figure 20-1*
*The Importance of the Trade Sector Has Grown*

Cause and effect regarding exchange rates and trade flows are sometimes difficult to decipher. However, the surging dollar from 1980 to 1985 had a pronounced negative impact upon the U.S. trade balance, as *Figure 20-2* clearly demonstrates. As the deficits widened to alarming proportions, actions taken by U.S. policymakers — along with economic fundamentals — served to effectively devalue the dollar. The dollar's retreat helped redress some of these imbalances, and the deficit shrank from 1986 through mid-1991. But this brings up another important point, which we address below.

**CHANGES IN THE VALUE OF THE DOLLAR HAVE AN IMPORTANT IMPACT ON THE TRADE DEFICIT**

*Figure 20-2* also shows that from mid-1991 through the end of 1994 the deficit once again surged and is beginning to approach its previous record high level. This happened *despite* a sharp decline in the value of the dollar. Why? The primary reason is that the United States emerged from recession in April 1991, and this triggered a surge in the demand for imported goods. At the same time Europe, which was at a different stage of the business cycle, dipped into recession. While U.S. exports continued to grow, they did so at a much slower pace. As a result, the trade deficit exploded. Looking ahead, most experts believe that growth in the United States will slow significantly as the business cycle matures and, at the same time, growth in Europe will accelerate as it continues to emerge from recession. If that happens, the trade deficit will shrink. The important point to remember is that while the value of the dollar can play a major role in determining the trade deficit, business cycle differences between the U.S. and its trading partners can *also* be important. Failing to recognize this point, one would conclude from recent experience that the dollar is greatly overvalued. But that does not seem to be the case. Most serious observers believe, after having carefully examined the various models comparing purchasing power in the United States with other countries, that U.S. firms are *very* competitive with the dollar at its current level. But when much of the rest of the world is in recession and growth in this country is robust, exports growth languishes while imports surge. Consequently, the trade deficit widens appreciably.

**THE TRADE DEFICIT IS ALSO DEPENDENT UPON BUSINESS CYCLE DIFFERENCES BETWEEN THE U.S. AND ITS TRADING PARTNERS**

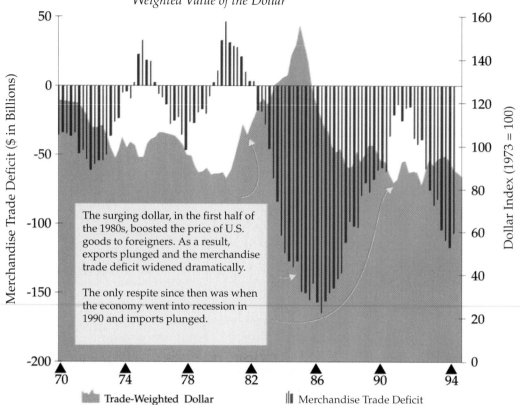

Figure 20-2 The U.S. Merchandise Trade Deficit Versus the Trade-Weighted Value of the Dollar

The surging dollar, in the first half of the 1980s, boosted the price of U.S. goods to foreigners. As a result, exports plunged and the merchandise trade deficit widened dramatically.

The only respite since then was when the economy went into recession in 1990 and imports plunged.

Trade-Weighted Dollar          Merchandise Trade Deficit

**TRADE BALANCE =**
**EXPORTS - IMPORTS**

Reduced to its essentials, the monthly trade balance is rather straightforward: It represents the dollar value difference between U.S. exports and imports on a seasonally adjusted basis. Recently, the deficit for goods and services *combined* has been running about $9 billion per month. But it is important to recognize that there is an enormous difference in the behavior of the *goods* and *services* portions of this report. For example, the monthly *merchandise trade deficit* in the United States is enormous, currently about $14 billion. Indeed, it is beginning to approach its previous record high level. But, at the same time, the United States is running a *service sector surplus* of about $5 billion per month, and this surplus has been relatively steady for the past several years. Even though America is in the midst of an export boom, imports continue to rise as well. Assuming *very* optimistic growth rates of 10% for merchandise exports and only 5% for merchandise imports, it would take about four years for the United States to register a trade surplus for goods and services combined and six years for the merchandise trade deficit to be eradicated. The reason is that the *absolute* amount of merchandise exports, currently about $45 billion each month, is swamped by merchandise imports of approximately $59 billion.

From a GDP accounting sense, exports *add* to GDP, while imports must be *subtracted* from GDP, since a portion of U.S. consumption and investment demand is satisfied by foreign — not domestic — producers. Thus, during periods of widening trade deficits, the United States registers slower growth than would otherwise be the case. Recently, hefty export demand has been outpaced by even faster growth in imports, and the trade deficit has widened. This has acted as a brake on GDP growth. So while GDP has been relatively rapid, it would have been *even faster* if the trade sector had remained stable. Specifically, 1994 GDP growth of 4.0% would have been 4.7% had it not been for the drag from trade. But, it is important to recognize that in *both* cases there would have been an enormous trade deficit. So what's critical from a GDP standpoint is not whether the overall trade balance is in surplus or deficit, but whether it is expanding or shrinking.

**WHAT'S IMPORTANT IS WHETHER THE DEFICIT IS EXPANDING OR SHRINKING**

Each month, the Census Bureau gathers data on total U.S. exports (wheat, computers, and tractors) and imports (Toyotas, fax machines, and caviar) (*Figure 20-3* and *Figure 20-4*). Even though the data are amazingly detailed, investors are advised to focus on the following broad groups of merchandise: food,

**THE TRADE DATA ARE EXTREMELY DETAILED**

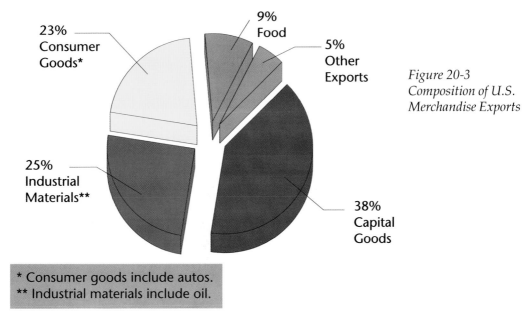

23%
Consumer
Goods*

9%
Food

5%
Other
Exports

25%
Industrial
Materials**

38%
Capital
Goods

*Figure 20-3
Composition of U.S.
Merchandise Exports*

\* Consumer goods include autos.
\*\* Industrial materials include oil.

industrial supplies (including oil), capital goods, and consumer goods (including autos). Trends in these categories are plotted and investment strategies adjusted accordingly. Exports and imports of services are growing rapidly, but are still dwarfed by the flows in manufacturing. As shown in *Figure 20-5*, during the fourth quarter of 1994, exports and imports of merchandise accounted for about three-quarters of the total. At this point, most services are rendered locally rather than internationally. However, that situation is likely to change in the years ahead. The principal service categories at the present time are travel and tourism and royalties and licensing fees. Because the services surplus remains quite steady on a monthly basis, it can largely be ignored. Rest assured that when the combined deficit for goods and services widens or shrinks, it does so as the result of changes in exports and imports of merchandise — not services.

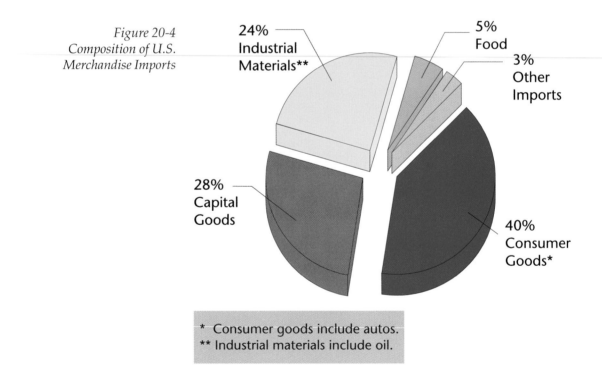

*Figure 20-4*
*Composition of U.S.*
*Merchandise Imports*

24%
Industrial
Materials**

5%
Food

3%
Other
Imports

28%
Capital
Goods

40%
Consumer
Goods*

\* Consumer goods include autos.
\*\* Industrial materials include oil.

The report also highlights trade flows between the United States and various countries, which are referred to as *bilateral* trade deficits and surpluses. For the record, America's largest trading partner is not Japan, Germany, or Britain; it is Canada. As indicated in *Figure 20-6*, our northern neighbor accounts for roughly 20% of total U.S. trade, followed closely by Japan with

EXPORTS                                    IMPORTS

Figure 20-5
*Exports/Imports of Services*

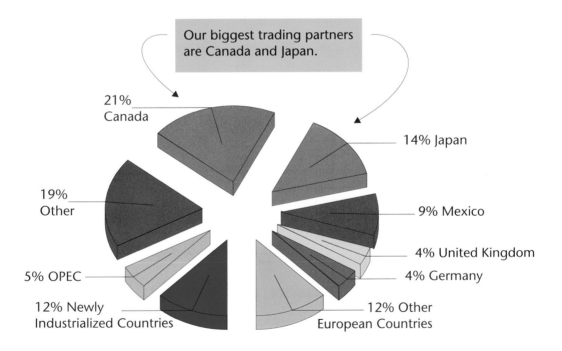

Figure 20-6
*U.S. Trading Partners: Exports Plus Imports*

about 15%. Mexico is a distant third with 9%, while Germany
and the United Kingdom each represent about 5% of the total.

It is important to recognize that there are three separate reports on trade, and market participants need to understand the differences *(Figure 20-7)*.

TRADE BALANCE FOR GOODS AND SERVICES
From a market viewpoint, the most valuable report is the monthly trade balance for goods and services because it is the most timely — the other two are released quarterly. This report became far more valuable in early 1994 when exports and imports of services were reported on a monthly basis for the first time. Previously, the monthly trade report was known as the *merchandise trade balance* because, as the name implies, it contained data only on exports and imports of goods. Services were available only on a *quarterly* basis. This new format made another change that eliminated the small, but annoying, distinction between data reported on a "Census" basis and a "balance of payments" basis. This latter method of reporting was crucial because GDP accounting used the trade data on the balance of payments basis. The major difference between the two methods of reporting involves the treatment of military aid and gold flows. This is not the place to discuss technicalities, but because there *was* a difference between these two methods of reporting, the Census Bureau (in the old days) had to release additional information — later in the month — which converted the trade data from the "Census" basis to a "balance of payments" basis. Fortunately, this new report eliminates all of these difficulties and allows us to focus on the data for goods and services that will flow directly into the GDP accounts. Having said this, the Census version will not fade away altogether, because many of the traditional geographic and product breakdowns are available only on a Census basis. For example, when we see data on oil imports, or on the trade deficit with Japan, we are seeing data on the Census basis. The good news is that it does not really matter!

NET EXPORTS
The second trade-related report, known as "net exports" is important because it is a part of the GDP data. This is the familiar (X - M) part of the GDP equation. These data are presented quarterly, in both nominal and real (inflation-adjusted) terms. But there is nothing new here. What goes into the GDP accounts is simply a quarterly average of the monthly data on goods and services. However, when we receive our first look at GDP growth for a particular quarter, we do not have trade data for the final month of the quarter; we must estimate it. This can sometimes create a problem. For example, in December 1994, we and most other analysts expected the trade deficit to narrow slightly from

$10.5 billion in November to about $10.0 billion. Indeed, the Commerce Department indicated in its "key source data" table (in which it tells market participants its assumptions about missing data), that it had a similar expectation. But the actual deficit for that month turned out to be $7.3 billion, or $2.7 billion below expectations. At the same time, the November deficit was revised downwards by $0.3 billion. This meant that the cumulative deficit for the fourth quarter was $3.0 billion less than expected ($0.3 billion less than expected in November plus $2.7 billion below expectations in December). Once these data were annualized (multiplied by four), it was clear that the net exports component of GDP would revise upwards (a smaller deficit) by $12.0 billion. By itself this piece added 0.8% to GDP growth in that quarter. This highlights how critical it is to forecast the missing data accurately! The important point is that once we have all of the monthly trade data, we essentially know what the net exports component of GDP is going to be.

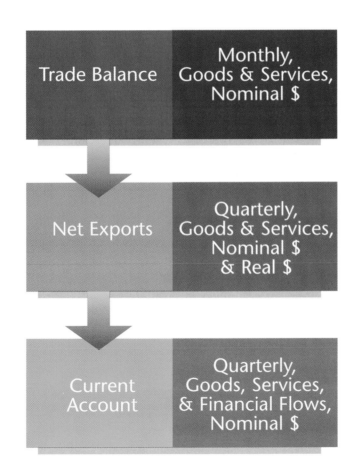

*Figure 20-7*
*The Three Separate*
*Reports on Trade*

CURRENT ACCOUNT

The final report is known as the "current account." Curiously, the markets tend to ignore this report. But, in fact, it is probably the most important of all trade data — it's the broadest measure of U.S. trade and includes both goods and services, as well as unilateral transfers (i.e., foreign aid) and financial flows. Current account data are crucial because they represent the amount of trade that must somehow be financed. Fortunately, when foreigners find U.S. investment attractive, and more funds flow in than flow abroad, this foreign investment finances a portion of our net exports deficit.

**TRADE DATA ARE DIFFICULT TO FORECAST**

Trade data are difficult to gather and to forecast, and we have learned to live with the many data collection problems. However, as described above, the Census Bureau figures are becoming more accurate and timely. Likewise, economists are improving their forecasts of imports by examining customs duties data — taxes collected on arriving goods. Yet the process is more difficult for exports. Analysts often take a "bottom up" approach, e.g., did Boeing actually deliver its jets within a certain month? Despite the uncertainties, a broad consensus is formed, against which the market judges a particular trade report.

**A DECLINE IN THE TRADE DEFICIT WILL BOOST THE DOLLAR**

How are the major markets affected *(Figure 20-8)*? Let us begin with the dollar since its response is usually the most direct. A decline in the deficit is always welcome news for holders of the greenback — one must *buy* dollars to purchase U.S. exports and *sell* dollars to buy imports. In this case, expectations play a major role. Suppose the Street consensus places the June trade deficit at $8 billion. A $3 billion shortfall would be viewed, perhaps even seized upon, as an opportunity to buy the dollar, short the yen, or sell sterling. We concede, however, that the foreign exchange market has become less impressed with trade reports than it used to be. Generally speaking, if the dollar has been trading within a well-defined range, the monthly trade figures tend to be ignored beyond a few hours. Conversely, if the dollar has just broken out of its recent boundaries, data on trade flows will have a greater impact.

The case for bond investors is a little more subtle. Suppose the trade deficit comes in less than expected. Bond investors are torn between two factors. First, a smaller deficit triggers a dollar rally — good news for bond market participants. But, if the trade deficit is shrinking, it simultaneously adds to GDP growth. A faster pace of economic activity is negative for bonds. What should an investor do? It is not always clear — the market reaction seems to be determined by the mood of the moment. In all candor, there are times when economists have had a hard time anticipating the market's response even if we had known the numbers in advance! Caveats aside, fixed-income analysts generally attach significance to the breakdown between exports and imports. Given a lower deficit scenario, the bond market prefers a reduction in imports to a surge in exports. The reason revolves around the bond holder's ever-present fear of a strong economy — and the possibility of higher inflation. Recall, exports increase GDP, whereas imports reduce GDP. In short, a dream report (again, taking into account expectations) for bond investors would be the following: (1) Prior to release, the Street assumes an $8 billion trade deficit. (2) The actual deficit narrows to $5 billion. (3) The dollar is immediately bid higher. (4) Upon examination, it turns out that exports *declined* $1 billion, while imports fell $4 billion. Softer exports imply less pressure on manufacturers' demand for credit to finance production, and lower imports suggest that consumer spending is slowing — a deceleration in economic activity is always welcome by holders of fixed-income instruments. A nightmare for bond investors would be the reverse — a higher-than-expected trade deficit, a dollar sell-off, strong exports, and even stronger imports.

**BONDS COULD GO EITHER WAY — DEPENDING UPON THEIR MOOD AT THE MOMENT**

Equity players are often torn between following the bond or foreign exchange markets. Many times a trade report is bullish for the dollar but bearish for bonds — or vice versa. In our experience, stocks generally end the day higher if the deficit narrowed, or lower if the deficit widened. The stock market's response is also a function of whether the "trade problem" is a major issue at the time. If not, the best strategy for long-term investors is to follow *industry trends*, both on the export and import side. This requires some study and cannot be acted upon in a half hour. But patience is sometimes rewarded. Those who caught the turning point in 1988 happily noted rising share prices of firms with export exposure. Many of the companies that had been pronounced "DOA" were busy recapturing overseas markets — and returning to profitability.

**AND THE STOCK MARKET WILL RALLY**

*Figure 20-8*
*Market Reaction to the*
*Merchandise Trade*
*Balance*

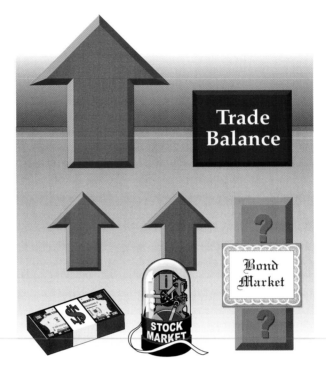

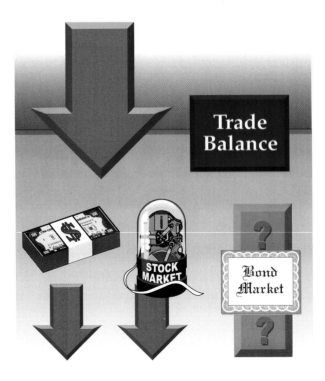

LAST, BUT NOT LEAST

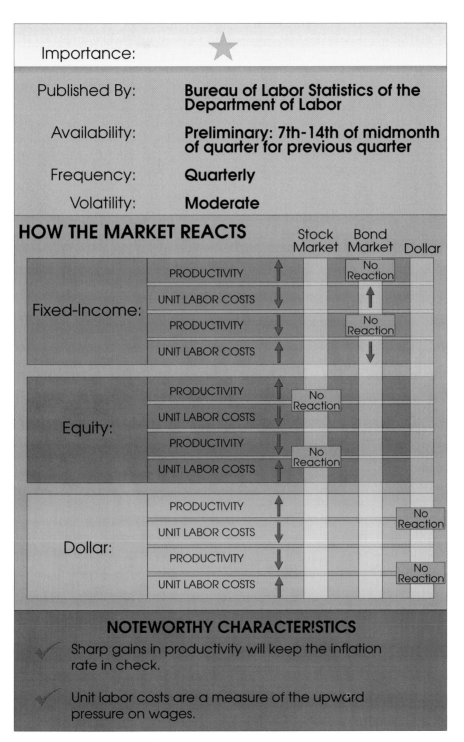

| Importance: ★ | | |
|---|---|---|
| Published By: | **Bureau of Labor Statistics of the Department of Labor** | |
| Availability: | **Preliminary: 7th-14th of midmonth of quarter for previous quarter** | |
| Frequency: | **Quarterly** | |
| Volatility: | **Moderate** | |

## HOW THE MARKET REACTS

| | | Stock Market | Bond Market | Dollar |
|---|---|---|---|---|
| **Fixed-Income:** | PRODUCTIVITY ↑ | | No Reaction | |
| | UNIT LABOR COSTS ↓ | | ↑ | |
| | PRODUCTIVITY ↓ | | No Reaction | |
| | UNIT LABOR COSTS ↑ | | ↓ | |
| **Equity:** | PRODUCTIVITY ↑ | No Reaction | | |
| | UNIT LABOR COSTS ↓ | | | |
| | PRODUCTIVITY ↓ | No Reaction | | |
| | UNIT LABOR COSTS ↑ | | | |
| **Dollar:** | PRODUCTIVITY ↑ | | | No Reaction |
| | UNIT LABOR COSTS ↓ | | | |
| | PRODUCTIVITY ↓ | | | No Reaction |
| | UNIT LABOR COSTS ↑ | | | |

## NOTEWORTHY CHARACTERISTICS

✓ Sharp gains in productivity will keep the inflation rate in check.

✓ Unit labor costs are a measure of the upward pressure on wages.

**PRODUCTIVITY IS DEFINED AS OUTPUT PER UNIT OF LABOR; IT IS A MEASURE OF EFFICIENCY**

Productivity is defined as output per unit of labor *(Figure 21-1)*. The Bureau of Labor Statistics begins by calculating the numerator — industry output measures produced by the Commerce Department in the quarterly GDP report, adjusted to suit its definitions. The labor denominator of the equation is really a measure of aggregate hours worked, i.e., the product of employment and the workweek. To derive the *growth rate* of productivity, the BLS takes the growth rate of output and subtracts the growth rate of aggregate hours worked. When productivity rises, the result is more output per unit of labor. The U.S. economy, therefore, is becoming more "efficient." An increase in productivity is widely regarded as a positive event.

*Figure 21-1*
*Calculation of Productivity*

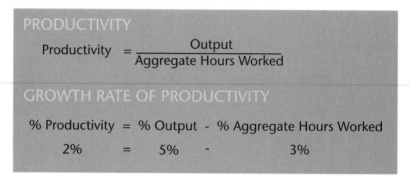

PRODUCTIVITY

$$\text{Productivity} = \frac{\text{Output}}{\text{Aggregate Hours Worked}}$$

GROWTH RATE OF PRODUCTIVITY

% Productivity = % Output - % Aggregate Hours Worked

2%　　=　　5%　　-　　3%

**PRODUCTIVITY STATISTICS ARE PROVIDED FOR SEVERAL SECTORS OF THE ECONOMY**

When productivity statistics are released, we find that data are provided for a number of different sectors of the economy — business, nonfarm, manufacturing, and nonfinancial. The business sector is obviously the broadest measure, but economists generally focus on nonfarm productivity. However, the farm sector is relatively small, and the reality is that there is generally not a lot of difference between the business and nonfarm measures. Some attention is also given to manufacturing productivity. As we will see in a minute, service sector productivity is difficult to measure; manufacturing productivity is not. By focusing on manufacturing, we can see what is happening to productivity in that portion of the economy that we can measure most accurately.

Potential GDP growth is the sum of the growth rates of the labor force and productivity *(Figure 21-2)*. In a sense, this can be regarded as our economic "speed limit." If we grow faster than potential for a sustained period of time, the economy will eventually overheat and the inflation rate will rise (see Chapter 23 for a more detailed discussion of potential GDP growth). During the 1980s this growth rate was generally considered to be about 2.5%, consisting of 1.5% growth in the labor force and a 1.0% gain in productivity. Because employment growth for the balance of the 1990s is likely to be significantly slower than in the expansion of the 1980s, probably only about 1.0%, productivity growth will have to carry more of the burden of boosting real incomes in this decade. Productivity growth will have to climb to 1.5% if potential growth is to remain at 2.5%. There is every reason to believe this can happen, since firms laid off thousands

INCREASES IN PRODUCTIVITY CAN BOOST THE ECONOMIC SPEED LIMIT AND RAISE INCOME GROWTH

*Figure 21-2*
*Calculation of Potential GDP*

POTENTIAL GDP

Potential GDP  =  % Labor Force  +  % Productivity

In the 1980s the labor force grew quickly, but productivity growth was slow.

    2.5%    =    1.5%    +    1.0%

In the 1990s the labor force will grow more slowly, but productivity growth will quicken.

    2.5%    =    1.0%    +    1.5%

or perhaps

    3.0%    =    1.0%    +    2.0%

upon thousands of workers in the early part of the 1990s in an attempt to become more efficient. At the same time, they invested billions of dollars in business equipment — computers in particular — in an effort to boost productivity. Indeed, it is not inconceivable that productivity growth could be 2.0% for the rest of the 1990s. If so, this 2.0% growth rate, combined with the expected 1.0% growth rate in the labor force, suggests that potential growth could be as high as 3.0%. This would raise the economic speed limit and allow the economy to grow more quickly without the fear of triggering a sustained surge in inflation.

## PRODUCTIVITY GAINS ARE VERY DIFFICULT TO MEASURE IN THE SERVICE SECTORS

Recent gains in productivity consisted primarily of rapid growth in the goods-producing sectors; the U.S. experienced disappointing results in service sector productivity. For example, in 1994, nonfarm productivity rose 1.4%, but productivity in the manufacturing sector climbed at a 4.6% pace. While no separate measure of service-sector productivity is provided, the implication is that it grew very slowly at best and may have actually declined. Given the increasing predominance of the service sector in our economy, the slow growth or decline in service-sector productivity is disquieting. As shown in *Figure 21-3*, service-related industries now account for 49% of GDP, but 79% of all nonfarm jobs in the United States. Thus, there are a lot of people employed in the service sector, but they are apparently producing far less output than they should. We do not know whether this sluggish performance in service-sector productivity is real or is simply the result of measurement problems. It is easy to measure productivity in manufacturing-related jobs because analysts can physically measure output. If a firm produces 1,000 refrigerators in this quarter with 100 workers, and next quarter it produces 1,020 refrigerators with the same work force, it is clear that productivity rose. But how does one measure output of services? Many measures of service output are based on proxies such as labor input, tonnage shipped, or the number of checking transactions. But if the trucking industry, for example, adopts advanced computer programs to reduce the number of miles traveled on some routes, that improvement in productivity will not be picked up by the current tonnage-shipped process. If checking transactions are processed more quickly in the banking industry, the current measurement system — based on the number of checking transactions — will miss the improvement in productivity. And faster service at a checkout counter will improve the quality of customer service, but will not be captured by the current measurement system. Is poor service-sector productivity growth real, or not? No one knows for sure. But given the increasing importance of this sector, it certainly matters.

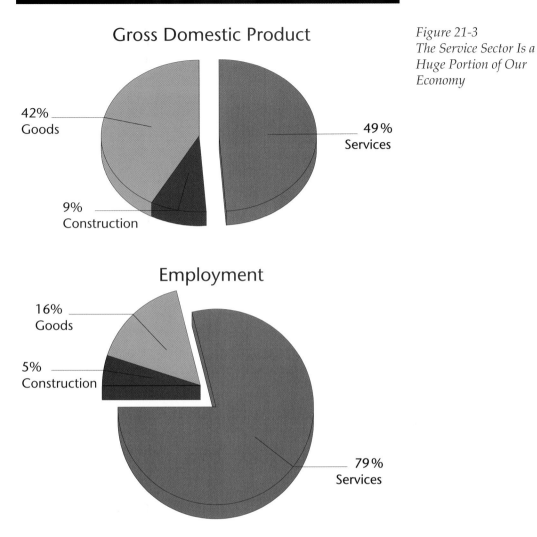

## Gross Domestic Product

42%
Goods

49%
Services

9%
Construction

## Employment

16%
Goods

5%
Construction

79%
Services

*Figure 21-3*
*The Service Sector Is a*
*Huge Portion of Our*
*Economy*

On the surface it would appear that a 5% increase in wages could lead a company to raise prices by 5%. But if productivity were to rise by that same 5%, then the firm's labor cost per unit of output has not changed. Hence, "unit labor costs," which are simply labor costs adjusted for gains in productivity, have not changed. The boss is paying his workers 5% more money, but is garnering 5% more output. In this situation, there is no pressure to raise prices — higher wages are offset by the gain in productivity. Thus, the markets should focus on unit labor costs, rather than wage gains, when trying to determine the likely upward pressure on the inflation rate.

**UNIT LABOR COSTS
ARE A MEASURE OF
LABOR COSTS
ADJUSTED FOR
PRODUCTIVITY
GAINS**

**THE INFLATION RATE IS HIGHLY CORRELATED WITH UNIT LABOR COSTS**

As shown in *Figure 21-4*, the inflation rate is closely linked to the year-over-year increase in unit labor costs. The reason for this is fairly obvious — labor costs represent about two-thirds of a corporation's total cost. The remainder is spent on raw materials and commodities. Given the importance of labor costs to the individual firm, it is not surprising that if those costs rise sharply, they are reflected quickly in product prices. Indeed, we have found that, as a rule of thumb, the inflation rate appears to be about 1.0% higher than the growth rate of unit labor costs. This difference presumably reflects profit margins. Once we know what is happening to unit labor costs, we can see whether our inflation forecast is in the ballpark.

*Figure 21-4*
*Unit Labor Costs Versus CPI*

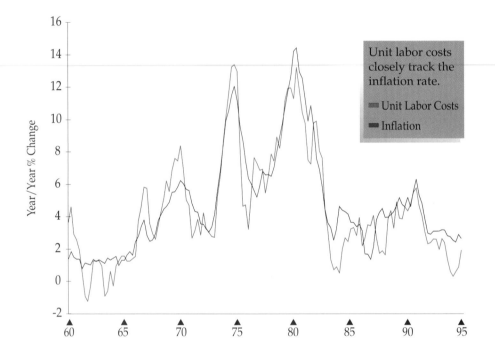

**PRODUCTIVITY GAINS CAN HELP HOLD DOWN THE INFLATION RATE**

The example cited above strongly implies that anything that can boost productivity will result in a lower rate of inflation. We learned earlier that higher productivity also boosts GDP growth. It is clear, therefore, that faster growth in productivity is truly a win/win situation.

In the end, the efficiency of U.S. workers is determined by the amount of capital that is available to each, the quality of the labor employed, and the efficiency of the production process. Thus, productivity growth can be greatly enhanced by more investment *(Figure 21-5)*. A cut in the capital gains tax rate, for example, would be helpful in encouraging businessmen to invest. An increase in the savings rate would boost the supply of savings that could fund that investment. Some of this may occur naturally during the course of the 1990s as the baby boomers age and move into their high savings years. But tax incentives to encourage savings, such as higher maximum amounts that can be invested tax-free each year in an IRA or 401(k) account would be helpful. Finally, a better educated work force would undoubtedly be more productive. In the 1990s the baby boomers will be older and wiser and, presumably, more productive. That should help to boost productivity. But one area crying out for immediate attention is our primary and secondary school system.

**PRODUCTIVITY GROWTH CAN BE BOOSTED BY A NUMBER OF FACTORS**

*Figure 21-5*
*How to Boost Productivity Growth*

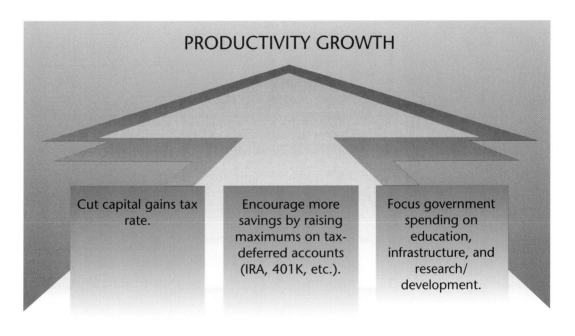

THE BOND MARKET
WILL PAY SOME
ATTENTION TO UNIT
LABOR COSTS, BUT
IGNORE
EVERYTHING ELSE

Productivity growth is not something that captures the attention of the fixed-income market. Unit labor costs, however, are generally noted and have been known to generate a modest amount of interest *(Figure 21-6)*. This is because market participants have become aware of the fact that unit labor costs are very important in determining the amount of upward pressure on the inflation rate. If they rise sharply, bond market participants will worry because they know that labor costs represent two-thirds of a firm's total costs. If those productivity-adjusted costs are going up, there is a good chance that the company will raise prices. Thus, an increase in unit labor costs will make the bond market nervous. A decline would be greeted favorably. In our opinion, the bond market *should* pay more attention to this report, but the reality is otherwise.

Neither the stock market nor the foreign exchange market pay any particular attention to this report.

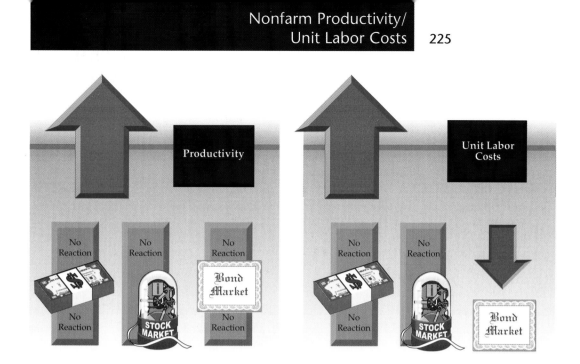

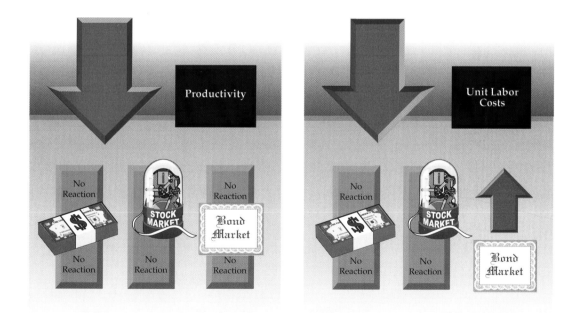

*Figure 21-6*
*Market Reaction to Productivity, Unit Labor Costs*

# PART III

## FEDERAL RESERVE OPERATIONS

In this book's introduction we pointed out that the Federal Reserve (the "Fed") has an enormous impact on the economy through its control of key interest rates. Combined with its power to create money, the Fed's policies greatly influence commodity prices, the value of the U.S. dollar in foreign exchange markets, government and corporate bond yields, mortgage rates, real estate prices, and stock market valuations. With the demise of coherent, counter-cyclical fiscal policies from Congress and the White House, the Federal Reserve has effectively taken over management of the business cycle. Unless you have some feel for monetary policy and a fundamental macroeconomic outlook, you will be forever "surprised" by events. Moreover, investing in the 1990s and beyond will require a global view. As the markets become increasingly interconnected, a better grasp of monetary policies overseas will be needed, especially if an investor wishes to diversify outside the home market. Understanding the Federal Reserve will help you comprehend the workings of other central banks, such as the Bundesbank and the Bank of Japan.

**ITS DETERMINATION AND IMPLEMENTATION**

The following two chapters focus on practical aspects of "Fed-watching" that can be utilized by those involved in the financial markets. Investors, traders, and speculators must understand exactly what the Federal Reserve does and does not control, what the federal funds rate means and its relation to other interest rates, how policies are implemented, and what economic data the Fed monitors.

Chapter 23 arms the reader with a working knowledge of the central bank and how it operates in the marketplace — its stated goals, the relationship between fiscal and monetary policy, the relationship between the Fed and Congress, the factors the central bank looks at to determine monetary policy, and how policy shifts affect the fixed-income market. A great deal of emphasis is placed on the macroeconomic environment because changes in monetary policy are based almost exclusively on economic variables. In the first part of this book we discussed a variety of economic indicators and how each of them provides us with information about either GDP growth or the inflation rate. In the next chapter we will see that it is GDP growth and the inflation rate that determine the Federal Reserve's monetary policy. Now that you are armed with a detailed knowledge of the economic indicators, from housing starts to the PPI, the next chapter serves to reinforce these concepts *because the Federal*

**MARKET PARTICIPANTS MUST UNDERSTAND HOW THE FEDERAL RESERVE DETERMINES MONETARY POLICY**

*Reserve follows these very same data! If you want to know what the Fed is up to, simply watch what it watches.*

**KNOWLEDGE OF HOW THE FEDERAL RESERVE IMPLEMENTS POLICY IS EQUALLY IMPORTANT**

In addition to monitoring factors that help *determine* Federal Reserve policy — overall economic activity, employment growth, the inflation rate, etc. — traders and investors need to know how the Fed *implements* monetary policy. In Chapter 24, we take a more detailed look at the "plumbing"—how the Fed attempts to hit its funds rate target, the nuts and bolts of the reserves market, and why the central bank may choose customer repos rather than system repos. Throughout the 1980s and early part of the 1990s, market participants needed an in-depth understanding of how the central bank implemented policy, because at that time the Fed was targeting bank reserves. You needed to know *exactly* how many reserves the Federal Reserve was required to add or drain in a given statement period to achieve its reserves target in order to determine whether it was being aggressive (trying to push the funds rate lower) or stingy (attempting to raise the level of the funds rate). If you understood the reserves targeting procedure, you could correctly interpret the constant signals the Fed was sending to the markets about the desired level of short-term rates. But that was then. This is now. Luckily, life has become much simpler because the Federal Reserve *tells us* exactly what it is doing! The central bank specifically followed a reserves targeting procedure from October 1979 through the latter part of the 1980s. At that point it reverted back to its old methodology of targeting the funds rate. Nonetheless, throughout that *entire* period you needed to follow its daily open market activity to determine when monetary policy was being changed. But then, on February 4, 1994, the Fed entered a new era whereby it tells us *specifically* what that funds rate target is. The mystery is gone. We no longer need "Fed watchers" to analyze the Fed's daily open market activity and tell us the desired level for the funds rate. The game has changed. Everyone *knows* what the Fed is doing, because the Federal Reserve *tells* us. The "Fed watchers" role today is not to determine *whether* a policy change has occurred, but rather to anticipate *when* the Fed is going to make its next move. That part of the game has not changed. Furthermore, our experience over the past decade indicates clearly that monetary policy is dynamic and changes over time. We cannot predict when the Fed might revert to its former ways or make other changes. For that reason we believe it is still important for market participants to have a basic understanding of Fed procedures, although we will concede that this knowledge is far less critical today than it was previously. Peruse Chapter 24 and try to understand the major concepts, but basically keep it for reference.

## THE BASICS

The ultimate objective of both fiscal and monetary policy is to achieve an economy characterized by rapid GDP growth, relatively full employment, and stable prices. In an ideal world, policymakers would like to see GDP growth of about 2.5%, an inflation rate no higher than 2.5%, and the unemployment rate at about 5.5%. Let's briefly examine each of these three so-called longer term economic objectives. With respect to growth, a 2.5% pace is generally viewed as the economic speed limit. Anything faster will eventually cause an uptick in inflation. Anything less means that the economy is not producing as many goods and services — and jobs — as it could. Concerning inflation, policymakers tell us they want to see a zero rate of inflation, but in reality they are probably willing to live with an inflation rate of about 2.5% for two reasons. First, to achieve a zero-inflation goal, one must accept a sharply reduced pace of economic expansion for a protracted period of time. During that period the unemployment rate will be quite high. This is *not* a politically acceptable situation. Second, if prices rise by 2.5% per annum, part of that price gain, perhaps 1.0-1.5%, reflects improvements in quality. Thus, the "true" inflation rate is a minimal 1.0-1.5%. It is simply not worth the cost to wring that last bit of inflation out of the economy. Finally, economists regard the "full employment" unemployment rate to be about 5.5%, at which point the only remaining unemployment is transitional. A certain number of people are always changing jobs and are temporarily unemployed. Any attempt to push the unemployment rate lower will ultimately result in an accelerating rate of inflation. Thus, it is clear that there are trade-offs among these long-term economic objectives. Attempts to stimulate GDP growth and create jobs may well boost the inflation rate. Efforts to curb inflation could push the economy into recession. Theoretically, policymakers would like to achieve all three of these economic objectives simultaneously. But pulling it off, in practice, is quite difficult!

By altering government spending and taxation, thereby influencing aggregate demand, *fiscal* policy can have a significant impact on economic activity, employment, and the rate of inflation. The responsibility for implementing fiscal policy is shared between the White House and Congress. In theory, lawmakers should run budget deficits to stimulate the economy when it dips into recession, but then produce budget surpluses when the economy is running at full speed to help keep growth in check. But in reality, the government has not run a budget surplus in more

ALL POLICYMAKERS SEEK RAPID GDP GROWTH, FULL EMPLOYMENT, AND STABLE PRICES

TO ACHIEVE THESE OBJECTIVES POLICYMAKERS CAN USE FISCAL POLICY than 30 years — and does not have the prospect for a surplus for another 30 years. Thus, fiscal policy as a tool for achieving the macroeconomic objectives outlined earlier is essentially nonexistent. Politicians can accomplish only one thing with fiscal policy at the moment — shrink the deficit. To intentionally boost the deficit to stimulate the economy is unthinkable given the sheer magnitude of budget deficits in the years ahead.

**POLICYMAKERS CAN ALSO USE MONETARY POLICY**

In 1913, Congress created the Federal Reserve System for the purpose of carrying out *monetary* policy. By regulating the volume of bank reserves through open market operations, the Federal Reserve influences interest rates — the level of which causes changes in the behavior of businesses and consumers *(Figure 23-1)*. Policy changes also affect the pace of money creation, ultimately influencing economic activity and prices. In a recession, defined as at least two consecutive quarters of negative GDP growth, the Federal Reserve acts to stimulate credit expansion by increasing bank reserves, prompting interest rates to fall *(Figure 23-2)*. An increased amount of loanable funds thus becomes available for corporate and consumer borrowing. As business activity picks up, firms increase hiring, and the unemployment rate falls. In an inflationary period, when the CPI is running at a 5% rate or higher and the economy is booming, the Federal Reserve acts to cool the economy by decreasing bank reserves. With fewer funds available, interest rates tend to rise. These higher rates discourage borrowers and retard economic activity. At some point, slower growth results in moderating price pressures.

**THE RELATIVE IMPORTANCE OF THESE LONGER TERM GOALS CAN CHANGE OVER TIME**

Depending on the economic environment, certain goals take precedence over others. For example, in the 1970s, the chief political worry was inflation. Even though unemployment trended higher for most of the decade, the public wanted "something done" about rising prices. This brought forth a host of quick fixes, such as Nixon's wage and price "freeze" and Carter's oil price "guidelines," but none of them seemed to do the trick. As the crisis came to a head in the summer of 1979, President Carter was more or less forced into appointing an inflation "hawk," Paul Volcker, to head the central bank. Acting swiftly, the new Federal Reserve chairman instituted what amounted to a frontal assault on spiraling prices. With inflation rates once again headed toward double-digits, Volcker signaled a dramatic change in policy on October 6, 1979. First, the Fed

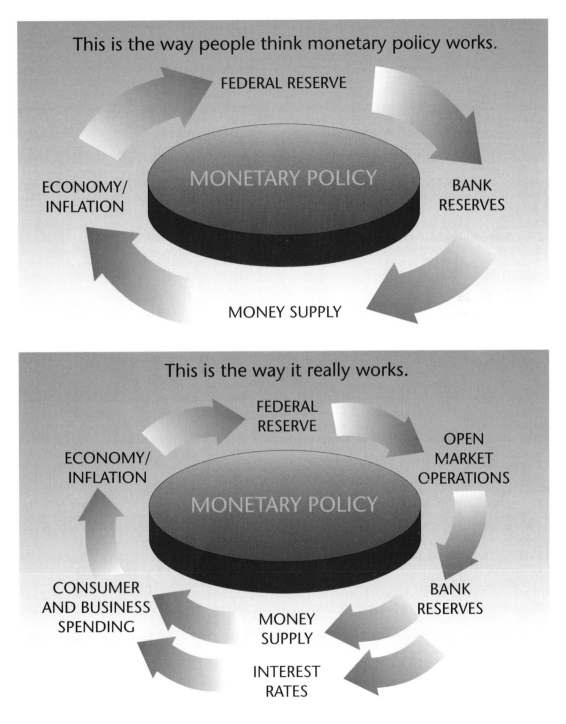

*Figure 23-1*
*How Federal Reserve Monetary Policy Affects the Economy and Inflation*

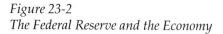

*Figure 23-2*
*The Federal Reserve and the Economy*

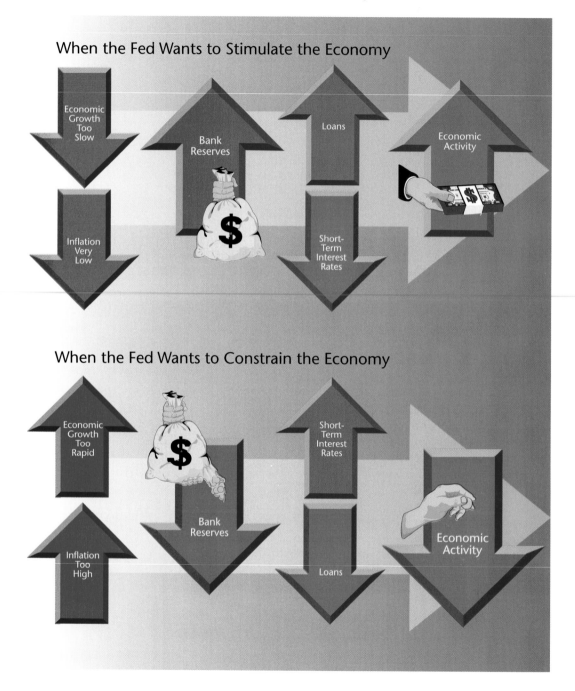

## When the Fed Wants to Stimulate the Economy

Economic Growth Too Slow

Inflation Very Low

Bank Reserves

Loans

Short-Term Interest Rates

Economic Activity

## When the Fed Wants to Constrain the Economy

Economic Growth Too Rapid

Inflation Too High

Bank Reserves

Short-Term Interest Rates

Loans

Economic Activity

hiked the discount rate by a full percentage point, from 11% to 12%. Second, the central bank established an 8% marginal reserve requirement on "managed liabilities," effectively halting a method by which banks had brought about rapid credit expansion. Finally (and perhaps most importantly), the Federal Reserve Board placed ". . .greater emphasis, in day-to-day operations, on the supply of bank reserves, and less emphasis on confining short-term fluctuations in the federal funds rate." In other words, the Fed began targeting (and squeezing) bank reserves and money growth directly — even if that meant substantially higher interest rates. All of this was done because, at the time, inflation had become a very serious problem.

By April 1980 the Federal Reserve's tighter monetary policy stance began to bite, the economy dipped into recession, and the unemployment rate rose sharply. At that juncture inflation was no longer the enemy. The focus of the Federal Reserves shifted towards restoring economic expansion and lowering the unemployment rate. Thus, depending upon the stage of the business cycle, the relative importance of these various long-term economic objectives shifts.

The experience in the late 1970s and early 1980s described above is a good example of the practical distinction between monetary and fiscal policy. Given the reality of politics, there was little chance that either Congress or the Administration — even if they had the power to do so — could have taken such unpopular steps and knowingly have risked a recession. This is not to say that the Federal Reserve is completely insulated from politics — it is not. The Federal Reserve system was created by Congress, and Congress can limit the Federal Reserve's freedom if it strays too far from an acceptable path. However, we should point out that the seven members of the Federal Reserve Board are appointed to 14-year terms. The chairman has a four-year guarantee at the helm. The closest analogy is the Supreme Court — members of both institutions righteously consider themselves "above politics," and both institutions will from time to time make very unpopular decisions. In the final analysis, the Federal Reserve is the only institution willing to bring about a full-blown recession to effectively counter accelerating inflation.

FEDERAL RESERVE POLICY IS INDEPENDENT OF BOTH CONGRESS AND THE ADMINISTRATION — BUT IT IS SENSITIVE TO THE WISHES OF BOTH

**MONETARY POLICY TODAY IS LARGELY DETERMINED BY THE PACE OF ECONOMIC ACTIVITY AND THE "OUTPUT GAP"**

Since early 1994 the Federal Reserve seems to be relying heavily on the output gap to determine monetary policy. To understand why, we must first explain the terminology. The output gap is defined as the difference between potential and actual GDP — basically the degree of slack in the economy. Potential GDP is simply a measure of how many goods and services the economy could produce if at full employment. In that situation everybody who wants a job has one, and factories are zipping along at their maximum sustainable pace. This is the straight line shown in *Figure 23-3* shown growing at about a 2.5% rate. The *growth rate* of potential GDP represents the sum of growth in the labor force (about 1%) and long-term growth in productivity (believed to be about 1.5%). See *Figure 23-4* and Chapter 21. When the economy slips into recession, workers are laid off and factory output declines sharply. Actual GDP falls far below potential and the output gap widens. In this situation there is *downward* pressure on the inflation rate. Once the recession ends the economy begins to expand vigorously and the gap narrows. Typically, two or three years into an expansion, actual GDP catches up to potential and the output gap disappears. If the economy *continues* to grow rapidly (i.e., at a rate in excess of the 2.5% growth rate of potential GDP), actual GDP will move above potential. But this is an unacceptable situation because now there is a tendency to get *upward* pressure on the inflation rate. Workers will seek higher

*Figure 23-3*
*GDP Gap —Actual Compared to Potential*

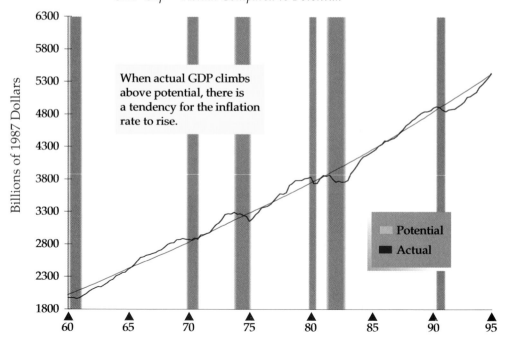

When actual GDP climbs above potential, there is a tendency for the inflation rate to rise.

wages, and companies will take advantage of the excessive demand for goods and services by raising prices. Thus, the object of the game for the Federal Reserve is to encourage the economy to expand rapidly from the end of a recession until the time that the output gap disappears. At that point it would like to have GDP growth slow magically to its long-run, noninflationary, potential growth pace. If the Fed gets it right, potential and

## POTENTIAL GDP

Potential GDP  =  % Labor Force  +  % Productivity

In the 1980s the labor force grew quickly, but productivity growth was slow.

| 2.5% | = | 1.5% | + | 1.0% |

In the 1990s the labor force will grow more slowly, but productivity growth will quicken.

| 2.5% | = | 1.0% | + | 1.5% |

or perhaps

| 3.0% | = | 1.0% | + | 2.0% |

*Figure 23-4*
*Calculation of Potential GDP*

actual GDP will track essentially on top of each other, and the economy will be at full employment. This means that the unemployment rate will be at the so-called full employment level of around 5.5%, and factory usage will be at its effective maximum level, which is generally believed to be about 85%. Furthermore, the inflation rate should be steady at a relatively low level of, say, 2% or so. Inflation will only accelerate if the Fed lets actual GDP climb above potential for a protracted period of time. If the Fed can actually *cause* potential and actual GDP to track together, it will have successfully achieved all of its longer term macroeconomic objectives — rapid GDP growth, full employment, and relatively stable prices.

In February 1994 policymakers at the Federal Reserve began to tighten despite ample slack in the economy. As shown in *Figure 23-3*, the output gap at that time was still quite wide. But the Fed could see that if it allowed the economy to expand at a 3.5-4.0% pace, which is well in excess of potential GDP growth, the output gap would disappear by the end of the year. Thus, its objective was to slow the economy to its long-run, noninflationary, potential growth rate of 2.5% by the time that the output gap disappeared. Recognizing that monetary policy works with a lag of

THIS FOCUS ON GDP GROWTH AND THE OUTPUT GAP SEEMS TO HAVE BEGUN IN 1994 nine to twelve months, the Fed knew it had to move quickly to prevent upward pressure on the inflation rate. Citing the rapid pace of economic expansion and the upward movement of the so-called "leading indicators of inflation," the Fed began to tighten. But to do so at this particular stage was unprecedented. In the past, the Fed usually waited until the output gap disappeared before it began to tighten. But because there is a nine-to-twelve month lag between the time the Fed raises interest rates and the time it impacts the economy, the inflation rate began to rise. The Fed would then panic. Almost invariably it would push interest rates too high and, ultimately, the economy would dip into recession. But by 1994 the FOMC members apparently had learned from their predecessor's mistakes and decided not to wait until the inflation rate actually began to rise before tightening. So in February 1994, this group began to push the funds rate up almost one full year before the time they expected the inflation rate to rise — far sooner than in the past. By so doing they hoped to achieve a so-called "soft landing." That is, they wanted GDP growth to slow to a noninflationary rate of 2.5% or a bit less, but they *did not* want growth to slow so much that the economy fell into recession. If they were able to nudge GDP growth down to a noninflationary rate by the time that the slack in the economy disappeared late that year, they thought that they could simultaneously achieve all three of their macroeconomic objectives. (By the time this book is published, you will know whether they succeeded or not.)

**IN ADDITION TO GDP GROWTH AND THE OUTPUT GAP, THE FED ALSO APPEARS TO BE FOCUSING ON THE "LEADING INDICATORS OF INFLATION"**

The output gap chart clearly indicates that the inflation rate is a lagging indicator of economic activity. For example, if GDP growth remains rapid for an extended period of time, actual GDP moves above potential and the inflation rate begins to rise. Similarly, if the economy falls into recession, actual GDP falls well below potential and the inflation rate declines. Thus, the pace of economic activity ultimately precedes changes in the inflation rate. For this reason, market participants need not focus a great deal of attention on the *current* rate of inflation — it is a lagging indicator. Rather, they should examine the pace of economic activity, the output gap, *and* the so-called *leading indicators of inflation* shown in *Figure 23-5* because these factors have become very important to the Fed in determining monetary policy. Having discussed GDP growth and the output gap previously, we will now briefly turn our attention to these leading indicators of inflation.

**Wages**: Wages are the single largest cost factor for almost every firm. Indeed, wages represent about two-thirds of a firm's total

## THE LEADING INDICATORS OF INFLATION

- •WAGE PRESSURES
- •COMMODITY PRICES
- •GOLD PRICES
- •SHAPE OF THE YIELD CURVE
- •EXCHANGE RATES
- •CAPACITY UTILIZATION
- •PRICES PAID BY MANUFACTURERS (NAPM)

*Figure 23-5*
*The Leading Indicators of Inflation*

costs.  As a result, any change in wages — up or down — is quickly passed along to the consumer in the form of higher or lower prices for that firm's product.  Average hourly earnings are one measure of wage pressures.  But the reality is that an increase in wages can be offset by an increase in productivity.  For example, if businesses pay people 3.5% more money, but they produce more goods and are 3.5% more productive, those firms do not worry about the higher wages.  Labor costs adjusted for productivity are known as *unit labor costs* and, not surprisingly given their importance, changes in them correlate well with the inflation rate.  (See Chapter 21 on Nonfarm Productivity/Unit Labor Costs and *Figure 21-4* in particular.)

**Commodity prices**: Commodity prices are a *cost* to the manufacturer. While the relationship between commodity prices and inflation is quite loose, the fact remains that if commodity prices rise far enough and for a long enough period of time, there will be a tendency for that manufacturer to raise prices. (For a more thorough discussion of commodity prices, refer to the chapter on the PPI.)

**Gold prices**: The price of gold is believed to be an indicator of inflationary expectations, which are as important to the Fed as the inflation rate itself. For example, if market participants are worried about a sharp rise in the inflation rate — which will cause the price of their security holdings to decline — they will probably want to hold "real" assets, such as gold and real estate, the prices of which rise as inflation accelerates. Moreover, if business people expect the inflation rate to rise, there is a tendency for them to raise prices to maintain their "real" profit margins. Thus, a rise in inflationary *expectations* can be self-fulfilling and actually bring about a pickup in the inflation rate itself.

**Shape of the yield curve**: The shape of the yield curve — which is simply the difference between long- and short-term interest rates — is another indicator of inflationary expectations. As described on the very first page of Chapter 1, an expected pickup in the rate of inflation will cause bond prices to fall and yields to rise. If investors expect the inflation rate to climb, bond yields will rise relative to short rates, and the yield curve will become more positively sloped. If investors expect the inflation rate to subside, bond yields will fall relative to short rates and the yield curve will become flatter. Thus, the shape of the yield curve can be a good barometer of inflationary expectations.

**Exchange rates**: If investors believe that the inflation rate in the United States is poised to rise, thereby eroding the value of their holdings of dollar-denominated securities, they are likely to sell some of their dollar-denominated assets. As they do so, the value of the dollar declines. If foreign investors expect the U.S. inflation rate to fall, they will want to buy dollar-denominated assets. In the process the dollar will rise. Thus, the foreign exchange value of the dollar can be a good indicator of foreign investors' views concerning the future rate of inflation.

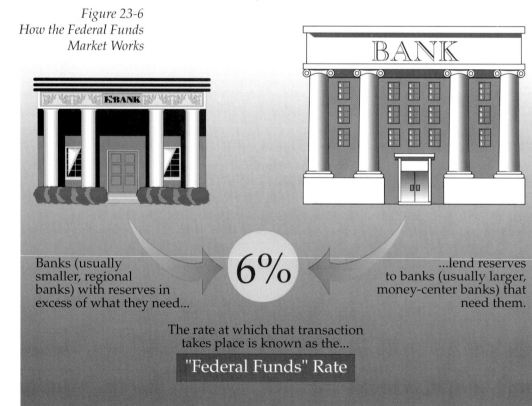

*Figure 23-6*
*How the Federal Funds*
*Market Works*

Banks (usually smaller, regional banks) with reserves in excess of what they need...

6%

...lend reserves to banks (usually larger, money-center banks) that need them.

The rate at which that transaction takes place is known as the...

"Federal Funds" Rate

**Capacity utilization**: Capacity utilization was described in the chapter on industrial production. The main idea is that if manufacturers experience strong demand for their products, they will boost the pace of production. At some point their factories will be running at full speed. If there continues to be excess demand for these products, manufacturers may be tempted to raise prices. This process seems to begin once capacity utilization climbs to about 85%.

**Prices paid by manufacturers**: Prices paid by manufacturers are basically a reflection of commodity prices. We can measure these price changes by examining the price component of the purchasing managers' report. If purchasing managers are paying more for their materials, they indicate this on their monthly survey — and we see the price component rise. (See the chapter on the Purchasing Managers' Report). Here again, if manufacturers indicate that their costs are going up, they will probably try to pass these higher costs along to their customers in the form of higher prices.

It is not always clear how the Fed will respond to various combinations of GDP growth, the output gap, and the leading indicators of inflation but, in general, the following guidelines should be helpful. First of all, if there is no slack in the economy (i.e., actual GDP is at or above potential), and the economy is expanding at a rate in excess of its 2.5% potential growth path, the Fed *is certain* to tighten. In a situation where there is still some slack in the economy but the economy is growing rapidly (i.e., in excess of its potential growth rate of 2.5%), and it can be determined that the output gap is going to disappear within nine to twelve months, the Fed is *likely* to tighten. The probability of a Fed tightening move will increase sharply if the leading indicators of inflation are rising. With the economy at full employment, the Fed must always worry about a sudden spurt of growth that could quickly result in some upward pressure on the inflation rate. In this situation, the Fed is unlikely to ease and could actually tighten if the leading indicators of inflation begin to rise. For the Fed to consider easing, it seems to us that the economy must both be slowing down and have at least *some* slack in it (i.e., the output gap is positive). In that event the Fed *could* ease if the leading indicators of inflation are relatively stable. The only situation in which the Fed *is certain* to ease is if the economy is slowing down, the output gap is widening, and the leading indicators of inflation are also turning downward. Then and only then will the Fed *surely* ease.

CHANGES IN THE FEDERAL RESERVE'S MONETARY POLICY WILL BE DETERMINED BY THE COMBINATION OF THESE THREE FACTORS

THE "FEDERAL FUNDS RATE" IS A GOOD GAUGE OF FEDERAL RESERVE POLICY

One of the best indicators of the Fed's monetary policy stance is the "federal funds rate." This is because the funds rate is an accurate barometer of the volume of bank reserves. Because bank reserves earn no interest, banks generally like to keep no more than the required minimum on deposit at their local Federal Reserve bank or in their vaults. However, because deposit flows are constantly shifting, reserves shortages and surpluses are routinely encountered. Banks with excess reserves lend them to banks with reserve deficits *(Figure 23-6)*. There is an active market for these loanable funds, and the "price" paid for their use — the interest rate charged — is known as the "federal funds rate." Because the Federal Reserve can precisely control the volume of bank reserves, it is able to manipulate the funds rate with a great deal of precision. Market participants use this (primarily overnight) rate as a gauge not only of existing conditions within the banking industry, but also of the Federal Reserve's position on credit and money growth. A rising funds rate is usually indicative of a contractionary monetary policy designed to decrease the availability of credit. A decline in this key rate suggests an expansionary policy.

BY PEGGING THE FUNDS RATE, THE FED EFFECTIVELY DETERMINES ALL SHORT-TERM INTEREST RATES

In addition to being an accurate indicator of the Federal Reserve's monetary policy stance, the funds rate is used to price almost all short-term U.S. interest rates *(Figure 23-7)*. Essentially, the funds rate is the bank's marginal borrowing rate. Banks constantly create liabilities to finance new loans. One such way is to issue CDs. If for some bizarre reason the CD rate is 8% and federal funds are 6%, the banks bypass the former and borrow at the latter. This action alone is sufficient to drive down CD rates. Other rates are linked as well. Take, for example, the prime rate — the rate banks charge their best corporate customers. It turns out that the banks add about 3% to the CD rate to determine the prime. Therefore, since banks fund a large portion of their loans with CDs, an adjustment here means a change in the prime rate. There are other examples; also linked to federal funds are rates on Treasury bills, commercial paper, bankers acceptances, money market rates, and Eurodollars. The point is that the funds rate is pivotal, as it affects virtually all other short-term instruments.

LONG-TERM INTEREST RATES DEPEND LARGELY ON INFLATIONARY EXPECTATIONS

Unfortunately, the analysis becomes more complicated when attempting to link the money markets with long-term securities. Since the relationship is less than perfect, we should think of them as two distinct entities. By definition, short-term securities mature in one year or less. As a result, expectations concerning inflation are not terribly important. How bad can inflation get during the next three to six months? The risk of owning these securities essentially rests with your assumptions regarding near-term Federal Reserve policy. This is not necessarily true of long-term bonds. Inflationary expectations play a much larger role, as future inflation rates must be discounted over a longer time horizon. Consequently, even though the Federal Reserve may be easing, lower short rates may not always drive down long rates *(Figure 23-8)*. The reason is that stronger economic growth can lead to increased borrowing by corporations and consumers. As borrowers come to the credit markets looking to finance a new factory or obtain a home loan, bond market rates can actually rise! But let's not get carried away here — if the Federal Reserve is *aggressively* easing or tightening credit, bond yields will certainly move in the same direction as short-term rates.

*Figure 23-7*
*Federal Funds Versus Selected Short Rates*

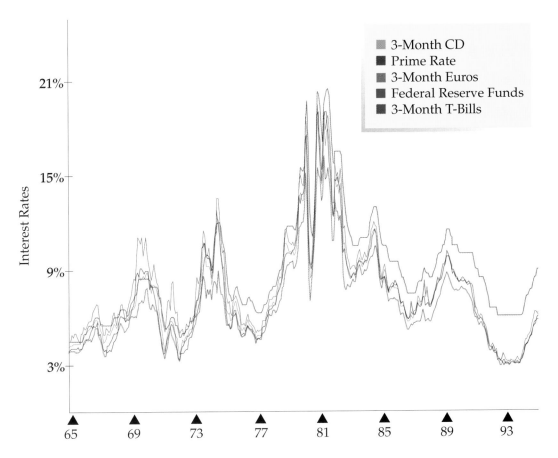

Figure 23-8 Federal Funds Versus AAA Corporate Bond Yields

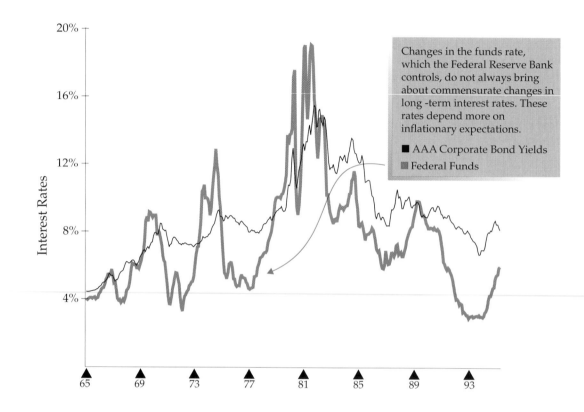

Changes in the funds rate, which the Federal Reserve Bank controls, do not always bring about commensurate changes in long-term interest rates. These rates depend more on inflationary expectations.

■ AAA Corporate Bond Yields
■ Federal Funds

**THE FED CAN PRECISELY CONTROL SHORT-TERM INTEREST RATES, BUT IT CANNOT CONTROL LONG RATES**

The Federal Reserve controls short-term rates through its ability to set the price of reserves — the federal funds rate. But it does not directly control long-term rates. These rates are market-determined and are based on a variety of factors, such as actual inflation, inflationary expectations, supply and demand conditions, the credit risk of a particular security, and so forth. Nevertheless, knowing which way the Fed will move next is extremely valuable to those investing in a variety of financial markets.

**THE *BEST* WAY TO GAUGE FED POLICY IS TO EXAMINE THE "REAL" FUNDS RATE**

We noted previously that the funds rate was a good gauge of Fed policy. There are a number of other ways to determine whether Fed policy is tight or easy. Some of these, such as discount window borrowings and the level of net free or borrowed reserves, will be discussed in the next chapter. But *the best way* to judge Fed policy, and the way that the Fed currently seems to determine whether its policy is tight or easy, is by looking at the "real funds rate," which is simply the funds rate adjusted for the rate of inflation (*Figure 23-9*). For purposes of this discussion we define the inflation rate as the year-over-year change in the CPI. Suppose, for example, that the funds rate rises from 6% to 9%. On the surface one would conclude that the Fed was being less accommodative and trying to tighten its monetary policy stance. But also suppose that, in that period of time, the inflation rate has climbed from 4% to 8%. This means that in real terms the funds rate has actually declined from 2% (6% - 4%) to 1% (9% - 8%). In this situation Fed policy has actually become *more stimulative*, not less. Admittedly, this is not a situation that happens too often, but the reality is that probably the *best way* to gauge Fed policy is to look at the funds rate in real terms. Indeed, Fed Chairman Greenspan has referred to the real funds rate on a number of occasions in the past several years. As shown on the chart, over the course of the last 40 years the funds rate has averaged about 175 basis points (or 1.75%) above the inflation rate. We would deem that to represent a "neutral" Fed policy stance. If the Fed wants to speed up the pace of economic activity, it will push the funds rate lower. If it wants to slow economic growth, it forces the funds rate higher. If, for example, the inflation rate is 3%, a funds rate that is 1.75% higher (or 4.75%) should be regarded as a roughly neutral Fed policy stance. In that same world with the inflation rate at 3%, a funds rate of 6%, or 3% in real terms (the 6% funds rate less a 3% rate of inflation), would be regarded as restrictive. If, in this situation, after examining the output gap and the leading indicators of inflation, the Fed should decide to ease, it will need to lower the funds rate by 1.25% (to 4.75%) to shift from a restrictive policy stance to one that is neutral. If, after having shifted back to a neutral policy stance, the Fed finds that the pace of economic activity does not soon show signs of picking up to the desired 2.5% pace, it may have to shift into an outright accommodative mode. But the first step is simply to move from being restrictive to neutral. Similarly, with the inflation rate at 3% and the funds rate also at 3%, or 0% in real terms — the situation in early 1994 — Fed policy would be accommodative. If the Federal Reserve decides to tighten, it will need to raise the funds rate by 1.75%, to 4.75%, to get back to a neutral posture. If that does not do the trick, it might be forced to tighten still further and shift into an outright restrictive stance.

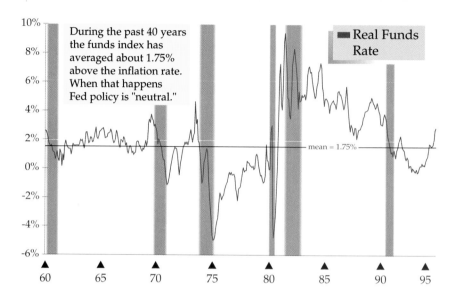

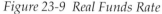

During the past 40 years the funds index has averaged about 1.75% above the inflation rate. When that happens Fed policy is "neutral."

*Figure 23-9  Real Funds Rate*

**IN ADDITION TO ITS IMPACT ON THE BOND MARKET, THE FEDERAL RESERVE'S ACTION ALSO AFFECTS THE FOREIGN EXCHANGE MARKET**

In addition to the money and bond markets, two more are affected by changes in the federal funds rate — the foreign exchange and equity markets. By its control of short-term interest rates, the Federal Reserve has some degree of influence over the U.S. dollar. Generally speaking, higher rates tend to boost the currency, as global investors seek the highest possible yield. Rising U.S. rates, relative to foreign rates, tend to encourage investment in dollar-denominated assets. When U.S. rates are declining relative to those overseas, investment will flow toward other countries and other currencies.

*Figure 23-10* indicates the historical relationship between interest rate spreads and the value of the U.S. dollar in deutsche mark terms. Short-term interest rates and the dollar were closely linked for many years, but in early 1994 this relationship broke down as other factors (such as the size of the current account deficit) became more important. The correlation between long-term interest rates and the dollar, however, held up fairly well in that period of time. In general, we can say that as the spread between U.S. and overseas interest rates narrows, the dollar weakens and vice versa. But this raises an obvious question: Does the Federal Reserve attempt to peg the exchange rate? Not really. Over the years, the Federal Reserve has consistently formulated interest rate policies that favor domestic concerns. Only in extreme cases does the dollar take first priority. Remember, the central bank really has only one tool — short-term

*Figure 23-10 Rate Spreads Between the United States and Other Countries Can Have an Impact on the Dollar*

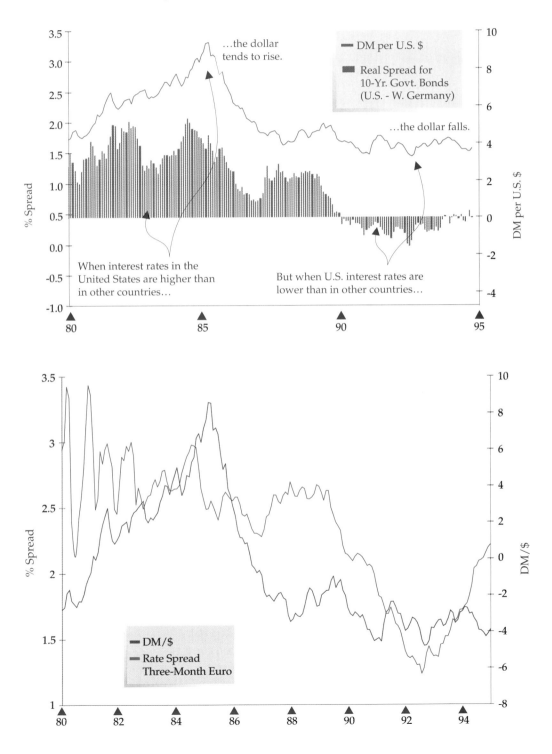

*Figure 23-11 S & P Versus Three-Month CD Interest Rate*

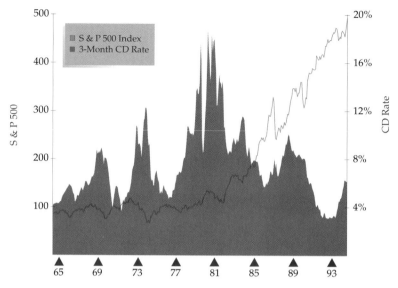

interest rates — with which to influence domestic demand, prices, economic activity, and employment. When push comes to shove, these domestic factors take precedence over imports and exports. And, indeed, that is as it should be since the trade sector only constitutes about 11% of the economy. If the domestic economy — 89% of the total — is behaving in an appropriate manner, why in the world would the Fed want to raise rates to support the dollar? If it were to do so, it would cause 89% of the economy to grow more slowly than it should. In a sense the Federal Reserve would be letting the tail wag the dog! Furthermore, as we can see from the experience in 1994, there is no assurance that even if the Fed were to raise rates that the dollar would rise.

**STOCK PRICES ARE ALSO INFLUENCED BY FEDERAL RESERVE POLICY CHANGES**

Stock market valuations are also dependent to some extent upon the level and direction of interest rates. Think of stocks the same way you would long-term bonds. Equity prices are a function of the present discounted value of future income streams. If rates decline, future earnings are "discounted" less — the present value moves higher. Alternatively, think of short-term rates as the "opportunity cost" of being in the equity market. For instance, if XYZ corporation pays a 3% dividend while a money market fund pays 9%, the opportunity cost of XYZ ownership is 6%. In order to break-even, XYZ's price must rise by 6%. If short rates are 5%, the stock price need only advance 2% for an investor to be satisfied. Of course, beyond these simple examples lies more complexity — in many cases, stock prices and interest rates are *not* inversely correlated. As *Figure 23-11* shows, stock prices can sometimes rise right along with interest rates. It really comes down to whether profit gains outpace rate increases. In the worst case (stagflation) poor earnings trot alongside higher rates. In this environment, you can bet the DOW is headed south. The best case occurs as the economy is coming out of recession — stocks are cheap, earnings are beginning to pick up, and interest rates are low. In this situation, you can bet the farm on higher equity prices. The bottom line is this: If the outlook for corporate profits rises, the stock market usually follows *(Figure 23-12)*.

*Figure 23-12*
*How the S&P Tracks Corporate Profits*

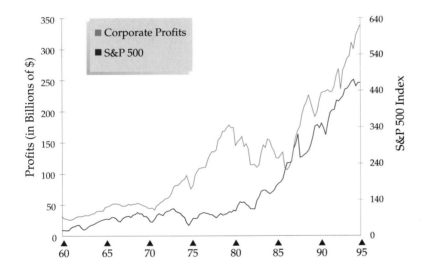

The U.S. central bank has two additional agendas aside from the macroeconomic goals we discussed previously. The first is its role as "lender of last resort"—the Federal Reserve is the ultimate backstop for the U.S. banking system. The second priority is to stand guard against *severe* currency depreciation. Beyond a certain point, it simply does not allow the "printing of money" to pay for economic ills. If monetary stringency sometimes results in high interest rates and recessions, so be it. Of course, this was not always the case. Prior to the 1950s, the Federal Reserve routinely purchased securities directly from the Treasury to unabashedly support the government bond market. For most of the 1960s and 1970s, the Federal Reserve was content to "lean against the wind" — tightening credit a bit when the economy overheated, but quickly loosening when activity slowed. Thus, this business of risking recessions is fairly new, having begun only in late 1979 when Paul Volcker took over the helm.

THE FED HAS TWO MAJOR FUNCTIONS ASIDE FROM ITS ATTEMPT TO MEET LONG-TERM GOALS

TRICKY BUSINESS

In this chapter we will attempt to explain how the Fed's open market desk in New York carries out the FOMC's wishes. But before getting into a discussion of how the Fed actually *implements* monetary policy, we would like to point out *interpreting* monetary policy has recently become a lot simpler. Previously, market participants had to spend a great deal of time analyzing the Fed's daily open market activity for signs of whether the Federal Reserve was changing its policy stance. But in February 1994, the Fed, for the first time, began to tell us *exactly* where they want the funds rate and the discount rate. Thus, for market participants, there is no longer any mystery about whether Fed policy has changed. However, economists and others in the market must still try to *anticipate* changes in Fed policy by examining the factors outlined in the previous chapter — the pace of economic expansion, the positions of actual and potential GDP, and the current and leading indicators of inflation. That part of the game has not changed.

**INTERPRETING MONETARY POLICY HAS BECOME A LOT SIMPLER FOR MARKET PARTICIPANTS**

The Fed must still follow a rather rigorous procedure to determine how many reserves it must add or drain every day through its open market activity. So, from the Fed's viewpoint the world is not very different. We intend to discuss that process in this chapter. We gave some thought to omitting this discussion when we were in the process of planning this book but, in the end, we decided that one can never be sure when the Fed might change its policy procedures again. If you understand how the Fed works, and how it implements monetary policy, you will be in a better position to understand how you should interpret its actions in the future should it make further changes in its procedures. But before we address how the Federal Reserve implements monetary policy, we must first understand the tools it has at its disposal.

**FROM THE FEDERAL RESERVE'S POINT OF VIEW THE GAME HAS NOT CHANGED AT ALL**

The textbooks tell us that the Federal Reserve has three tools at its disposal to implement monetary policy — open market operations, the discount rate, and changes in reserve requirements *(Figure 24-1)*. The reality is that the first — open market operations — is far and away the most important. Through its Federal Open Market Committee (FOMC) the Federal Reserve controls a portfolio of government securities, mainly U.S. Treasury bills, notes, and bonds. At the simplest level, a purchase of securities in the open market adds reserves to the banking

**OPEN MARKET OPERATIONS ARE EFFECTIVELY THE FEDERAL RESERVE'S ONLY MONETARY POLICY TOOL**

system. A sale drains reserves. To see how it works, let's follow a Federal Reserve purchase *(Figure 24-2)*. In the modern era, banking assets consist primarily of loans and government securities. The majority of their liabilities are demand deposits (checking accounts) and certificates of deposit (CDs). When the Federal Reserve buys a Treasury issue from a bank, it pays by crediting that bank's reserve account at the Federal Reserve. The bank now has money available to support a new loan if it wishes. New loans mean new deposits. Moreover, since M-1 (the narrowest measure of the money supply) is defined as demand deposits plus currency in circulation, new deposits mean new money. In effect, the Federal Reserve creates money by deciding to increase its portfolio holdings of securities. In the process, interest rates decline. If the "supply" of money increases, the "price" of money — the interest rate — falls. Viewed another way, the Federal Reserve — by reducing the "supply" of bonds trading in the market— causes their prices to rise. Because price is inversely proportional to yield, interest rates drop.

| OPEN MARKET OPERATIONS | DISCOUNT RATE | RESERVE REQUIREMENTS |
|---|---|---|
| Expansionary Buy U.S. Treasury securities and increase reserves | Expansionary Lower discount rate | Expansionary Lower reserve requirements |
| Contractionary Sell U.S. Treasury securities and decrease reserves | Contractionary Raise discount rate | Contractionary Raise reserve requirements |

*Figure 24-1*
*The Three Tools that the Federal Reserve Uses to Implement Policy*

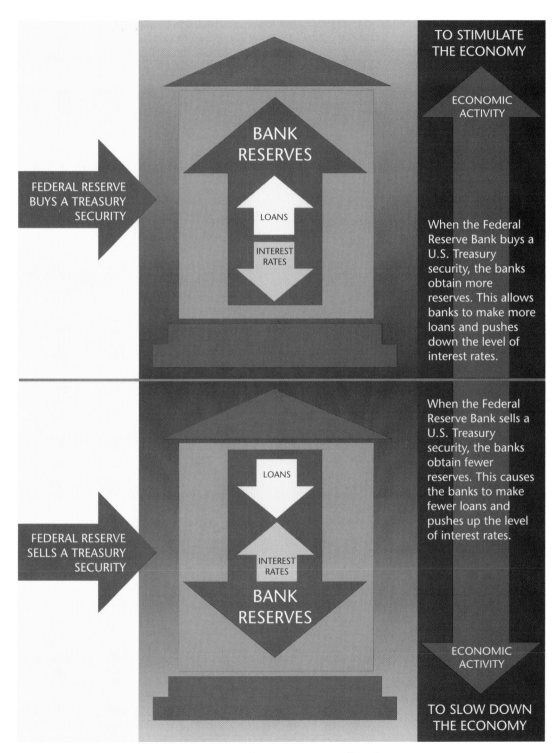

TO STIMULATE
THE ECONOMY

ECONOMIC
ACTIVITY

BANK
RESERVES

LOANS

INTEREST
RATES

FEDERAL RESERVE
BUYS A TREASURY
SECURITY

When the Federal
Reserve Bank buys a
U.S. Treasury
security, the banks
obtain more
reserves. This allows
banks to make more
loans and pushes
down the level of
interest rates.

When the Federal
Reserve Bank sells a
U.S. Treasury
security, the banks
obtain fewer
reserves. This causes
the banks to make
fewer loans and
pushes up the level
of interest rates.

LOANS

INTEREST
RATES

BANK
RESERVES

FEDERAL RESERVE
SELLS A TREASURY
SECURITY

ECONOMIC
ACTIVITY

TO SLOW DOWN
THE ECONOMY

*Figure 24-2 How Open Market Operations Affect the Economy*

## THE DISCOUNT RATE IS NO LONGER A MAJOR MONETARY POLICY TOOL

Although a great deal of publicity is generated when the discount rate is changed, it is not terribly important. The discount rate is the interest rate charged to member banks when they borrow directly from the Federal Reserve. In the old days the Federal Reserve was very secretive. Changes in the federal funds rate and reserves targets were never announced, but changes in the discount rate were. Therefore, a discount rate adjustment received considerable attention because it was the most visible of the Federal Reserve's monetary policy tools. When the central bank altered the discount rate, it wanted to make a major policy statement. Accordingly, changes in the discount rate made front page headlines on every newspaper in the country. But today the Federal Reserve tells the markets whenever it is making a change in policy. It is currently targeting the federal funds rate (which we will discuss in a moment), and it tells us what that target is. Because the funds rate is a market rate, and all other short-term interest rates are based upon it, attention should be focused upon the federal funds rate, not the discount rate.

## RESERVE REQUIREMENT CHANGES HAVE NOT BEEN A POLICY TOOL FOR YEARS

The textbooks tell us that raising or lowering the reserve requirement — the percentage of deposits that banks are required to hold as non-interest-bearing assets — is another way the Federal Reserve can influence the level of interest rates. If banks are forced to maintain a larger portion of their assets as reserves, they have less money to make mortgages or other loans. This tool of monetary policy is talked about a lot in theory but is rarely used. In fact, the last time reserve requirements were changed *at all* was in April 1992 when the Federal Reserve lowered the reserve requirement on transactions deposits from 12% to 10%. Furthermore, most market participants do not understand that whenever the Federal Reserve changes its reserve requirements, it offsets the impact via its open market operations. For example, if the Fed lowers the reserve requirement on demand deposits and frees up $3 billion of reserves which *could* support additional loan growth and a faster pace of economic activity, the Fed simply absorbs an equivalent amount of reserves through its open market activity. It puts the reserves in on one side and takes them out on the other. Nothing changes. While in theory changes in reserve requirements *could* be a tool of monetary policy, the fact is that they are not used in this way. Rather, investors should focus attention on the federal funds rate, which is primarily determined by the Federal Reserve through its open market operations. Since 1982, adjusting the funds rate has been the Fed's main policy lever. Later on, we will see how the Fed's New York "Desk" — the central bank's trading arm — darts in and out of the reserves market to control this key short-term rate.

For all practical purposes, then, the Fed has only one tool with which to accomplish its objectives — its open market operations. We noted earlier that by altering the volume of bank reserves, the Fed can affect both the growth rate of the money supply and the level of the Federal funds rate.

In the good old days — prior to the early 1980s — there was a respectable relationship between the growth rate of nominal GDP in one year and the nominal aggregates M-1 and M-2 a year or two earlier. *Figure 24-3* suggests that if the Federal Reserve were able to regulate money growth, particularly the rate of expansion of M-2, it would have reasonable control over the rate of economic expansion. Similarly, *Figure 24-4* compares the rate of money growth and inflation two years later. Here again, money growth seems to have some impact on the inflation rate, but with a considerable lag.

HISTORICALLY, MONEY SUPPLY GROWTH HAS INFLUENCED THE PACE OF BOTH ECONOMIC ACTIVITY AND THE INFLATION RATE

However, these relationships have become less impressive since the mid-1980s. While everyone seems to have an opinion on the subject, we believe the major turning point was the Monetary Control Act of 1980. Among other things, this act phased out Regulation Q. As interest rate ceilings on deposits were lifted, a rapid growth of "near money" took place. Innovations, such as money market deposit accounts, allowed depositors to earn interest on bank balances. The net result was a blurring of what "money" actually meant. Was it cash? Or was it savings?

THESE RELATIONSHIPS HAVE BECOME LESS CLEAR IN RECENT YEARS

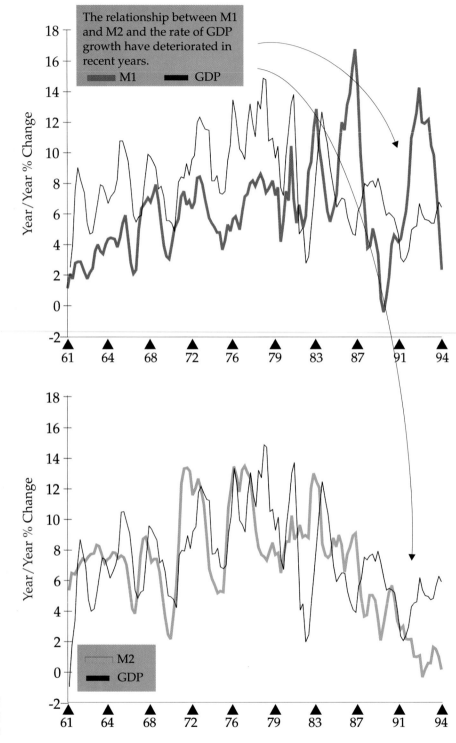

The relationship between M1 and M2 and the rate of GDP growth have deteriorated in recent years.

M1   GDP

M2   GDP

Figure 24-3
The M1 and
M2 to GDP
Relationship

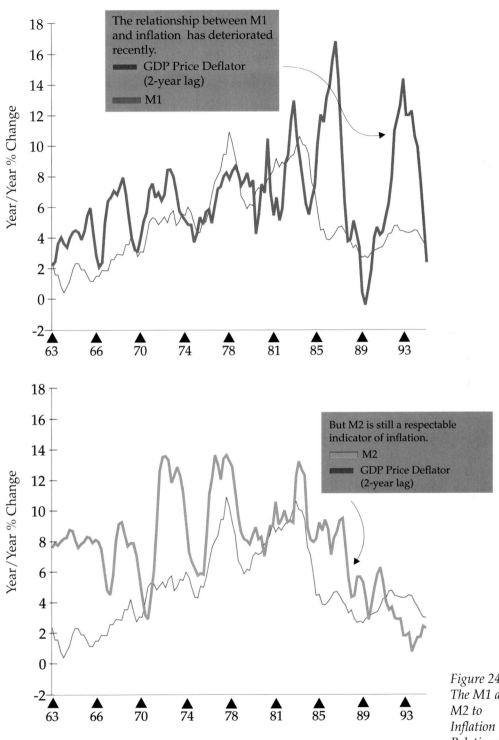

The relationship between M1 and inflation has deteriorated recently.
- GDP Price Deflator (2-year lag)
- M1

But M2 is still a respectable indicator of inflation.
- M2
- GDP Price Deflator (2-year lag)

Figure 24-4
The M1 and
M2 to
Inflation
Relationship

**WHAT IS MONEY?**

### M-1 INCLUDES ANYTHING THAT CAN BE USED TO CARRY OUT TRANSACTIONS

Virtually all economists agree that money represents anything that can be used to carry out transactions *(Figure 24-5)*. Such a definition certainly includes currency and travelers checks. It also includes a variety of checkable deposits, since most businesses accept payment in the form of a check. These checkable deposits consist primarily of demand deposits, NOW accounts, and credit union drafts. The items noted above are all included in a measure of money the Federal Reserve refers to as M-1.

### M-2 STARTS WITH M-1 AND ADDS OTHER VERY LIQUID ASSETS

There are alternate ways, however, of holding liquid assets. These other assets can be accessed quickly, although in many cases cannot be used directly as means of payment. The Federal Reserve has lumped M-1 together with a variety of these instruments into a broader definition of money it calls M-2 *(Figure 24-6)*. Passbook savings deposits fall into this category, as do small denomination CDs. Money market mutual fund shares (MMMFs) at brokerage houses and money market deposit accounts (MMDAs) at banks and thrifts are also incorporated into M-2. These two definitions of money, M-1 and M-2, are by far the most common, even though the Federal Reserve has an even broader measure it calls M-3 *(Figure 24-7)*.

**IT IS NOT ENTIRELY CLEAR WHICH MONETARY AGGREGATE IS MOST IMPORTANT**

The most important point is that there is no clear-cut definition of money. In many cases, only minute differences exist between the various types of financial instruments; whether a particular asset should be included in M-1 or M-2 is not always obvious. This has bothered economists and policymakers for years. For example, how should the Federal Reserve respond when M-1 and M-2 provide entirely different pictures of money growth? Of economic growth? Of inflation? These problems are not likely to disappear in the near future. In the meantime, much to the chagrin of "monetarists," monetary policy relies heavily upon the judgment of Federal Reserve officials.

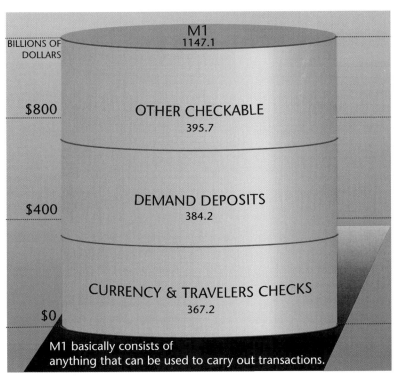

*Figure 24-5*
*The Components of M1*

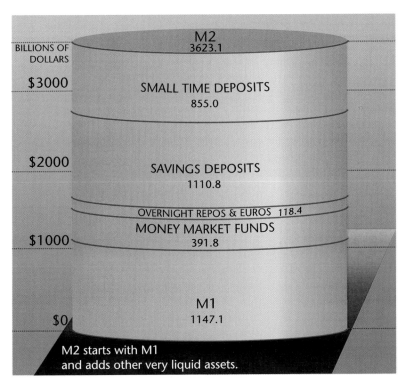

*Figure 24-6*
*The Components of M2*

*Figure 24-7*
*The Components of M3*

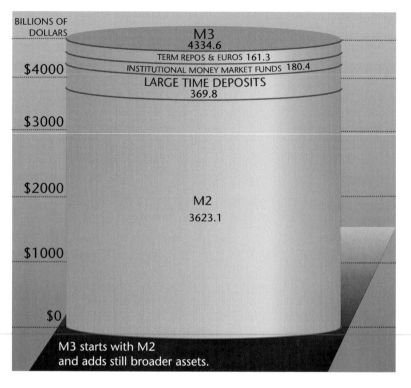

THE IMPLEMENTATION OF FEDERAL RESERVE POLICY IS A FOUR-STEP PROCESS.

The process is depicted in Figure 24-8.

STEP 1. ESTABLISH TARGETS FOR THE VARIOUS MS

As noted previously, the Federal Reserve has developed a number of different monetary measures — each of which presumably bears some relationship to the level of economic activity. The first step in the policy process is to identify the linkages between the various monetary aggregates and nominal GDP growth and to specify an annual "target" growth range for M-2 and M-3. The Federal Reserve can then calculate reserve levels that it believes will be consistent with achieving the monetary aggregates' objectives.

SPECIFYING THE ANNUAL TARGET RANGES IS ITSELF A THREE-STEP PROCESS

First, the Federal Reserve decides upon a desired growth rate for real GDP and an "acceptable" rate of inflation to determine the target rate for expansion of nominal GDP *(Figure 24-9)*. For example, long-term sustainable growth of real GDP appears to be about 2.5%. If the Federal Reserve decides that it wants to reduce the inflation rate to, say, 2.0%, the desired or targeted rate of nominal GDP growth would be approximately 4.5%.

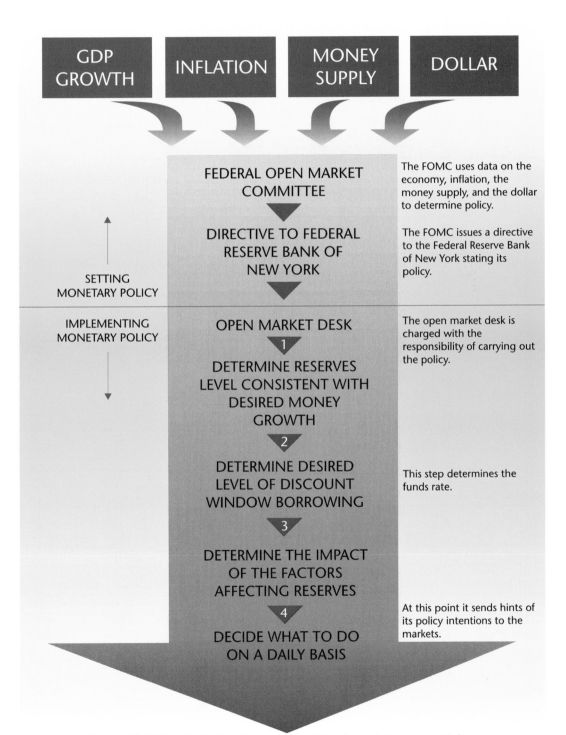

Figure 24-8 How the Federal Reserve Bank Implements Monetary Policy

**SELECT GROWTH RATE FOR GDP AND ADD DESIRED RATE OF INFLATION TO DETERMINE TARGET FOR NOMINAL GDP**

| GROWTH RATE | | INFLATION | | NOMINAL GDP |
|---|---|---|---|---|
| 2½% | + | 2% | = | 4½% |

**USING HISTORICAL RELATIONSHIPS BETWEEN NOMINAL GDP GROWTH AND GROWTH IN THE MONEY SUPPLY (M2 IN THIS EXAMPLE), ESTIMATE VELOCITY GROWTH**

| NOMINAL GDP | | VELOCITY GROWTH | | TARGET GROWTH |
|---|---|---|---|---|
| 4½% | - | 1½% | = | 3% |

**ESTALISH A BAND AROUND THIS TARGETED GROWTH RATE TO FORM A TARGET RANGE FOR M2**

**TARGET RANGE**
**1% - 5%**

Next, the Federal Reserve compares the historical growth rates of nominal GDP to the growth rate of money to determine the proper relationship between the two. This relationship is known as "velocity." The Federal Reserve has concluded that, over a long period of time, nominal GDP grows about 1.5% faster than M-2. Thus, in this example, given desired nominal GDP growth of 4.5%, M-2 should grow at roughly a 3% pace to achieve the desired objective.

Finally, the Federal Reserve then establishes a band on either side to obtain its target range. Currently, the targets are 1%-5% for M-2 and 0%-4% for M-3. (Note: In the past, the Federal Reserve spent thousands of manhours trying to figure out the velocity of M-1 and whether or not it was "stable." A few years ago, the central bank gave up and conceded that M-1 velocity was not constant after all; it now concentrates on M-2. At about the same time as the Federal Reserve noted the velocity problem, it "downgraded" M-1 for policy-making purposes. As a result, M-1 is no longer targeted).

Even after specifying these growth rates for M-2 and M-3, the
Federal Reserve is still unable to directly control money growth.
All it can hope to do is provide reserves to the banking system in
sufficient quantity to cause the federal funds rate, and thus most
other short-term interest rates, to rise and fall. These rate changes
cause businesses and consumers to alter their behavior —
ultimately affecting the pace of money expansion. Step two in the
process of implementing monetary policy, therefore, is to determine the volume of reserves consistent with achieving the
desired pace of monetary growth.

**STEP 2. DETERMINE THE VOLUME OF RESERVES NECESSARY TO ACHIEVE THE DESIRED PACE OF MONEY GROWTH**

## "REQUIRED RESERVES" REPRESENT THE AMOUNT OF RESERVES THAT BANKS ARE REQUIRED TO HOLD

At present, the banking system operates in a world of (almost)
contemporaneous reserve accounting (CRA). Avoiding the gory
details, CRA implies the following: Every other Wednesday, the
banks must come up with their *required reserves* based on the
amount of deposits held. Currently, the average reserve requirement on transaction-type deposits is around 8%; 3% on the first
$54 million and 10% on anything over that amount. Because M-1
consists entirely of transactions deposits — and transactions
deposits are a meaningful portion of the broader aggregates — it
is clear that by specifying growth targets for money, the Fed
effectively determines desired levels of deposits. By working
backward, it can calculate the levels of required reserves that are
consistent with achieving both the targeted rates of money
growth and the implied level of deposits.

**TOTAL RESERVES CONSIST OF BOTH "REQUIRED" AND "EXCESS" RESERVES**

## "EXCESS RESERVES" REPRESENT THE ADDITIONAL RE-SERVES THAT BANKS WANT TO HOLD

While the levels of required reserves provide the link between
reserves and money, the Federal Reserve is actually more interested in total reserves, which represents the total amount of
reserves that the banking system demands. Required reserves
can be held either in a special reserve account at the Federal
Reserve or in the form of vault cash. Every business day, the
central bank sends each bank a statement indicating its reserve
account balance from the previous day. As the maintenance
period progresses from Thursday through Wednesday (two
weeks hence), the bank is able to monitor its reserve account and
compare its balance to its requirements. If the bank is running
behind, it can purchase additional reserves from other banks in
the federal funds market. Conversely, if it has surplus balances, it

sells those in the funds market. On the final day of the two-week period, the bank has 13 days (e.g., Thursday the 1st through Tuesday the 13th) of data from its reserve account on hand. It then makes an estimate of the reserve account balance on the 14th day. A prudent banker does not want to risk falling short in the reserve account because he or she erroneously estimated the reserve balance on that final Wednesday. As a result, each individual bank wants to hold reserves above and beyond the required amount. Those additional balances are called *excess reserves*. The sum of required reserves and excess reserves is called *total reserves (Figure 24-10)*. It represents the total demand for reserves by the banking system — the amount that is required to be held, plus the small amount of additional reserves that banks want to hold.

THE KEY EQUATIONS:

$$TR = RR = ER$$
$$40,000 = 39,000 + 1,000$$

$$NBR = RR + ER - DWB$$
$$39,700 = 39,000 + 1,000 - 300$$

$$(+)NFR \text{ OR } (-)NTB = ER - DWB$$
$$700 = 1,000 - 300$$

TR=TOTAL RESERVES
RR=REQUIRED RESERVES
ER=EXCESS RESERVES
NBR=NONBORROWED RESERVES
DWB=DISCOUNT WINDOW BORROWINGS
NFR=NET FREE RESERVES
NTB=NET BORROWED RESERVES

*Figure 24-10*
*Calculating Net Free Reserves and Net Borrowed Reserves*

If the Fed desired, it could choose to supply the banking system with all the reserves it needs. But, in doing so, it loses control over the funds rate. In this situation, funds could trade at 2% or 20%—there are simply no constraints. To avoid potentially large swings in the funds rate, the Fed deliberately withholds some of the reserves that the banking system needs. It forces some banks to borrow from the discount window and ensures that, toward the end of the two-week period, the funds rate will rise at least as high as the discount rate. For example, in the middle of a maintenance period, funds could trade at 6% with a discount rate of 8%. But if the banking system as a whole does not have an adequate quantity of reserves, individual banks soon begin to feel the shortage. Because of a natural tendency to avoid borrowing from the discount window (repeated borrowing brings out the Federal Reserve's auditors) some banks will have to aggressively bid for needed reserves, placing upward pressure on the funds rate. Should the funds rate rise far above the discount rate, banks will eventually drop out of the funds market and get the necessary reserves from the Fed's discount window. This mechanism establishes an effective upper and lower limit on the funds rate. By deliberately shortchanging the banking system and not supplying all of the necessary reserves via open market operations, the central bank establishes a degree of control over the federal funds rate.

THE FEDERAL RESERVE NEVER PROVIDES THE BANKING SYSTEM WITH ALL THE RESERVES IT NEEDS THROUGH ITS OPEN MARKET OPERATIONS — IT FORCES THEM TO BORROW AT THE DISCOUNT WINDOW

KEY POINT:

- The Federal Reserve Bank never provides all the reserves the banking system needs through its open market operations.

- By deliberately shortchanging the banking system, the Federal Reserve establishes some control over the funds rate.

If we subtract the desired amount of discount window borrowings from total reserves, we obtain a reserve aggregate known as *nonborrowed reserves*. It is this aggregate that the Federal Reserve Bank is attempting to control *(Figure 24-10)*.

THE FED ACTUALLY TARGETS "NONBORROWED RESERVES" — TOTAL RESERVES MINUS DISCOUNT WINDOW BORROWINGS

"NET FREE (OR BORROWED) RESERVES" MEASURE ALMOST THE SAME THING

We should point out that at the close of a two-week maintenance period, the level of required reserves is virtually known (data for 13 of the 14 days is already available). Thus, the only two items that can change are excess reserves and discount window borrowings. This means that prior to 1994 one important clue to Federal Reserve policy was the difference between excess reserves and borrowings. This difference is known as "net borrowed" or "net free reserves" (again, see *Figure 24-10*). If the difference is positive, i.e., excess reserves are greater than borrowings, it is called *net free reserves*. If borrowings are larger than excess reserves, it is called *net borrowed reserves*. Net free and net borrowed reserves are exactly the same thing — the only difference is whether the difference is a positive or a negative one. If we focus exclusively on nonborrowed reserves, it is difficult to detect changes in policy because of the fluctuation in required reserves. However, net free or net borrowed reserves will normally remain constant unless the Federal Reserve changes policy.

*Figure 24-11*
*Federal Funds Versus Discount Rate*

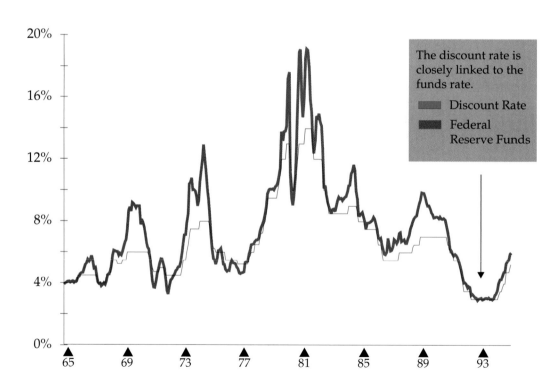

The discount rate is closely linked to the funds rate.
  Discount Rate
  Federal Reserve Funds

On many previous occasions, the Fed changed policy by altering the amount of borrowings from the discount window. If reserves are ample, the funds rate can be expected to trade close to the discount rate *(Figure 24-11)*. However, the Federal Reserve always gets some discount window borrowings because a few banks invariably overdraw their reserve account and are forced to the window. In practice, $100 million is generally considered to be the minimum (frictional) level of borrowing.

If the Federal Reserve wished to ease further, and if borrowings were already at very low levels, the central bank could not reduce the level of borrowing — the only alternative was to lower the discount rate. But normally, the Fed initiated an easing move by first reducing the desired level of discount window borrowing. If borrowings declined from, say $600 million to $400 million, the banking system was short fewer reserves than had been the case previously. Instead of withholding $600 million of necessary reserves from the banking system, the Federal Reserve was now shortchanging it by only $400 million. As the relative degree of "shortness" declined, the funds rate fell. Conversely, the Fed could have tightened policy by increasing the level of discount window borrowings, which would cause the funds rate to rise.

IN ADDITION TO THE FUNDS RATE, ANOTHER GAUGE OF FEDERAL RESERVE POLICY WAS THE LEVEL OF DISCOUNT WINDOW BORROWINGS

As the Federal Reserve tightened, borrowings increased — causing the net reserves position to move from net free reserves, to zero, to progressively deeper levels of net borrowed reserves. The larger the negative number, the tighter policy was, and the higher the funds rate was relative to the discount rate *(Figure 24-12)*. When the central bank was in the process of easing, the level of borrowings declined and net borrowed reserves become less deep, and the funds rate fell. Thus, two key measures of Fed policy were discount window borrowings and the net reserves position. In practice, most professional "Fed watchers" routinely monitored both because there were occasions when either measure individually could have distorted.

WE COULD ALSO GAUGE FEDERAL RESERVE POLICY BY THE NET RESERVES POSITION

*Figure 24-12*
*Discount Window*
*Borrowings and the*
*Net Reserves Position*
*— Two Gauges of the*
*Tightness of Federal*
*Reserve Policy*

**INITIAL POLICY**

| NET EXCESS RESERVES | | DISCOUNT RESERVES | | WINDOW BORROWING |
|---|---|---|---|---|
| 700 | = | 1,000 | - | 300 |

**FEDERAL RESERVE BANK TIGHTENS**

| NET RESERVES* | | EXCESS RESERVES | | DISCOUNT WINDOW BORROWING |
|---|---|---|---|---|
| 500 | = | 1,000 | - | 500 |

WHEN THE FED TIGHTENS, THE NET RESERVES POSITION IS REDUCED.

WHEN THE FED TIGHTENS, DISCOUNT WINDOW BORROWINGS INCREASE.

* NOTE: WHEN THE DIFFERENCE BETWEEN EXCESS RESERVES MINUS BORROWINGS IS POSITIVE, IT IS KNOWN AS "NET FREE RESERVES."

EVERY $100 MILLION INCREASE IN DISCOUNT WINDOW BORROWING IMPLIED A ¼% RISE IN THE FUNDS RATE, AND VICE VERSA

The above discussion suggests that there was some relationship between the funds rate/discount rate spread and the targeted level of net borrowed reserves. Unfortunately, the linkage was not airtight. There are still a number of technical factors that can affect the level of reserves. If these factors collectively drain (or supply) reserves, the funds rate is subject to some upward (or downward) pressure. Also, banks' demand for excess reserves can fluctuate over time, which causes net borrowed reserves to change. Nevertheless, despite all of these potential difficulties, a rule of thumb that worked reasonably well was to assume that a change in the Federal Reserve's net borrowed reserves target of $100 million caused a change in the funds rate of 20-25 basis points. Thus, a shift from $600 million to $400 million of net borrowed reserves caused the funds rate to fall 40-50 basis points.

How do all these changes in reserves affect the rate of money growth? The answer is that the mechanism works entirely through changes in interest rates. As the Federal Reserve tightens, the funds rate rises — prompting all short-term rates (including the prime) to rise and discouraging individuals and corporations from borrowing. The reduction in loan demand causes a slowdown in deposit creation, thereby slowing money growth.

CHANGES IN THE FUNDS RATE ARE IMPORTANT BECAUSE MONETARY POLICY WORKS THROUGH CHANGES IN INTEREST RATES

Summing up, the Fed attempted to regulate money growth by altering the level of discount window borrowings and net borrowed reserves. This gave rise to changes in interest rates, which ultimately had an impact on the demand for money. It should be pointed out that the linkages in the process were quite loose, and furthermore, the mechanism worked with a lag. The Federal Reserve simply does not have the ability to control money growth with a high degree of precision. But if the Fed forces interest rates high enough, economic activity slows along with money growth. If the central bank allows rates to slide, eventually the economy and money growth begin to rebound.

THE FED TRIED TO REGULATE ECONOMIC GROWTH BY ALTERING THE LEVEL OF DISCOUNT WINDOW BORROWING

As mentioned above, the Federal Reserve tries to indirectly regulate money growth by changing the level of net free or net borrowed reserves. But once a target level has been established, there are additional problems — other factors can affect the level of reserves in any given week. If the Fed takes its eye off the ball, the funds rate can fluctuate wildly as the combined effect of the factors swing about. For instance, let's assume certain technical factors are about to drain $1 billion of reserves during a one-week period. If the Fed did not intervene, the funds rate surges as the reserves shortage is translated into more aggressive bidding for available funds. Ultimately, discount window borrowings increase by the same $1 billion because the banking system cannot obtain the necessary reserves elsewhere. If the operating factors then turn around the next week and provide $1 billion of reserves, the funds rate plummets along with discount window borrowings. To avoid these disruptive gyrations, the Federal Reserve offsets the effects of these factors through open market operations. If the operating factors drain $1 billion of reserves, the Fed will attempt to add $1 billion via open market operations, and vice versa.

STEP 3. THE CENTRAL BANK MUST CONTEND WITH A VARIETY OF FACTORS THAT CAN CAUSE RESERVE LEVELS TO FLUCTUATE

THERE ARE MANY FACTORS AFFECTING RESERVES

These so-called "operating factors" are all items on the Federal Reserve's balance sheet apart from its own holdings of securities and reserve balances. There are 15 of these factors, but only four will be discussed — currency in circulation, float, Treasury deposits, and foreign central bank deposits.

CURRENCY IN CIRCULATION IS PROBABLY THE EASIEST TO UNDERSTAND

The easiest factor to explain is "currency in circulation." As individuals cash checks, a bank will eventually need to obtain additional currency. To do so, it goes to its local Federal Reserve Bank and "pays" for it by drawing upon its reserve account balance. Therefore, changes in currency affect the level of bank reserves (Figure 24-13). For instance, during the December holidays, we all run to our automatic teller machines for cash. This has the effect of reducing reserves in the banking system, which must be put back via open market operations.

FLOAT IS MORE VOLATILE

Perhaps the most volatile operating factor is "Federal Reserve float." The problem of float usually arises because foul weather or a computer glitch interferes with the normal check clearing process — yet another job handled by the Fed. Essentially, two banks claim credit for a deposit, when in reality only one deposit was made. To understand this, assume that, for whatever reason, there is a delay from the time Bank A's reserve account at the Fed is increased and when Bank B's account is reduced. For a while, both banks actually hold the same deposit — and thus the reserves. During this delay, reserves are temporarily increased by a rise in float. In response, the Fed steps in and removes the surplus reserves.

THE TREASURY'S CASH BALANCE IS ALSO IMPORTANT

A third annoyance that can upset the level of reserves is "Treasury deposits at the Federal Reserve." The U.S. Treasury holds its funds (your taxes) in two types of accounts. Its equivalent of a "checking account" is maintained at the Federal Reserve. All checks issued by the Treasury, whether they are to Social Security recipients or defense contractors, are drawn on this account. Normally, the Treasury keeps a working balance of about $5 billion at the Fed. Any additional funds are deposited in what are known as "tax and loan" or "TT&L" accounts at commercial banks. Whenever the Treasury makes a payment, its balance falls below the $5 billion level. To bring the balance back up, the Treasury routinely transfers funds from the TT&L accounts at banks to its account at the Fed. Problems arise when the Treasury's cash balance at the Federal Reserve suddenly or

*Figure 24-13 Impact on Reserves of Various Factors*

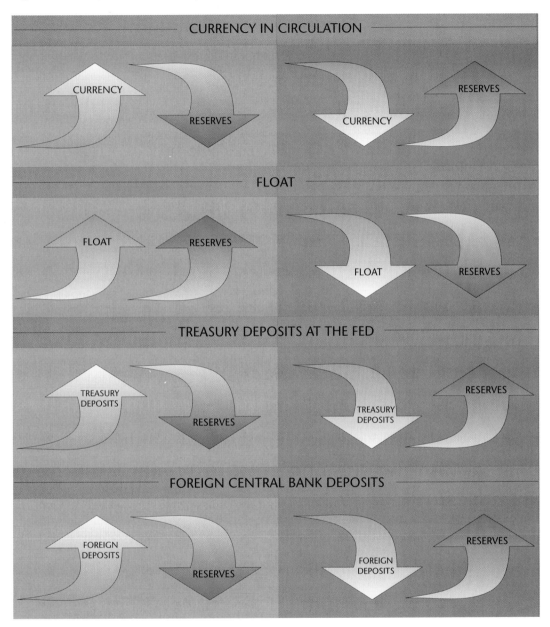

unexpectedly rises above or falls below the $5 billion level. For example, if its balance suddenly surges to $8 billion, there would be $3 billion fewer reserves in the banking system than the Federal Reserve expects. Conversely, if the cash balance dips far below $5 billion, there will be surplus reserves in the system.

Dislocations with the Treasury's cash balance can become particularly acute following a large inflow of tax receipts — funds involuntarily flow out of the TT&L accounts into the Treasury's account at the Fed. This situation arises because banks generally establish an upper limit on the amount of TT&L balances they are willing to accept. They do so for two reasons. First, these accounts are not particularly profitable, since the banks must pay the Treasury an interest rate close to the federal funds rate. Second, tax and loan account balances must be "collateralized" — fully backed by security holdings. Sizable inflows into these TT&L accounts will result in banks reaching capacity. When this happens, any additional receipts are automatically remitted to the Treasury's account at the Federal Reserve. Currently, "capacity" is around $35 billion. If during the height of tax season the Treasury's total cash balance reached $43 billion (and only $35 billion can be maintained in tax and loan accounts), the remaining $8 billion will reside in the Treasury's Federal Reserve account. Thus, the balance at the Fed is $3 billion higher than normal. The banking system is short that same $3 billion of reserves — reserves that must be replaced by the Fed.

FOREIGN CENTRAL BANKS ALSO HOLD DEPOSITS AT THE FEDERAL RESERVE TO SERVICE THEIR FOREIGN EXCHANGE OPERATIONS

The final operating factor to be discussed is "foreign central bank deposits." Foreign central banks maintain accounts at the Federal Reserve primarily to service their foreign exchange operations. If, for example, the Bank of England purchases dollars, funds are transferred from the overseas branch of a U.S. bank to the U.K. central bank account at the Federal Reserve. This action serves to decrease the level of reserves in the banking system. The Fed quickly attempts to replenish lost reserves, because otherwise pressures will develop in the federal funds market.

WHAT IS IMPORTANT IS THE NET EFFECT OF ALL THESE FACTORS

The operating factors — currency in circulation, float, Treasury deposits, and foreign central bank deposits — are the major ones that affect the level of reserves in any given period. To determine the volume of necessary open market operations (the amount of reserves it must add or drain), the Federal Reserve essentially starts with the level of nonborrowed (or net borrowed) reserves from the prior period and adds the net effect of the operating factors to determine the level of reserves that would be in the

system if it did nothing. It then compares this result to the
desired or targeted level of nonborrowed (or net borrowed)
reserves that was previously determined. The difference between
these two figures represents the amount of reserves that the Fed
must add or drain via open market operations for that particular
two-week maintenance period.

Once the Federal Reserve calculates the volume of necessary
open market operations, how does it actually inject or drain
reserves? To supply reserves, the Fed basically has four options:
 · An outright purchase of securities
 · A purchase internally from a foreign central bank
 · A system repo; or
 · A customer repo.

To drain reserves, the Federal Reserve Bank can choose among
the following:
 · An outright sale of securities
 · A sale internally to a foreign central bank
 · A reverse repo (matched-sale/purchase agreement)

STEP 4. DECIDE
WHAT TO DO ON A
DAILY BASIS

FIRST THE FED
MUST FIGURE OUT
HOW IT IS GOING
TO ADD OR DRAIN
THE NECESSARY
VOLUME OF
RESERVES

It is important to understand that when the Federal Reserve
purchases securities, either from the "Street" or from a foreign
central bank, it is permanently adding reserves to the banking
system *(Figure 24-14)*. This will be important to us later on when
we discuss how the Fed actually carries out its day-to-day
operations. When the Federal Reserve buys a government
security from a dealer, the dealer gives up the security, but in
exchange gets a credit to its checking account — and the dealer's
bank gains reserves. When the Fed buys a security from a foreign
central bank, the process is a bit more circuitous, but the end
result is the same.

WHEN THE
FEDERAL RESERVE
BUYS SECURITIES,
IT ADDS RESERVES
TO THE SYSTEM
*PERMANENTLY*

The mechanics of a "system repo" (or repurchase agreement) are
essentially the same, but in this case reserves have temporarily
been added to the banking system. The dealer community sells a
government security to the Federal Reserve, but with a simulta-
neous agreement to repurchase it at a later date (at a slightly
higher price). These repos can be done on either an overnight
basis (one business day) or for a period of time up to seven days
depending upon the needs of the Fed. Because system repos are
essentially a secured form of dealer borrowing, the rate is
normally just under the federal funds rate — the rate that applies
to unsecured borrowing.

WHEN THE FED
DOES A SYSTEM
REPO, IT ADDS
RESERVES ON A
*TEMPORARY* BASIS

| | PERMANENT | TEMPORARY |
|---|---|---|
| **ADD** | | |
| OUTRIGHT PURCHASE OF SECURITIES | X | |
| OUTRIGHT PURCHASE OF SECURITIES FROM A FOREIGN CENTRAL BANK | X | |
| SYSTEM REPO | | X |
| CUSTOMER REPO | | X |
| **DRAIN** | | |
| OUTRIGHT SALE OF SECURITIES | X | |
| OUTRIGHT SALE OF SECURITIES TO A FOREIGN CENTRAL BANK | X | |
| REVERSE REPO (MATCHED-SALE/PURCHASE) | | X |

*Figure 24-14*
*The Federal Reserve Can Add (or Drain) Reserves on Either a Permanent or Temporary Basis*

CUSTOMER REPOS ALSO ADD RESERVES TO THE SYSTEM ON A *TEMPORARY* BASIS

The final method that the Federal Reserve uses to add reserves to the banking system is a "customer repo." The mechanics of a customer repo are nearly identical to that of a system repo. And, as is the case with a system repo, a customer repo temporarily adds reserves to the banking system. Thus, the Fed has two ways to provide temporary reserves to the banking system. To understand the concept of a customer repo, take another look at the role of foreign central banks. Earlier, we noted that these banks have accounts at the Fed to service their foreign exchange transactions. As intelligent bankers, they recognize that if money sits idle in a deposit account, it earns no interest. Therefore, these banks leave instructions with the Federal Reserve to invest those funds overnight. Normally, the Fed routinely sells them a security out of its own portfolio on an overnight basis, which allows the foreign central bank to earn interest. But the Fed can choose (for reasons we describe in a moment) to let the "Street" sell the foreign central bank the security. In this case, the Fed arranges a customer repo. We say "arrange" because the Federal Reserve is essentially facilitating a transaction between a dealer and a foreign central bank. If you have always wondered who the "customer" was, now you know — it is a foreign central bank.

An outright sale of securities permanently drains reserves from the banking system. A "matched-sale/purchase agreement" (or reverse repo) drains reserves from the banking system on a temporary basis. The Federal Reserve chooses between these operations in accordance with its needs.

WHEN THE FEDERAL RESERVE NEEDS TO DRAIN RESERVES, ITS CHOICES ARE ENTIRELY ANALOGOUS

Now we are ready to see what the Federal Reserve does on a daily basis. Recall, there are always operating factors adding or draining reserves from the banking system that the Federal Reserve — actually the Federal Reserve Bank of New York's trading "Desk" — attempts to counterbalance with open market operations. In understanding Fed operations, it is crucial to recognize that in the old days (pre-1994) about 90% of the Fed's actions were designed to do nothing more than offset the impact of the operating factors. If the Fed did repurchase agreements, it was not necessarily signaling an easing of policy. Similarly, reverse repos did not always imply that the Fed was tightening. But from time to time in the past the Fed *did* use open market operations to signal a policy change. In today's world, 100% of the Fed's open market activity is purely technical and meant only to offset the impact of the operating factors. But the process of implementing monetary policy is quite fluid, and one can never be certain that today's method of operation will continue in the future. In the discussion that follows, we will try to give you some hints for separating the wheat from the chaff should the Fed revert back to its old ways. We will focus on situations in which the Fed must add reserves to the banking system — simply because the Fed is in an "add mode" most of the time. But the discussion can just as easily be applied to those situations in which the Fed must drain reserves.

NEARLY ALL FEDERAL RESERVE OPERATIONS ARE DESIGNED TO OFFSET THE IMPACT OF THE OPERATING FACTORS

| TO ADD RESERVES | PROBABLE FEDERAL RESERVE ACTION |
|---|---|
| LARGE AND EXTENDED NEED | BILL OR COUPON PASS |
| SMALL AND EXTENDED NEED | SECURITY PURCHASE FROM FOREIGN CENTRAL BANK |
| TEMPORARY NEED | SYSTEM REPOS AND/OR CUSTOMER REPOS |
| TO DRAIN RESERVES | PROBABLE FEDERAL RESERVE ACTION |
| LARGE AND EXTENDED NEED | BILL SALE |
| SMALL AND EXTENDED NEED | SECURITY SALE TO A FOREIGN BANK |
| TEMPORARY NEED | MATCHED-SALE/PURCHASE AGREEMENT |

*Figure 24-15*
*How the Federal Reserve Decides What To Do on Any Given Day*

TO DECIDE WHAT TO DO ON ANY GIVEN DAY, THE FEDERAL RESERVE MUST ANTICIPATE RESERVES NEEDS FOUR TO SIX WEEKS IN ADVANCE

If it sees a need to add a sizable quantity of reserves for an extended period of time, usually an amount in excess of $4 billion per day for four consecutive weeks, the Federal Reserve will consider an outright purchase of securities *(Figure 24-15)*. It then buys T-bills or Treasury notes and bonds — called a "bill pass" or "coupon pass" — and adds those securities to its own portfolio. As noted previously, this will add an equivalent amount of reserves to the banking system on a permanent basis.

IF IT EXPECTS A SIZABLE ADD NEED FOR AN EXTENDED PERIOD OF TIME, THE FED INJECTS RESERVES TO THE SYSTEM ON A PERMANENT BASIS

For our purposes, these outright purchases of securities are generally regarded as purely technical operations and have no policy implications. The only other point that should be noted here is that these transactions are not done very often, usually only four or five times a year.

If the Fed anticipates a somewhat smaller add requirement (that also extends for a number of weeks), it can choose to buy some government securities from a foreign central bank *(Figure 24-15)*. This adds a more modest amount of reserves to the banking system on a permanent basis. As was the case above, this action is devoid of policy significance.

IT MIGHT ALSO BUY SOME SECURITIES FROM FOREIGN CENTRAL BANKS

More often, however, the Federal Reserve's add requirement varies. It may need to add a large amount of reserves for a week or two, only to be followed by a period in which its add requirement shrinks dramatically or even turns into a drain requirement. In these situations, the Fed opts for one of the methods by which it can add reserves to the system temporarily, i.e., system repos (either overnight or multi-day) or customer repos *(Figure 24-15)*.

IF RESERVES NEEDS ARE SMALLER OR LESS PROTRACTED, THE FEDERAL RESERVE ADDS RESERVES ON A TEMPORARY BASIS

At this point, it should be noted that the Federal Reserve can provide exactly the same amount of temporary reserves to the system in a variety of ways *(Figure 24-16)*. If, for example, it sees a need to inject $2 billion of reserves per day for four consecutive days, it can do $2 billion of overnight system repos on each of the four days. Alternatively, it can execute a $2 billion four-day system repo, or it can opt for a $2 billion customer repo on each of the four days. Every one of these operations supplies exactly the same amount of reserves.

IT CAN PROVIDE THE SAME AMOUNT OF TEMPORARY RESERVES IN A NUMBER OF WAYS

Overnight system repos were generally considered to be the most aggressive action the Fed could take *(Figure 24-17)*. They told the Street that the funds rate was at least 25 basis points higher than what the Fed intended. Thus, overnight system RPs were frequently indicative of a change in policy. Term (multi-day) repos were usually regarded as technical and implied that the Fed faced a fairly sizable add requirement. In addition, multi-day system repos indicated that the funds rate may have been a bit on the high side, but not high enough to trigger overnight repos. Customer repos indicated a more modest add requirement and were also generally viewed as technical. When the Federal Reserve arranged customer repos, the funds rate was relatively in line with its objective.

PRIOR TO 1994 EACH OF THESE OPERATIONS WOULD CONVEY A VERY DIFFERENT MESSAGE TO THE MARKETS IN TERMS OF POLICY

THERE WAS NO
INHERENT LOGIC
IN THE MARKET'S
INTERPRETATION
OF THESE
VARIOUS
OPERATIONS

As shown above, there was no inherent logic behind the market's interpretation of these various operations from a reserves viewpoint — the Fed can provide exactly the same amount of reserves in any number of different ways. But in the pre-1979 period when the Fed was explicitly targeting the federal funds rate, traders quickly learned that when the Fed executed each of these various operations, it was trying to tell the market something about policy. As a result, the above interpretations became widely accepted. In the 1980s, when the Fed was less explicitly targeting the funds rate, the same connotation was attached to these various types of repos. The Fed was well aware that the market interpreted different operations in different ways, and it used that to its advantage when it wanted to convey a particular policy message. Since February 1994, when the Fed began to *tell* us its funds rate objective, this game of guessing the significance of a particular Fed operation ceased to exist. If you *know* that the funds rate target is 6%, it no longer matters whether the Fed is doing customer or system RPs, or matched sales for that matter. You are safe in concluding that these operations are purely technical and have no policy significance. But because the method of carrying out Fed policy has changed several times in the past 20 years, we can never be sure when or if it will change again. For that reason, we feel it is important to understand the significance that the market *used to* attach to

*Figure 24-16*
*The Federal Reserve Can Provide Exactly the Same Amount of*
*Temporary Reserves to the System in a Variety of Ways*

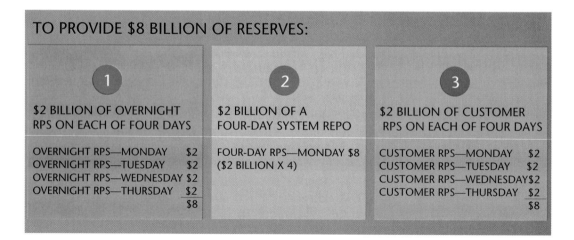

**TO PROVIDE $8 BILLION OF RESERVES:**

| **1** | **2** | **3** |
|---|---|---|
| **$2 BILLION OF OVERNIGHT RPS ON EACH OF FOUR DAYS** | **$2 BILLION OF A FOUR-DAY SYSTEM REPO** | **$2 BILLION OF CUSTOMER RPS ON EACH OF FOUR DAYS** |
| OVERNIGHT RPS—MONDAY $2<br>OVERNIGHT RPS—TUESDAY $2<br>OVERNIGHT RPS—WEDNESDAY $2<br>OVERNIGHT RPS—THURSDAY $2<br>$8 | FOUR-DAY RPS—MONDAY $8<br>($2 BILLION X 4) | CUSTOMER RPS—MONDAY $2<br>CUSTOMER RPS—TUESDAY $2<br>CUSTOMER RPS—WEDNESDAY $2<br>CUSTOMER RPS—THURSDAY $2<br>$8 |

| OPERATION | MESSAGE SENT |
|---|---|
| OVERNIGHT REPOS | Very aggresssive, funds rate too high, possible sign of easier policy stance |
| TERM REPOS | Technical, sizable add requirement |
| CUSTOMER REPOS | Technical, smallish add requirement |

*Figure 24-17*
*Each of these Operations Would Convey a Different Message to the Markets*

these various operations. It just might become important again at some point down the road.

Let us see how the Fed might have chosen between the various methods of providing reserves to the system on a temporary basis. History suggests that the Fed's selection of one operation over another was based on three factors:
· The size of the add requirement;
· The level of the funds rate; and
· The policy message the Fed wants to send.

**HOW WOULD THE FED CHOOSE BETWEEN THESE VARIOUS OPERATIONS?**

When the add need was sizable but temporary, the Fed selected some type of system repo because foreign central banks hold a total of only about $5 billion in their accounts. If the Fed needed to add $8 billion of reserves on a given day, it could not satisfy that reserves need via customer repos. The maximum it could do was $5 billion and, typically, customer repos do not exceed $3 billion. Thus, size became one criterion in the decision-making process. In this case, the Federal Reserve was called upon to execute some type of system repos.

**IF THE ADD NEED WAS SIZABLE, BUT ONLY TEMPORARY, THE FEDERAL RESERVE WOULD HAVE TO SELECT SOME SORT OF SYSTEM REPOS**

THE CHOICE BETWEEN OVERNIGHT AND TERM REPOS WAS GENERALLY DETERMINED BY THE LEVEL OF THE FUNDS RATE

As noted above, if funds were 25 basis points higher than the Fed desired, it would usually select overnight repos rather than multi-day to signal the markets that the rate was considerably higher than it intended. If faced with a sizable add requirement, but the funds rate was less than 25 basis points higher than desired, the central bank most likely would choose multi-day system repos. In each instance, the Fed considered the size of the add requirement, but then looked at the level of the funds rate and picked the operation that best reflected its policy objective.

THE SAME TYPE OF CONSIDERATIONS APPLIED WHEN THE FEDERAL RESERVE WAS FACED WITH A MORE MODEST ADD REQUIREMENT

When the add need was modest, the choice was generally between overnight system repos and customer repos. Once again, the Fed examined the level of the funds rate. If it was 25 basis points higher than intended, the Fed most likely opted for overnight system repos to convey the message that the funds rate was on the high side. At a somewhat lower funds rate level, the Fed would probably opt for customer repos. If, for whatever reason, the funds rate was on the low side, even though the central bank needed to add reserves, it generally decided not to intervene on that day rather than risk sending the market an inappropriate signal. For example, if the Fed arranged customer repos with the funds rate at a lower level than on other recent days when it did customer repos, the market may have erroneously concluded that the Fed was easing. Thus, as had been the case all along, the Fed first looked at the size of its add need, checked the level of the funds rate, and picked the operation that seemed most appropriate for the policy it was pursuing at that particular point in time.

IN THE OLD DAYS, IF THE FEDERAL RESERVE WANTED TO CHANGE ITS POLICY STANCE, IT WOULD ALTER THE LEVEL OF DISCOUNT WINDOW BORROWINGS

Prior to February 1994, when the Federal Reserve looked at the economic situation — GDP growth, employment, inflation, and so forth — and decided that it wanted to adopt an easier policy stance, it reduced the amount of discount window borrowings and increased the net reserves level slightly. This meant that it had to provide more reserves to the market through its open market operations. For instance, if it wanted to reduce discount window borrowings by $200 million, then it had to add an extra $200 million of reserves via open market operations. This process, presumably, caused the funds rate to trade lower. If the Fed wanted to tighten, it boosted the amount of discount window borrowing.

To facilitate the transition, the Federal Reserve would want to send a signal of an easier policy stance to the markets. If the add need was sizable, it might have chosen overnight repos rather than multi-day repos to convey that message. With a smaller need to supply reserves, it could have chosen overnight system repos rather than a customer repo operation. Occasionally, it would send an easing signal by arranging customer repos with funds at a particularly low level. But the Fed *never* signaled a policy change with multi-day repurchase agreements.

THE FED WOULD ALSO WANT TO SEND A SIGNAL TO THE MARKETS OF AN EASIER POLICY STANCE

The key to detecting a change in policy in the earlier environment was determining when the Federal Reserve was being more aggressive than it had been previously for any particular add requirement. The problem was that the Fed has much more accurate data on the actual volume of banking system reserves than is publicly available. Each day it learns what happened to reserves levels on the previous day. Those of us on the Street receive an update only once a week. If the Fed did something differently than expected, the obvious dilemma that an analyst faced was deciding when the Fed was simply reacting to an unexpected change in one or more of the factors affecting reserves and when it was trying to signal a policy change. We found that there were several useful guidelines.

TO DETECT A CHANGE IN POLICY, MARKET PARTICIPANTS WOULD TRY TO DETERMINE WHEN THE FEDERAL RESERVE WAS BEING MORE AGGRESSIVE THAN IT HAD BEEN PREVIOUSLY

FIRST, DECIDE IF *YOU* WOULD EASE POLICY

The first thing that a Fed watcher did was look at the recent economic statistics and decide whether, from his or her viewpoint, a change in policy was warranted (Figure 24-18). *Chances are if the analyst would not make a change in policy, the Federal Reserve would not either.*

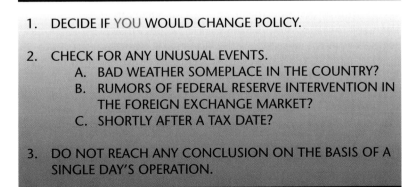

1.  DECIDE IF YOU WOULD CHANGE POLICY.

2.  CHECK FOR ANY UNUSUAL EVENTS.
    A.  BAD WEATHER SOMEPLACE IN THE COUNTRY?
    B.  RUMORS OF FEDERAL RESERVE INTERVENTION IN THE FOREIGN EXCHANGE MARKET?
    C.  SHORTLY AFTER A TAX DATE?

3.  DO NOT REACH ANY CONCLUSION ON THE BASIS OF A SINGLE DAY'S OPERATION.

*Figure 24-18*
*How the Market Used to Detect Federal Reserve Policy Changes*

## SECOND, BE ON THE LOOKOUT FOR ANY UNUSUAL EVENTS THAT COULD ALTER RESERVE LEVELS

The second thing the Fed watcher did was see whether there were any unusual events that could alter reserves levels. If, for example, the analyst noted that there had been a major snowstorm in the Midwest, he or she would be alerted to the possibility that float could rise and provide more reserves to the banking system. Or the Fed watcher might have heard that there had been a considerable amount of foreign exchange intervention. (When the Federal Reserve sells foreign currencies to support the dollar, banking system reserves decrease). Or perhaps it was a period shortly after one of the big tax dates when it becomes much more difficult to estimate the level of the Treasury's cash balance at the Fed. If there were some unusual events taking place, an analyst would be reluctant to conclude that an unexpected action was indicative of a change in policy.

## THIRD, NEVER REACH A CONCLUSION ON THE BASIS OF A SINGLE DAY'S ACTIVITY

One final point — we could rarely reach a conclusion about Federal Reserve policy on the basis of a single day's operation. Generally, all that could be done on that day was to note that this action seemed unusual and could be indicative of a change in policy. We wanted to track the behavior of the funds rate over the rest of that day and waited to see some confirmation of an easier policy stance reflected in Fed activity on subsequent days.

ABOUT 90% OF THE FED'S OPEN MARKET OPERATIONS WERE PURELY TECHNICAL

We have seen that in the pre-February 1994 period about 90% of the Federal Reserve's open market operations were designed to do nothing more than offset the impact of the operating factors. The very fact that the Fed was doing repos or matched sales did not necessarily indicate a policy change. What was important was the level of the funds rate and the particular operation that the Fed selected. Furthermore, it should be understood that the Fed tried very hard not to send misleading signals to the market although, occasionally, the message that the Fed thought it was sending was not the signal that the market received.

Because the Federal Reserve used open market operations to signal a change in policy about 10% of the time, "surprise" repos or reverses would ring a bell on Wall Street. Since early detection of a policy shift was of supreme importance to the financial markets, the professional Fed watcher's primary function was knowing *when the bell's ring was true or hollow.*

THE REMAINING 10% OF THE TIME THE FEDERAL RESERVE USED ITS OPEN MARKET OPERATIONS TO SIGNAL A POLICY CHANGE

To implement monetary policy in today's world, the Fed still follows the four-step process that was outlined earlier. It decides upon a desired rate of growth for nominal GDP and, making as good a guess as it can about velocity growth, comes up with a desired rate of growth for each of the monetary aggregates. It then works backwards from those monetary aggregates targets to determine the appropriate levels of bank reserves. It must then contend with the influence of all those factors that can cause the level of bank reserves to fluctuate. And, finally, it still has to add or drain reserves on a daily basis. In choosing between the various methods of adding or draining reserves, the Fed still follows the same basic guidelines that we discussed previously. So from the Fed's viewpoint the world has not changed a great deal.

IN TODAY'S WORLD THE FED STILL FOLLOWS THIS SAME GENERAL PROCEDURE

In the past, the Fed watcher's primary responsibility was not only to examine the economic landscape and determine *when* the Fed might change policy, but to religiously analyze the Fed's daily open market activity in an attempt to determine *whether* there was any policy significance to a particular operation. In short, the job was to determine if the Fed was changing its funds rate objective. But in today's world the Fed *tells* us exactly where it wants the Federal funds and discount rate. The wizard has been revealed — there is no longer any mystery about this aspect of Fed policy! Thus, the Fed watcher's role today is more focused on determining *when* — after looking at the combination of growth in the economy, the positions of actual and potential GDP, and the current and leading indicators of inflation — the Fed is likely to announce a change in policy. Final note: In the first year since the Fed began announcing the results of its FOMC meetings, the Fed tightened eight times. Seven of those moves occurred at FOMC meetings. Thus, market participants generally

THE DIFFERENCE IN TODAY'S WORLD IS THAT THE MARKET NO LONGER HAS TO GUESS AT THE SIGNIFICANCE OF A PARTICULAR OPERATION do not have to pay much attention except on those eight days a year when the committee is scheduled to meet. However, there is no *guarantee* that in the future the Federal Reserve will continue this pattern, so stay alert!

# Contents

The attached software is a 15-minute demonstration of the Global Portfolio Manager™ simulation software marketed by International Financial Training & Technology, Inc., the parent company of International Financial Press, Ltd. Global Portfolio Manager™ provides a simulated market environment in which you can:

- •Increase your familiarity with unfamiliar investment vehicles and strategies.
- •Experiment with alternative hedging and risk management strategies.
- •Hone your ability to predict, interpret, and react to news announcements.

This simulation is the same software used by many of the world's major investment banks to train their capital markets personnel.

In this simulation exercise you assume the role of a portfolio manager. You are competing against an unmanaged globally diversified Benchmark Portfolio. Your objective is to outperform the Benchmark Portfolio on a risk-adjusted basis. Assume the following are the results at the end of the simulation:

|  | Return | Risk |
|---|---|---|
| Benchmark Portfolio | 10% | 20% |
| Your Portfolio | 12% | 26% |

Given these results, your return is 120% (12%/10%) of the benchmark's return, but your risk level is 130% (26%/20%) of the benchmark's level. You have *underperformed* the Benchmark Portfolio on a risk-adjusted basis.

However, if your portfolio's return is 90% (9%/10%) of the benchmark's return while your risk level is 80% (16%/20%) of the benchmark's risk level, you have *outperformed* the benchmark on a risk-adjusted basis.

|  | Return | Risk |
|---|---|---|
| Benchmark Portfolio | 10% | 20% |
| Your Portfolio | 9% | 16% |

When the simulation begins, your portfolio will exactly mirror the Benchmark Portfolio. If during the entire simulation you make no changes to your portfolio, your risk adjusted performance will exactly equal the Benchmark Portfolio's risk-adjusted performance. In order to outperform the benchmark, you will have to follow and interpret both the news stories and the market indicators and use your analysis to periodically reallocate your portfolio.

By underweighting those market sectors that you expect to underperform and overweighting those market sectors you expect to outperform, you can attempt to outperform the benchmark. Keep in mind that:

> •Trading is not free and that the simulation incorporates a realistic schedule of transaction costs.
>
> •The market sectors will not always move the way that classic economics would suggest. Sometimes the market moves in the wrong direction for no explicable reason. In this simulation the market sectors move the way they would be expected to move approximately 80% of the time.

Because this simulation incorporates both fixed income and equity market sectors from around the world, you will be able to make a wide variety of different types of bets including:

> •FX bets
> •Duration bets
> •Equity sector bets
> •Fixed-income sector bets
> •Spread bets

The directions that follow will provide you with information on how to install and operate the simulation as well as how to interpret your results. Good luck!!

P.S. By acquiring this software, you have the opportunity to become part of our design and development team. Almost every feature incorporated into our simulations was a result of a customer request or comment. At IFT&T, Inc., we are dedicated to continually improving our software and welcome your comments, requests, and suggestions.

IFT&T's Global Portfolio Manager™ is divided into two components:

**PRODUCT OVERVIEW
TWO COMPONENTS**

1. **Program Module** is the computer instructions to run the Scenario Modules. A program can run an unlimited number of scenarios.

2. **Scenario Module** contains the data (newswire, security prices, market indicator values, etc.) that allow the Program Module to replicate a specific market environment.

**System Requirements**

To install the Global Portfolio Manager™ for Windows simulation software, you will need the following hardware and software:

• An IBM-PC® or fully compatible personal computer with:
  • 486SX processor running at 33 MHz or higher
  • 16-bit VGA graphics adapter
  • 3½" Floppy drive
  • 3 MB of free disk space for Program Module
  (Each scenario installed requires an additional 1-2 MB.)
  • 4 MB of RAM (8 MB recommended)
• Color monitor
• Windows 3.1, Windows for Workgroups, Windows 95 (Available Spring 1996)
• Mouse

**Software Installation**

1. Start Windows.
2. Insert the simulation program disk #1 into the diskette drive on your computer.
3. From the Windows Program Manager:
   Select the File menu option.
   Select the Run option from the drop-down menu.
4. Key **A: Setup** in the Command Line box.
5. Click **OK**. After a brief pause while the installation program initializes, you will see the following Setup screen:

| WinGPM Setup |
|---|
| If you want to install WinGPM in a different directory and/or drive, type the name of the directory. |
| Install To:  `C:\WINGPM` |
| To quit Setup, choose the Exit button. |
| **Continue**    **Exit Setup** |

The installation will install the program into the C:\WinGPM directory when you click on the Continue button. To install the program in a different directory and/or drive, type the name of the new directory in the install box.  Then click on the Continue button to proceed.

The setup installation will begin copying files from the install disk to the directory you specified. The progress of the installation will be shown.

6. When disk #1 is completely installed, if necessary, you will be prompted to insert additional diskettes. After all disks are installed, the screen will display the following message "WinGPM installation is complete." Click on the **OK** button to continue.

Then the Program Manager will reappear with the WinGPM icon in its own window. Double-click on this icon to begin the simulation.

DEMO LIMITATIONS

The demo version of our simulation product is fully functional with all the features of our actual product except:
• The report writing section has been omitted.
• The run time has been reduced to approximately 15 minutes.

 An actual scenario will run approximately 2 hours.

The demo can be copied and distributed to others to allow them to evaluate the product.

TYPOGRAPHIC
CONVENTIONS

| Example | Description |
|---------|-------------|
| [Enter] | When you see brackets [ ] around a word, this indicates a key to be pressed on the keyboard. For example: [Enter]. You should press the Enter key. |
| File | Underlined letter identifies the key you can select in conjunction with the [Alt] key to execute this option. For example: [Alt] + F would select the file option. |
| "Exit" | When you see quotations ("") around a word, this indicates a toolbar button should be pressed. For example: "Exit." You should press the Exit toolbar button. |

STARTING THE
SIMULATION

This manual has the following typographic conventions:

To start the simulation:

1. Open the WinGPM program group.
2. Double-click on the WinGPM icon. The program title screen will appear briefly.
3. The Open Scenario File window will appear with a listing of the installed scenarios shown. An example follows:

Open Scenario File

Select scenario file:

| | |
|---|---|
| Individual Stocks | (GEB30001) |
| Global Fixed Income Market | (GFB30001) |
| International Mix | (GMB3D999) |
| Riskless Arbitrage | (TMT30001) |

OK

Cancel

You can select a scenario file by using one of the following methods:

• Double-click on the scenario file.
• Single-click on the scenario file you want and then click the **OK** button or press the **[Enter]** key.
• Use the up or down arrow keys to highlight the scenario file you want and then click the **OK** button or press the **[Enter]** key.

If you click on the **Cancel** button, the Open Scenario File window will close. You can use one of the following methods to reopen the Scenario File window:
• Single-click on the "Open Scenario File" toolbar button.
• Select the **File** menu option. From the pull-down menu, select the **Open Scenario File** option.

After a scenario file has been selected, the Scenario Options window will appear with a blinking cursor in the box beneath the instruction "Enter your name:".

4. Type your name. (**Note:** The simulation will not allow you to proceed unless you enter a name in the box.)

5. Select a **Difficulty Level.** A darkened circle next to Level 1 identifies it as the default level. To accept the selected level, click on OK.  If you want to run the scenario at another difficulty level, single-click on the circle next to the new level. The level determines what strategies can be employed during the scenario. The following strategies will be available at each level:

|  | Level 1 | Level 2 | Level 3 |
|---|---|---|---|
| Ability to hold long positions | X | X | X |
| Ability to take short positions |  | X | X |
| Ability to hedge long positions |  | X | X |
| Ability to speculate with derivative instruments |  |  | X |
| Ability to use margin to leverage up the portfolio |  |  | X |

6. Select a **Performance Measure**. A darkened circle next to Relative to Benchmark identifies it as the default measure. If you want to run the scenario using another performance measure, you need to single-click on the circle next to the new measure.

**Performance Measure Definitions**

*Absolute Return*
The most common but least accurate way to measure performance is absolute return. For example, if a $100 million portfolio increases to $110 million, the absolute return is 10%. This  measure only indicates that some good—perhaps even lucky — trades were made, not that the portfolio was managed with any care or consistency.  In the real world, where investment choices are made with careful consideration of the risks involved, lucky trades are often meaningless since they are often impossible to replicate on a regular basis.

*Risk-Adjusted Return*

With risk-adjusted return, the absolute performance number is adjusted to reflect the degree of risk taken to obtain it. Let's suppose that two portfolio managers started with $100 million and that Manager A ended with $105 million and Manager B ended with $110 million. In absolute terms, B did better than A, turning in a 10% as opposed to a 5% return. However, if Manager B took THREE times the risk of Manager A in order to achieve those results, then Manager A outperformed B on a risk-adjusted basis. Simply put, given the risks, Manager B would have required a return of 15% in order to have equaled the performance of Manager A. This is a far more realistic way to evaluate the investment performance of a given portfolio.

*Relative to a Benchmark*

The most realistic way that portfolio performance is measured is relative to a benchmark, and this should be the preferred choice for the scenario. Professional investors and portfolio managers often utilize investments that mirror a particular benchmark of investments, such as the S&P 500, the Lehman Brothers Bond Index, the FTSE 100, and others. As they continue to invest, their performance is compared both in return and in risk to that underlying Benchmark Portfolio. In the simulation, the Benchmark Portfolio will be the original, fully invested portfolio given in the beginning. In other words, by using this measure of performance, users will know whether or not their investing skills provided any real value to the portfolio.

7. To continue, click on the **OK** button. Now all the scenario information has been selected and you can begin.

You can use either of the following methods to start the scenario:
• Single-click on the "Go" toolbar button.
• Select the **File** menu option. From the pull-down menu, select the **Start Simulation** option.

The word "Loading...." will appear in the information panel as the data are loaded.

USING THE
SIMULATION

### Selecting Menu Options

The menu options appear beneath the title at the top of the screen. The main menu options are:

Each menu option has a letter underlined. To select a menu, you can choose either of the following methods:
• Single-click on the file menu option.
• Press **[Alt]** + underlined letter.

To select an item from the drop-down menu, you can choose either of the following methods:
• Press the underlined letter of the item you want to select.
• Use the up and down cursor key to highlight the item you want, then press the **[Enter]** key.

Some menu options may be dimmed. This indicates that this menu option is not available for selection, and nothing will happen if you try to select it.

### Selecting Toolbar Options

The toolbar is located beneath the menu options on the left side. To select a toolbar option, single-click on the appropriate button.

The toolbar buttons are:

 "Open scenario file"

 "Start simulation"

 "Exit simulation"

"Performance graph"

"Display hint"

The toolbar buttons are a shortcut to menu options. For example, the "Start simulation" toolbar button is equivalent to selecting the **File** menu option and the **Start Simulation** item from the drop-down menu.

If a toolbar button is dimmed, this means it is not available to be selected.

## Information Panel

The information panel is located on the same line as the toolbar buttons but on the other side of the IFT&T logo.

| WinGPM - International Mix | | |
|---|---|---|
| File  Transactions  Graphs  Reports  Window  Help | | |
| [toolbar buttons]  IFT&T | Hint available | 8/45 |

This panel will display the following messages throughout the simulation:

| | |
|---|---|
| Loading... | Displays while the selected scenario data is loaded into the appropriate window. |
| Hint Available | Displays when the information currently being shown in the Newswire window has significant value. To display the hint associated with the newswire story, you can either: |
| | ·Press [F1]. |
| | ·Single-click on the "Display Hint" toolbar. |
| | ·Select the Help menu option and select the Hint F1 item from the drop-down menu. |
| PAUSE/Hint Available | Displays while you are viewing the hint. Once you have exited from the Hint window, the PAUSE will no longer be displayed. |
| Simulation Over | Displays at the end of the simulation. No additional trades can be performed. |

## Datapoint Panel

The datapoint panel is located on the same line as the toolbar buttons at the right edge of the screen.

| WinGPM - International Mix | | |
|---|---|---|
| File  Transactions  Graphs  Reports  Window  Help | | |
| [toolbar buttons]  IFT&T | | 4/45 |

This panel displays the following two numbers at all times:

• *First Number* indicates the current datapoint within the simulation. This number changes approximately every two seconds.

• *Second Number* indicates the total datapoints within the simulation.

In most simulations, 360 trading days (more than one full year of market activity) are compressed into two hours. The datapoint panel identifies which day you are viewing. For example, 26/360 means you have reached day 26 of a 360-day scenario.

EXPLANATION OF
THE WINDOWS

When reviewing this section, it may be helpful to start the simulation so that you can refer to the windows indicated.

The screen is divided into a number of separate and distinct windows. We will discuss each of these windows and the information each contains.

## Market Window

The large window at the top of the screen contains the portfolio, with specific market information for each sector or instrument. The screen size permits you to view only 18 instruments at one time. If your portfolio consists of more instruments, you must click on the arrow beneath the Market window to view the other instruments. A down arrow would indicate additional sectors or instruments are below those you are currently viewing. An up arrow would indicate additional sectors or instruments are above those you are currently viewing.

An explanation of each column in the Market window is listed below:

**Sector**
This column contains the name of each security or market sector in your portfolio.

**Bench Alloc** (Benchmark Allocation)
This column is the Benchmark Portfolio's allocation in this investment, expressed as a % of the total portfolio.

For example, 3.25% of the Benchmark's Portfolio is in 90 Day T-bills.

**Port Alloc** (Portfolio Allocation)
This column is your portfolio's current allocation in this investment (% of total portfolio). Green indicates a long position; red, a short position.

**Div Yield or YTM** (Dividend Yield or Yield-to-Maturity)
For a fixed-income portfolio, this column is current yield-to-maturity of a fixed-income security/sector based on its current market price (%). In an equity portfolio this column is the dividend yield of an equity security/sector.

**.01 or Beta**
This column measures the volatility or risk of the security/sector. The dollar value of .01 is the change in price this instrument will have for every one basis point change in market yields. This is the best measure of volatility for each security in the portfolio. The greater the .01, the more sensitive this investment is to changes in interest rates movements.

For equity sectors, this value is the beta of the security/sector. Beta measures the volatility of the security relative to the volatility of the S&P 500.

**Cnv** (Convexity)

Convexity measures the change in a bond's duration. It is only shown for fixed-income instruments.

**OAS** (Option-Adjusted Spread)

The option-adjusted spread uses a Monte Carlo based analysis to determine the true yield spread of a bond to the equivalent Treasury security after the value of any embedded options are subtracted.

**TR** (Total Risk)

For equity instruments, this is a comprehensive measure of risk that incorporates beta, alpha (if applicable), liquidity, and FX risk. For Fixed-income instruments, this is a comprehensive measure of risk that incorporates interest rate, spread, liquidity, credit, and FX risk.

**Curr Value** (Current Value)

This column is the current market quote for this investment. As stories come across the newswire and affect the price of securities, this will constantly change throughout the simulation. Current Value should be monitored closely for those securities in which you take positions that are different from those of the benchmark.

**Avg Cost** (Average Cost)

This column reflects the current cost basis for the position currently held in this investment. If multiple purchases or sales have been made, it will provide the average cost basis. Only when a position is sold out completely, (i.e., zeroed out) will a completely new cost basis be established.

**Port G/L** (Portfolio Gain/Loss)

This column shows how your investment in this instrument is performing on an absolute basis. This is where to look to find out if an individual position is making a profit (% gain or loss). Green numbers indicate a capital gain; red, a capital loss.

**T** (Technical Indicator)

This column indicates technical research opinions. Since many firms offer their own research departments' technical opinions, we've included them, too. The arrow indicates the "short-term" technical opinion (3 months or less). An up arrow indicates that the technicals favor an upward trend in the price. A down arrow indicates that the technicals favor a downward trend in the price. Here's a hint: Just as in the real world, they're pretty good, but not always right. Use your best judgment.

**Note:** Technical and fundamental research do not always agree.

**R** Research
This column provides fundamental research on the opinions of Wall Street analysts for this security, with a "**B**" meaning a buy signal and an "**S**" meaning sell. The column provides your firm's opinion.

## Futures/Options Window

Directly beneath the Market window is the screen containing derivatives. The screen size permits you to view only six derivatives at a time. If your portfolio consists of more derivatives, you must click the arrow on the side of the Futures/Options window to view the other derivatives. A down arrow would indicate additional derivatives are below those you are currently viewing. An up arrow would indicate additional derivatives are above those you are currently viewing.

An explanation of each column is listed below:

**Contract**
This column lists the derivative instruments.

**T** (Type)
This column indicates what type of derivative it is. For example:

> **F** = Futures Contract
> **C** = Call Option
> **P** = Put Option
> **S** = Swap Option

**Theor Val** (Theoretical Value)
This column is the theoretical value of a contract expressed in dollars.

**Mkt Value** (Market Value)
This column is the current price of each contract expressed in dollars.

**Val .01** (Value .01)
This column measures the volatility/risk of the derivative as a dollar value of a basis point. A negative value indicates that the

price will fall when the value of the underlying rises, while a positive value indicates the price will rise as the value of the underlying rises.

**Pos** (Position)
This column identifies the number of contracts you currently hold. A negative number indicates a short position, meaning your transaction is a sale. A positive number indicates a long position.

**Avg Price** (Average Price)
This column identifies the average price of the contract expressed in dollars.

**Gain/Loss**
This column is the current profit or loss that the position is generating expressed in dollars. The number will appear in green if there is a gain; in red, if there is a loss.

## Market Indicators Window
To track the broad market environment and to give you a context in which to make changes to your portfolio, the window on the upper-right screen provides ever-changing market indicator data. To follow this information, compare the initial market indicator data with the current market indicator data (directly underneath). **For a quick look at a specific trend, move the mouse cursor directly to a specific market indicator, then double-click to bring up its graph.** (Graphs will be discussed in greater detail in a later section.)

The market indicators are scenario specific. While many indicators may vary between scenarios, certain key indicators such as the FED Funds and the S&P 500 will be available in all scenarios.

## Newswire Window
The scrolling Newswire window is located in the lower right-hand side of the screen. The simulation is formulated as an event-driven market. Close scrutiny of the newswire, which will give clues to interest rate trends by providing stories about economic data, headlines about the actions of the FED, the economy, and the markets.

*Since time is compressed during the simulation, there are many more important events in this newswire than one might find in your average two hours in the real world. It pays to keep a sharp eye on the news.*

The newswire will scroll at approximately one line every two seconds. As the news comes across, you need to determine whether or not the story has a direct or indirect impact on the portfolio performance. If you have decided that the story has some relevance, you should read the entire story before you act since a headline may not give an accurate picture of the entire text. Once you are sure that your interpretation of events requires action, quickly move to the transaction screen to adjust your portfolio.

For more information, refer to the section *Making a Trade*.

**Remember:** The time and newswire continue to scroll while you are making trades. If you spend too much time in the transaction screen, you are probably missing important news stories.

## Performance Window

This window, located in the lower left-hand side of the screen, is where your portfolio performance is tracked throughout the simulation. To ensure a proper interpretation of performance, familiarize yourself with the following three measurement components:

*Current Risk (as measured by your portfolio AT THIS MO-MENT)*

### Absolute Current Risk

This number measures the *current* total risk level of your portfolio at this moment. It is a comprehensive measure that includes:
- Interest rate risk (duration and convexity)
- Spread risk
- Credit risk
- FX risk
- Beta risk
- Alpha risk
- Liquidity risk

| | Performance | |
|---|---|---|
| | **Absolute** | **Relative** |
| Current Risk | 52,039 | 100.00% |
| Wgt Avg Risk | 52,502 | 100.00% |
| Return / RAR | -0.38% | 0.00% |

### Relative Current Risk

This is your portfolio's total risk relative to the total risk of the Benchmark's Portfolio. When the simulation begins, your portfolio mirrors the Benchmark's Portfolio, so your portfolio has 100% of the risk level of the Benchmark's Portfolio. As you overweight or underweight the various market sectors in your portfolio relative to the benchmark, the relative risk level of your portfolio will change.

### Wgt Avg Risk (current risk categories as averaged since the beginning of the scenario)

### Absolute Wgt Avg Risk

The weighted average risk is the average of all the current absolute risk levels of your portfolio since the beginning of the simulation. It shows, on average, how much risk you have been taking on an absolute basis.

### Relative Wgt Avg Risk

As above, but on a relative basis.

### Return/RAR (Risk-Adjusted Return)

### Absolute Return/RAR

The percentage increase or decrease in your portfolio's value. For example, if your portfolio increases in value from 100MM to 105 MM, this number will be +5.00%.

### Relative Return

The percentage increase or decrease in your portfolio's value relative to the increase or decrease in the benchmark's portfolio value, adjusted for the risk difference between two portfolios. If this number is positive, your investment decisions have added value to the portfolio on a risk-adjusted basis. If this number is negative, your investment decisions have cost the portfolio on a risk-adjusted basis. Note this number is "all inclusive" at all times so transaction charges, fines etc. are immediately reflected in this number. The higher this number, the better your performance.

## Graphs

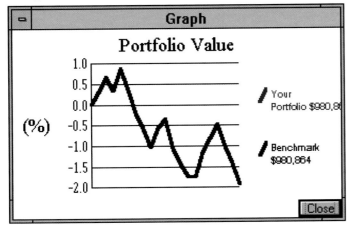

To provide additional tools to make informed portfolio changes, we have included a full range of graphs, including market indicators, performance, and others specific to the scenario. Graph windows, once opened, will NOT continuously update. You must first close then reopen a Graph window to see any updates.

All graphs, with the exceptions of the Yield Curve and Performance graphs, will include both the current trendlines and the moving average line. General technical analysis guidelines can be used when interpreting the graphs.

All graphs are available via the **Graphs** menu option, including:

**Yield Curve**
The Yield Curve graph compares the yield curve at the beginning of the simulation (in black) to the current yield curve (in blue). Additional Yield Curves (1,2,3 and 4) are drawn as a reference point.
> Yield 1 = yield curve one fifth mark through simulation
> Yield 2 = yield curve two fifths mark through simulation
> Yield 3 = yield curve three fifths mark through simulation
> Yield 4 = yield curve four fifths mark through simulation

For example, the graph might show that interest rates are increasing at the long end of the curve while decreasing at the short end, also called a *steepening yield curve*. This could suggest that changes to the portfolio might be appropriate.

### Performance

The absolute performance of your portfolio vs. that of the Benchmark Portfolio is shown by this graph and can be useful to show you *HOW* your performance differs from the benchmark.

### Indicators

### Indicators Graphs

Each market indicator can be graphed, showing the trend of the market indicator since the beginning of the simulation.

### Currency Graphs

The performance of the U.S. dollar relative to other currencies is illustrated by the currency graphs. The exchange ratio starts at 1.000. As the value goes up, the dollar is getting stronger relative to the other currency.

The currency graphs available are determined by the foreign instruments within the scenario and may include:

- British Pound
- Japanese Yen
- German Deutsche mark
- French Francs
- Canadian Dollars
- Australian Dollars

## Reports

There are two types of reports you can obtain from the Reports menu:

### Trade Blotter

This is a running record of every trade you made during the simulation. When the simulation has been completed, you may wish to look back to see how you reacted to various changes in the markets. The Trade Blotter tells you at what datapoint you made the trade, what instrument was traded, the volume of the transaction, and the price the transaction was executed at.

```
=                          Trade Blotter
┌──────────────────────────────────────────────────────────────────────┐
│ Data                         Transaction    Trans                      │
│ Point  Instrument            Type           Volume           Price     │
├──────────────────────────────────────────────────────────────────────┤
│   21  90 Day T-Bill          Sell            1.30            986.40     │
│   21  1 YR T-Bill            Sell            1.32            944.80     │
│   21  2 YR T-Note            Sell            1.34          1,014.90     │
│   21  5 YR T-Note            Sell            1.40          1,033.25     │
│   21  10 YR T-Note           Sell            1.48          1,056.32     │
│   21  10 YR Mex. T-Bond      Buy             1.58          1,038.71     │
│                                                                        │
│                                                                        │
│                         [  E xit  ]                                    │
└──────────────────────────────────────────────────────────────────────┘
```

## Scenario Profile

This screen displays all of the relevant details of the scenario, including a running total of your fines, margin interests, and commission costs.

```
=                          Scenario Profile
┌──────────────────────────────────────────────────────────────────────┐
│ Scenario: GMB3D999      Level: [1]   ┌─Active Features──────────────┐  │
│ Type:     Portfolio Mixed            │ [X] Scrolling News Wire      │  │
│ Player:   JOE SMITH                  │ [X] Long Positions           │  │
│                                      │ [ ] Short Positions          │  │
│ ┌─Current Performance────────────┐   │ [X] Sector Constraints       │  │
│ │                                │   │ [X] Benchmark Constraints  +/- 25% │
│ │ Interest on Investments  $603  │   │ [ ] Hedging With Derivatives │  │
│ │ Margin Interest          $20   │   │ [ ] Speculating With Derivatives │
│ │ Total Fines              $0    │   │ [ ] Imposes Overhead Costs   │  │
│ │ Total Commissions        $0    │   │ [ ] Imposes Commission Costs │  │
│ │ Portfolio Value     $1,009,323 │   │                              │  │
│ │ Benchmark Value     $1,008,820 │   │ Starting Capital:  $1,000,000│  │
│ └────────────────────────────────┘   │ Leverage Capital:      (NA)  │  │
│                                      │ Performance Measurement:     │  │
│            [  E xit  ]                │ Risk Adjusted Relative to Benchmark │
│                                      └──────────────────────────────┘  │
└──────────────────────────────────────────────────────────────────────┘
```

MAKING A TRADE **Sector Trade Market Window**

To change your portfolio's allocation of a specific security, you may select any of the following methods:

**Menu Method**
Select the **Transaction** file menu. From the drop-down menu, select the **Change Allocations** menu option. The Change Allocations window will appear showing the key market

---

**Change Allocations**

| Sector | Beta Or .01 | Bench Alloc | Current Alloc | New Alloc | G/L |
|---|---|---|---|---|---|
| 90 Day T-Bill | 0.03 | 3.30 | 3.30 | 2.00 | 0.21 |
| 1 YR T-Bill | 0.10 | 3.32 | 3.32 | 2.00 | 0.87 |
| 2 YR T-Note | 0.18 | 3.34 | 3.34 | 2.00 | 1.49 |
| 5 YR T-Note | 0.42 | 3.40 | 3.40 | 2.00 | 3.37 |
| 10 YR T-Note | 0.73 | 3.48 | 3.48 | 2.00 | 5.74 |
| 20 YR T-Bond | 1.10 | 3.57 | 3.57 | 3.57 | 8.54 |
| 30 YR T-Bond | 1.28 | 3.62 | 3.62 | 3.62 | 9.79 |
| 20 YR Corp AA | 1.03 | 3.55 | 3.55 | 3.55 | 7.94 |
| 20 YR Corp A | 1.01 | 3.55 | 3.55 | 3.55 | 7.77 |
| 20 YR Corp BBB+ | 0.96 | 3.54 | 3.54 | 3.54 | 7.40 |
| 20 YR Corp BB | 0.78 | 3.49 | 3.49 | 3.49 | 6.07 |
| 10 YR German Bund | 0.74 | 3.49 | 3.49 | 3.49 | 5.84 |
| 10 YR Japanese JGB | 0.81 | 3.50 | 3.50 | 3.50 | 6.40 |
| 10 YR British Gilt | 0.71 | 3.48 | 3.48 | 3.48 | 5.59 |
| 10 YR Mex. T-Bond | 0.49 | 3.42 | 3.42 | 5.00 | 3.90 |
| US Auto Index | 0.51 | 2.81 | 2.81 | 2.81 | -14.80 |
| US Banking Index | 0.16 | 3.15 | 3.15 | 3.15 | -4.33 |
| US Housing Index | 0.11 | 3.20 | 3.20 | 3.20 | -2.69 |
| US Transport Index | 0.74 | 2.54 | 2.54 | 2.54 | -22.80 |
| US Oil Gas Index | 0.19 | 3.11 | 3.11 | 3.11 | -5.47 |
| US Semi-Cond Index | 0.27 | 3.04 | 3.04 | 3.04 | -7.65 |
| US Telecomm Index | 0.51 | 2.78 | 2.78 | 2.78 | -15.66 |
| US Paper Index | -0.29 | 3.56 | 3.56 | 3.56 | 8.20 |
| US Health Index | -0.30 | 3.60 | 3.60 | 3.60 | 9.28 |
| US Defense Index | -0.31 | 3.62 | 3.62 | 3.62 | 9.99 |
| Canadian Index | 0.00 | 2.93 | 2.93 | 2.93 | -10.93 |
| China Index | 0.00 | 2.72 | 2.72 | 2.72 | -17.49 |
| Emerging Mkt Index | 0.00 | 2.62 | 2.62 | 2.62 | -20.50 |
| British Index | 0.00 | 3.00 | 3.00 | 3.00 | -8.75 |
| Mexican Index | 0.00 | 2.37 | 2.37 | 2.37 | -28.15 |
| Japanese Index | 0.00 | 2.64 | 2.64 | 2.64 | -16.59 |

**% Allocated**   94.48%
**Current Cash**   54,143.68
**Estimated Risk**   96.77%

[ **OK** ]   [ **Cancel** ]

[ **Reset to Benchmark** ]

---

information. You can make multiple trades from this window. The highlight can only move within the New Alloc column. Upon entering this window, the New Alloc column values will be the same as the Current Alloc column values until you make changes. To change an allocation value:

1. Highlight New Alloc value of the security you wish to change.
2. As you key in the new value, it will automatically replace the existing value.

To delete an allocation value:

1. Highlight New Alloc value of the security you wish to delete.
2. Press the **[Delete]** or **[Backspace]** or **[Space Bar]** to remove New Alloc value.

To undo all changes to the portfolio and mirror the benchmark:

1. Single-click on the "Reset to Benchmark" button at the bottom right side of the screen.

As you change the allocation for each security, the total portfolio adjusts immediately and is reflected in the % Allocated, Current Cash, and Estimated Risk values shown that are in the upper right-hand corner.

Once you have completed all the changes you wish to make, single-click on one of the following buttons:

- **OK**. To accept and save your allocation changes and return to the main screen.
- **Cancel**. To ignore the changes you just made and return to the main screen.

**Port Alloc Column Method**
Double-click on the value you wish to change within the Port Alloc column in the Market window. A pop-up window will appear showing the current portfolio value for the security you have selected. You can only make a single trade using this method.

To change the allocation value:

1. With the value highlighted, key a new value. The new value will automatically replace the existing value.
2. Single-click on the up or down arrow on the right side. The value will jump to the closest value in .05 increments.

To delete the allocation value:

1. With the value highlighted, Press the **[Delete]** or **[Backspace]** or **[Space Bar]** to remove the value.

Single-click on one of the following buttons:

- **OK**. To accept and save your allocation changes. You will return to the main screen.

• **Cancel.** To ignore the allocation change. You will return to the main screen.

### Market Window Method

If you double-click anywhere within the Market window, except the Port Alloc column, the Change Allocations window will appear showing the key market information. You can make multiple trades from this window by following the instructions as listed in the menu method above.

### Values

At the top of the Change Allocations window are the following values:

### % Allocated

The percent of your portfolio that is distributed among the investments. At the beginning, your portfolio will be 100% invested.

### Current Cash

The amount of your current cash can be positive or negative. Cash balances are automatically invested at the Federal Funds rate. Cash debts are financed at the Federal Funds rate plus 1%.

### Estimated Risk

Expressed as a percent, estimated risk is the amount of risk you are taking relative to the benchmark. RED number indicates you are taking less risk than the benchmark.

A number greater than 100% indicates you are taking more risk than the benchmark. Most scenarios contain volatility constraints. Therefore, the estimated risk becomes an important information since most scenarios will impose fines for exceeding these constraints.

### Derivative Trade Futures/Options Window

To change your portfolio allocation of a specific derivative, you may select any of the following methods:

### Menu Method

Select the **Transaction** file menu. From the pull-down menu, select the **Futures/Options Transactions** menu option. The Futures/Options Transaction window appears showing the key derivative information. You can make multiple trades from this window.

The highlight can only move within the New Position column where contracts are bought and sold. Upon entering this window, you will find that the New Position column values will be the same as the Current Position column values until you make a change.

**Note:** The benchmark never has a derivative position. You are limited to +/- 100 contracts for any one derivative.

To buy a derivative contract:

1. Highlight New Position value of the derivative you wish to change.

2. Key in the position you wish to have. Long positions are entered as positive numbers, and short positions are entered as negative numbers. The new position will automatically replace the existing value.

To sell a derivative contract:

1. Highlight the New Position value of the derivative you wish to change.

2. Press the **[Delete]** or **[Backspace]** or **[Space Bar]** to remove New Position value.

To reset your derivative portfolio position to zero:

1. Single-click on the "Reset: Close All Points" button.
The changes you make are immediately reflected in the Estimated Risk Value shown. The estimated risk must be within the scenario volatility constraints.

Once you have made all the changes you wish to make, single-click on one of the following buttons:
• **OK**. To accept and save your allocation changes. You will return to the main screen.
• **Cancel**. To ignore all your allocation changes and return to the same derivative positions prior to the current changes. You will return to the main screen.

**Pos Column Method**
Double-click on the value you wish to change within the Pos Column in the Futures/Options window. A pop-up window will appear showing the current position value for the derivative you have selected. You can make a single trade using this method.

To buy a contract:

1. With the value highlighted, key a new value (i.e., buy a contract). Your new position in this derivative will automatically replace the existing value.

2. Or, single-click on the up or down arrow on the right side, and the value will jump to the next value in increments of 1.

To sell a contract:

1.With the value highlighted, press the **[Delete]** or **[Backspace]** or **[Space Bar]** to remove the value.
Single-click on one of the following buttons:
•**OK**. To accept and save your allocation changes. You will return to the main screen.
•**Cancel**. To ignore all your allocation changes. You will return to the main screen.

### Futures/Options Windows Method
If you double-click anywhere within the Futures/Options window, except the Pos column, and the Futures/Options Transaction will appear showing the key derivatives information. You can make multiple trades from this window by following the instructions as listed in the menu method above.

### Values
At the bottom of the Futures/Options Transactions window is the following value:

### Estimated Risk
Similar to the portfolio changes, all purchases/sales of derivatives will affect the portfolio's risk. The number at the bottom of this screen indicates the risk you are incurring relative to the benchmark. Since most scenarios contain volatility constraints, the estimated risk must be monitored when changes to the portfolio are made. Most scenarios impose fines for exceeding volatility constraints.

HINTS    If a significant story appears in the newswire window, the information panel at the top of the computer screen will display the message, "Hint Available."

The hint provides additional information and suggested actions to consider in managing your portfolio. Viewing a hint is optional.

```
┌─────────────────────────────────────────────────────────────┬───┬───┐
│ —                              Hint                          │ ▼ │ ▲ │
├─────────────────────────────────────────────────────────────┴───┴───┤
│  File   Edit   Bookmark   Help                                       │
├──────────────────────────────────────────────────────────────────────┤
│ │Contents│ │Search│ │Back│ │History│ │Exit│                          │
└──────────────────────────────────────────────────────────────────────┘
```

# Home Sales Dropping

## Economic Indicator

**Chapter 16   New Home Sales - The Heartbeat of America**

HOME SALES ARE A LEADING INDICATOR OF ECONOMIC ACTIVITY

New home sales are an important indicator of the degree of strength or weakness in the key housing sector of the economy. Housing is a crucial segment of the economy because, historically, changes in consumer spending patterns have shown up first in autos and housing. Therefore, if the selling pace of new homes begins to slacken, eventually housing starts begin to slow, and employment in the construction industry declines. Once the housing sector begins to slide, numerous related industries -- like lumber and home furnishings -- also begin to suffer. **Thus, a dropoff in home sales can be a leading indicator of an impending recession.** Similarly, when the economy begins to rebound, the housing and automobile sectors are usually the first to experience recovery.

## Related Topics:

Newswire Story

Suggested Action

To view a hint, you can select one of the following methods:

• Press **F1**.

The simulation is temporarily placed in PAUSE mode while you are viewing the hint.

• Select the **Help** menu option. From the drop-down menu, select **Hint F1** option.

• Click once on "Display Hint" toolbar button.

To exit the Hint window, single-click on the "Exit" button.

**ENDING THE SIMULATION**

At any time during the simulation you wish to end, simply click on the "Exit" button on the toolbar.

**Note:** Once you exit the simulation, all trades and information are gone. When you begin again, you will start with the same portfolio as the benchmark.

**Allocation Error.**
**Your position must be in the range X% to Y%.**

Explanation:
Some scenarios place restrictions on the minimum and/or the maximum percentage that your portfolio can be allocated to any one security or market sector.

Corrective Action:
Change the allocations of each market sector that is outside the specified range.

**Can't load font: 'WinGPM.FON'.**

Explanation:
The program cannot find the file WinGPM.Fon to load.

Corrective Action:
Check the directory you specified at the time of installation and verify the file WinGPM.FON exists. You may need to manually add this font by selecting the Windows Control Panel Font resource.

**No scenario data files found.**

Explanation:
The program cannot find the data files in the directory you specified during the installation.

Corrective Action:
Reinstall the simulation. If this error still occurs, call technical support.

**Over-Allocation Error.**
**You may not allocate more than X% of your capital.**

Explanation:
If you have tried to allocate more capital to your portfolio than the scenario permits, an error message will flash on the screen telling you the capital constraints of the portfolio. For example, "X" can range from 100% in the case of an unleveraged scenario to a multiple of 100% for a leveraged scenario (i.e., 200% for leverage of 2:1). Your capital is initially invested at 100%.

Corrective Action:
While you are still in the Change Allocations window, you will need to reduce your allocations to bring your portfolio into compliance with the scenario's guidelines.

**Position Out of Range.**
**Your position must be in the range +/- 100 contracts.**

Explanation:
Many scenarios limit the size of the derivative positions you are permitted to build.

Corrective Action:
Change the number of derivative contracts to an acceptable number.

**Prohibited Transaction.**
**You have attempted to execute a prohibited transaction. Short positions are not allowed.**

Explanation:
Either the scenario you are running does not permit the attempted transaction or the difficulty level you selected prohibits the attempted transaction.

Corrective Action:
You need to find an alternative way of accomplishing your objective.

**Protection Check Failed!**

Explanation:
The software requires the security plug be correctly attached to the parallel port or the software will not run.

Corrective Action:
Check to make sure the security plug is securely attached to the parallel port and then try to restart the simulation.

**Please enter your name.**

Explanation:
You did not enter a name in the Scenario Options window.

Corrective Action:
Enter your name.

**Transactions Not Allowed.**
**Futures/Options transactions are not allowed at this difficulty level.**

Explanation:
A simulation must be run at a Level 2 or 3 before derivative transactions are allowed, even though the derivatives will show on the screen at a Level 1.

Corrective Action:
Exit the simulation and restart the simulation. In the Scenario Options window, select a Level 2 or Level 3.
**Note**: Once you have exited a simulation, you will lose your current portfolio settings.

**Volatility of your portfolio has exceeded the maximum of "X" to 100% relative current risk.**

Explanation:
Most scenarios have a specific maximum risk tolerance when the performance is being measured on either an absolute or risk-adjusted basis. The transactions you tried to execute would create a portfolio that would exceed the maximum risk level. This can happen when you are changing the allocation of your portfolio, OR given market conditions your portfolio can drift outside the constraints. Therefore, it is important to monitor the current relative risk to ensure you are within the constraints.

Corrective Action:
None required; the attempted transactions have automatically been canceled.

**Volatility of your portfolio is more than +/- X% from the Benchmark Portfolio volatility.**

Explanation:
Many scenarios require that you maintain an overall volatility level that is within "X" percentage of the benchmark's volatility when you elect to have performance measured against a benchmark. Violating this restriction will result in the imposition of a fine, "$Y" every 20 seconds, until the portfolio is brought back into balance.

Corrective Action:
Change the portfolio's allocations until the portfolio is +/- X% constraints.  Example: Volatility constraints of +/- 20% means the

portfolio relative risk must remain between 80% and 120%.

*Alternatively:*
If the scenario includes derivatives, use derivatives to bring the overall volatility of the portfolio within "X"% of the benchmark.

**You have been fined $X.**

Explanation:
This message will appear with the volatility errors if the scenario allows fines.

Corrective Action:
Change the portfolio's allocations until the portfolio is +/- X% constraints. Example: Volatility constraints of +/- 20% means the portfolios relative risk must remain between 80% and 120%.

*Alternatively:*
If the scenario includes derivatives, use derivatives to bring the overall volatility of the portfolio within "X"% of the benchmark.

reserves, calculating net free and net borrowed, *illus.*, 266; central bank contends with variety of factors that cause levels of to fluctuate, 271-275; customer repos add reserves to system on temporary basis, 276-277; determine volume of necessary to achieve desired pace of money growth, 265-271; excess, 265-266; Fed can add or drain on either permanent or temporary basis, *illus.*, 276; Fed figures whether to add or drain necessary, 275; Fed must anticipate needs four to six weeks in advance, 278; Federal Reserve does not provide banking system with all it needs but forces system to borrow at discount window, 267; Federal Reserve provides temporary in number of ways, 279; if needs smaller, Federal Reserve adds on temporary basis, 279; if sizable, extended need expected, then injected permanently into the system, 278; impact on of various factors, *illus.*, 273; many factors affecting, 272; nonborrowed, what the Fed targets, 267; required, 265; total consists of required and excess, 265-266; when Fed buys securities, it adds reserves to system permanently, 275; when Fed does system repo, it adds reserves on temporary basis, 275; when Federal Reserve needs to drain, its choices entirely analogous, 277

residential construction, one of the most important categories of construction spending, 185

retail sales, 107-115; are quite difficult to forecast, 110; can be a major market mover—strong report is negative for bonds, 114; car sales data help estimate automobile component of and consumption, 65-66; composition of, *illus.*, 113; consumption data rely heavily on report, 162-164; excluding autos, most important part of report, 108; first solid indication of strength or weakness in consumer spending, 108; 40% are durable goods, 60% are nondurable goods, 112-113; how

to forecast, *illus.*, 110; Johnson Redbook data are not very helpful, 111-112; market reaction to, *illus.*, 115; must also rely on unit car sales, 110; must rely on chain store sales, 111; neutral for the dollar, 114; positive for stocks, 114; report has several drawbacks, 108-110

retail sales report, contains data on purchases of goods only—no services, 108; data are extremely volatile, 109-110; data reported in nominal terms—not adjusted for inflation, 108-109; excluding autos, most important part of, 108; has a few problems, *illus.*, 109; has several drawbacks, 108-110

## S

S&P, how it tracks corporate profits, *illus.*, 251; versus three-month CD rate, *illus.*, 250

savings rate, good indication of consumers' willingness to spend, 162; United States, *illus.*, 163

securities, Federal Reserve may buy from foreign central bank, 279; when Fed buys these, it adds reserves to system permanently, 275

services, exports/imports of, *illus.*, 211; GDP: goods versus, *illus.*, 118; retail sales report excludes, 108; trade balance for goods and, 212

service sector, huge portion of our economy, *illus.*, 221; productivity gains difficult to measure in, 220

simulation (Global Portfolio Manager), ending the, 315; starting the, 294-297; using the, 298-300

single-family dwellings, report provides data on both multi- and, 138-139

stock market, could go up or down depending on the business cycle (durables), 157; factors affecting the, *illus.*, 15; faster production can trigger a rally, 125; if CPI rises, it will fall, 149; if NAPM rises, it should improve, 74; prices also influenced by Federal Reserve's policy